A HIST

Jane Austen's
Family

A HISTORY OF

Jane Austen's Family

George Holbert Tucker

SUTTON PUBLISHING

First published in 1983 by Carcanet New Press

This revised edition published in 1998 by
Sutton Publishing Limited
Phoenix Mill · Thrupp · Stroud · Gloucestershire · GL5 2BU

A catalogue record for this book is available from the
British Library.

ISBN 0-7509-1663-X

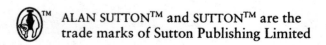 ALAN SUTTON™ and SUTTON™ are the
trade marks of Sutton Publishing Limited

Printed in Great Britain by
Guernsey Press Company Ltd
Guernsey, Channel Islands

To Elizabeth

Contents

Foreword

IN the days after World War II when I embarked on the career of a professional librarian, it was the golden rule to give the right book to the right reader at the right time. One can be forgiven, I trust, for wishing that this golden rule applied to authors and, in particular, to biographers. How many times have the sins and errors of past authors been perpetuated by present authors, and fresh errors perpetrated by the unwary or hasty biographer?

George Holbert Tucker has, I think, avoided this; he has skipped neatly round the quagmire of hearsay and rumour and presented to the literary world a volume, the very pages of which reflect hours and hours of painstaking research, fastidious attention to detail, and the assiduous checking and collation of known evidence.

In the vast world of Jane Austen (albeit her corpus is small) — the amount of literature about her and her style of writing — what a blessing it is to have a volume of precise, careful scholarship. Mr Tucker has given to the literary world a volume of true worth and an essential reference tool for future scholars. After the publication of this very human and most interesting study of the Austen family, no other writer on the subject of Jane Austen should be guilty of presumption or waste time in the pursuit of vague theories, incorrect facts or literary gossip.

I wish this book well and heartily commend it.

Paul Yeats-Edwards
Fellows' Librarian
Winchester College

Preface

TO WRITE a book about Jane Austen and not to include her as the principal character seems like preparing a banquet in honour of a celebrity and leaving his or her name off the guest list. With most authors this would be a case of cultural as well as social bad manners. With Jane Austen, however, the matter is somewhat different; she was probably the most modest and family-oriented writer of all the literary great, and it may be safe to assume that she would welcome the shifting of the spotlight from herself to those who directly or indirectly contributed to her greatness.

From the time of her happy childhood at Steventon Rectory until her untimely death forty-one years later, Jane Austen was a beloved member of a cheerful and cultured family. Whether she was ever fully aware of the extent of her talent is a matter for conjecture. If she was, she never let it interfere with being an agreeable member of a closely related group that regarded loyalty to one another as one of the chief virtues.

Even though we now know a great deal more concerning the day-to-day life of Jane Austen than was realized at the time her first biography appeared in 1870, there are many who still regard her as a talented amateur who lived a retired life in a remote Hampshire village where she somehow managed to write six of the best novels in the English language.

Nothing could be further from the truth. By birth and training, Jane Austen was an outstanding example of the social class that she depicted so discerningly — the landed gentry of England. This heritage was enriched by the many benefits she received from the members of her immediate family. From her father and brother James she derived her appreciation of English literature as well as an acquaintance with clerical life. From her clever mother she inherited wit. The social position of her wealthy brother Edward enabled her to mix familiarly with, and to observe the manners of, the people she used as characters in her novels. Association with her favourite brother Henry, a London banker, gave her the polish and advantages of Regency society; while sisterly interest in the careers of two naval brothers, Francis and Charles, kept her in constant touch with the stirring events of the Napoleonic wars. To these was added the abiding devotion of her only sister Cassandra, whose protective sympathy created the ideal atmosphere in which her great natural abilities reached fruition.

Frank and helpful criticism from all her family had been a part of her literary life since childhood, when she first began to write. It is also a matter of record that as she matured she continued to welcome the opinions of those whom she held in high esteem. In the end, she weighed what was offered in the balance of her genius, retaining the gold, but discarding the dross.

This book is an effort to indicate the family influences that helped to shape Jane Austen as a writer. It is my hope that it will shed a clearer light on the author who in *Northanger Abbey* characterized the novel as a literary form in which 'the greatest powers of the mind are displayed, in which the most thorough knowledge of human nature, the happiest delineation of its varieties, the liveliest effusions of wit and humour are conveyed to the world in the best chosen language.'

George Holbert Tucker

The Austen background

AUSTEN

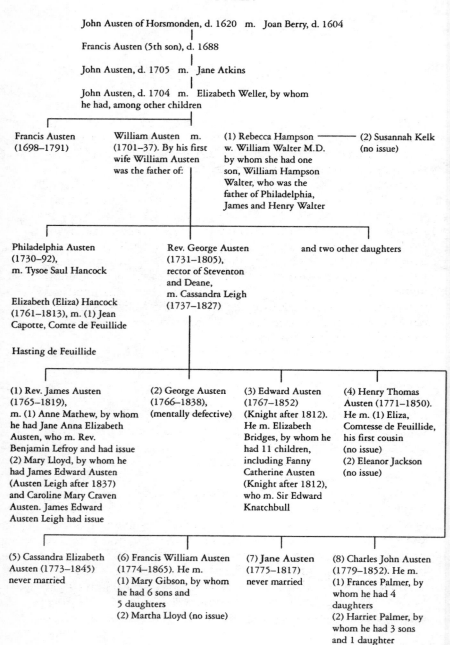

John Austen of Horsmonden, d. 1620   m.   Joan Berry, d. 1604

Francis Austen (5th son), d. 1688

John Austen, d. 1705   m.   Jane Atkins

John Austen, d. 1704   m.   Elizabeth Weller, by whom he had, among other children

Francis Austen (1698–1791)

William Austen m. (1701–37). By his first wife William Austen was the father of:

(1) Rebecca Hampson ——— (2) Susannah Kelk w. William Walter M.D. by whom she had one son, William Hampson Walter, who was the father of Philadelphia, James and Henry Walter

(2) Susannah Kelk (no issue)

Philadelphia Austen (1730–92), m. Tysoe Saul Hancock

Elizabeth (Eliza) Hancock (1761–1813), m. (1) Jean Capotte, Comte de Feuillide

Hasting de Feuillide

Rev. George Austen (1731–1805), rector of Steventon and Deane, m. Cassandra Leigh (1737–1827)

and two other daughters

(1) Rev. James Austen (1765–1819), m. (1) Anne Mathew, by whom he had Jane Anna Elizabeth Austen, who m. Rev. Benjamin Lefroy and had issue (2) Mary Lloyd, by whom he had James Edward Austen (Austen Leigh after 1837) and Caroline Mary Craven Austen. James Edward Austen Leigh had issue

(2) George Austen (1766–1838), (mentally defective)

(3) Edward Austen (1767–1852) (Knight after 1812). He m. Elizabeth Bridges, by whom he had 11 children, including Fanny Catherine Austen (Knight after 1812), who m. Sir Edward Knatchbull

(4) Henry Thomas Austen (1771–1850). He m. (1) Eliza, Comtesse de Feuillide, his first cousin (no issue) (2) Eleanor Jackson (no issue)

(5) Cassandra Elizabeth Austen (1773–1845) never married

(6) Francis William Austen (1774–1865). He m. (1) Mary Gibson, by whom he had 6 sons and 5 daughters (2) Martha Lloyd (no issue)

(7) Jane Austen (1775–1817) never married

(8) Charles John Austen (1779–1852). He m. (1) Frances Palmer, by whom he had 4 daughters (2) Harriet Palmer, by whom he had 3 sons and 1 daughter

The Austens of Kent

JANE AUSTEN came of a goodly heritage. By birth, and with the added gift of genius tempered with amused ironic detachment, she was the ideal delineator of her particular class — the English country gentry of the late eighteenth and early nineteenth centuries. On her father's side she was descended from six well-documented generations of respectable Kentish landowners who had gradually achieved eminence in their corner of England by way of the broadcloth trade.[1] That, and ironworking, had been the leading industries of the Weald of Kent for many generations. The Leighs of Cheshire, her mother's family, were much more aristocratic. Not only was their social position higher than the Kentish Austens', but their distinguished pedigree, extending back into the mists of the Middle Ages, had ramifications that connected them with some of the most memorable names in English history.[2]

Many years after Jane Austen's death, in an undated letter to his nephew, the Reverend James Edward Austen-Leigh, her brother, Henry evaluated his paternal ancestry thus: '... it is no scandal to say that my aforesaid relations of West Kent never raised any alarming fears of their setting even the Medway on fire.'[3] Significantly, he did not feel it necessary to draw a contrast between his Austen and Leigh backgrounds.

The Weald of Kent, the home of Jane Austen's paternal forebears, derives its name from the Anglo-Saxon word meaning *forest*.[4] It is now used to denote that part of England lying between the North and South Downs, including a fair-sized part of West Kent, a greater part of Sussex, and fragments of Surrey and Hampshire.[5] For centuries before the Roman occupation of Britain it was an almost impenetrable woodland, traversed only by ancient trails, inhabited by robbers, wolves, wild boar and deer, and regularly visited in season by swineherds to fatten their flocks. The region remained remote even after the Romans brought their legions and made roads. But by the sixteenth century, when Jane Austen's ancestors rose to prominence there, much of the timber had been felled, and the area was dotted with clearings, where farming, cloth-weaving, and iron-smelting activities clustered around the square-towered medieval churches that still grace the Wealden countryside.

The surname Austen, variously spelled Austen, Austin, Astyn, and Awsten, before standardization settled on the first two, is still fairly common in the Weald.[6] The 1978 Tunbridge Wells telephone directory, covering a radius of a little less than fifty miles including much of the Kentish Weald, listed fifty Austen families and seventy-one Austins. Both surnames are diminutives of Augustine, the Old French version of the Latin Augustinus, the usual Middle English form of a saint's name.[7] The saint in this particular instance was St Augustine (d. AD 604), the 'Apostle of the English' and first Archbishop of Canterbury, whose name often was shortened to St Austin.

Jane Austen's confirmed paternal ancestry begins during the reign of Elizabeth I with her fourth great-grandfather, John Austen I of Horsmonden, Kent, who was born around 1560 and died in March 1620. Reputable genealogists, including Sir Anthony Wagner, Clarenceux King of Arms (later Garter Principal King of Arms), have speculated that John Austen I of Horsmonden was a great-grandson of a William Astyn, who lived at Yalding, a Wealden town a few miles to the north of Horsmonden. His will was proved in the Prerogative Court of Canterbury in 1522, during the reign of Henry VIII. However, no conclusive proof for this assumption has so far been established.[8]

John Austen I married Joan, a daughter of Jeffrey Berry of Midley, Kent, in September 1584. After bearing him eight sons and one daughter, she died in December 1604, in giving birth to twin sons, Thomas and Richard, who survived. She is buried beneath the nave of the sandstone church dedicated to St Margaret of Antioch in Pisidia, that stands in lonely Gothic dignity some two miles from the present village of Horsmonden. Her gravestone bears a brass representing a Jacobean lady, her hands clasped in prayer, wearing a great beaver hat and a high, pleated ruff. Above her effigy is a small brass plate with a Latin sentence that roughly translated says: 'O friend, if you seek the grave of the one who prepared it, it was John my husband by the name of Austen.' Beneath her effigy is a larger brass plate recording, among other things, that Joan Austen 'DIED IN CHILDBED OFTEN VTTERING THESE / SPEACHES LET NETHER HVSBAND NOR CHILDREN NOR / LANDS NOR GOODS SEPERATE ME FROM THE MY GOD.[9] It is not as dramatic as Jane Austen's last words, 'I want nothing but death', but its sincerity and directness expresses the deep-rooted, unpretentious piety that characterized Joan Austen's famous descendant.

John Austen I outlived his wife by sixteen years, and is buried beside her. His will shows he was a man of means, owning property in both Kent and Sussex. He was succeeded by his eldest son, John Austen II (1585-1650), who, dying without issue, was succeeded by his eldest surviving brother, Francis (1600-88), Jane Austen's third great-grandfather.

John Austen I had been content to fill the role of a prosperous farmer, but by the time his surviving sons reached maturity they began to designate themselves as 'clothiers', that is, the fabricators of woollen cloth. Kent had been famous for its broadcloth since the fourteenth century, at which time Edward III invited Flemish weavers to come 'into our kingdom of England for the purpose of working wools there and otherwise exercising their mystery'.[10] Many of these Flemish weavers settled in the Weald of Kent, where water for finishing the heavy cloth was plentiful. By the fifteenth century the occupation of clothier had become so profitable that the fortunes of many former agricultural families like the Austens had been made in wool. The clothier provided the capital and the wool for the over-all operation, and the broadcloth, woven on looms by skilled weavers in cottages surrounding the clothier's more pretentious dwelling, was then processed in workrooms attached to his house. After that it was sold to London factors, who distributed it throughout England and on the Continent. For centuries Kentish broadcloth enjoyed an enviable reputation, but by the early eighteenth century, when Jane Austen's ancestors had turned to other occupations, its production was practically extinct in the Weald, the manufacture of finer types of cloth having shifted to other parts of England, particularly the Cotswolds. Even so, the industry had built up fortunes and a sturdy independence in many Wealden farming and sheep-breeding families.

Daniel Defoe has this to say concerning the social class from which Jane Austen's paternal ancestors were descended:

These clothiers and farmers, and the remains of them, upon the general elections of members of parliament for the country, show themselves still there, being ordinarily 14 or 1500 freeholders brought from this side of the county; and who for the plainness of their appearance, are called the gray coats of Kent; but are so considerable, that who ever they vote for is always sure to carry it, and therefore the gentlemen are very careful to preserve their interest among them.[11]

In this connection it is interesting to note that in a book formerly owned by Jane Austen and now belonging to the Jane Austen Memorial Trust,[12] in commenting on a woollen works at Wootton-under-Edge 'belonging to Messrs. Austin' someone has written 'A branch of the Austens — the "Gray Coats of Kent"', showing that the Hampshire Austens were well aware of their Wealden clothier background.[13]

To return to the Austen chronicle: it was Francis, the younger son of John Austen I, who acquired the two many-gabled, half-timbered Tudor manor houses (still extant) of Grovehurst and Broadford near Horsmonden in 1647, that were subsequently occupied by many generations of his family. At his death in 1688 Francis left a handsome inheritance to his only son, John Austen III, Jane Austen's great-great-grandfather, who was born around 1629 and married Jane Atkins of Brightling, Sussex. By her he had two sons, John Austen IV and Francis who died young, and three daughters, Jane, Ellen, and Anne. Only John Austen IV and his sister Jane had any direct connection with Jane Austen's family. In the case of the earlier Jane Austen, the benefits were unforeseen, but long-lasting.

Jane, the daughter of John Austen III, married Stephen Stringer, gentleman, of Triggs, Goudhurst, Kent, in May 1680. They were the parents of Hannah, who married William Monke, whose daughter, Jane, married Thomas May of Godmersham, Kent, in 1729. He had been born Thomas Brodnax but having inherited the estates of his mother's cousin, Sir Thomas May of Rawmere, Sussex, in 1727, he had taken the surname of May by Act of Parliament. A few years later, when he succeeded to the estates of Mrs Elizabeth Knight of Chawton, Hampshire, he again applied to Parliament for permission to change his name from May to Knight. This was also allowed but not before a Member of Parliament wryly remarked, 'This gentleman gives us so much trouble, that the best way would be to pass an act for him to use whatever name he pleases.'[14]

The present magnificent Palladian country house at Godmersham was built in 1732 for Thomas (Brodnax, May) Knight (1702-81). As he also inherited the gift of the living of Steventon when he came into the Knight properties in 1738, he was able to present it to his second cousin, the Revd George Austen, in 1761. But that was not the end of the benefits Jane Austen's family derived from the marriage of the earlier Jane Austen of Horsmonden to Stephen Stringer. Later in the eighteenth century, Thomas Knight II of Godmersham (1736-94) (son and heir of Thomas Knight I), being childless, adopted Edward, one of Jane Austen's elder brothers, to whom Knight's widow, Catherine (Knatchbull) Knight, handed over the Kent and Hampshire properties in 1797.[15]

With Jane Austen's great-grandfather, John Austen IV, we encounter tribulation for the first time in the Austen chronicle. It also serves to introduce his plucky widow, Elizabeth, whose sterling character and strong sense of duty towards her orphaned children enabled them to survive a serious social and financial setback. Fortunately a family document, 'Memorandums for mine and my Children's reading, being my own tho'ts on our affairs 1706, 1707, a rough draft in a retired hour', written by Elizabeth Austen, has been preserved; it sheds a revealing light on Jane Austen's paternal forebears.[16] After reading it, one must conclude that John Austen III of Grovehurst, Elizabeth Austen's father-in-law, was not a particularly likeable man.

John Austen IV became the master of Broadford upon his marriage to Elizabeth Weller of Chauntlers, Tonbridge, Kent, in December 1693. (A member of an old Tonbridge family, Elizabeth was a grand-daughter of Thomas Weller (1602-70), chief parliamentary agent for the Tonbridge area during the Civil War. His house had been sacked by Royalists, even though his family later protested he had lamented the unhappy fate of Charles I 'and had as much resentment against Cromwell's usurpation as any of his Majesty's subjects.'[17]) Playing the classic role of spendthrift son of tight-fisted father, John made the great mistake of concealing from his wife debts contracted during his carefree bachelorhood, trusting the wealth he would inherit at the death of his father would enable him to satisfy his long-suffering creditors. In the meantime he and his wife lived the good life of persons of their station. They fitted up the old gabled house with handsome furniture, plate and linen, and dispensed generous hospitality throughout the neighbourhood. Meanwhile John Austen IV staved off his creditors sufficiently to keep his personal affairs a secret from his unsuspecting wife. After he had fathered seven children, fate caught up with him in 1704, when he was stricken with consumption. With only a short time to live belatedly he took his wife into his confidence.

Faced with an appalling situation, Elizabeth proved under duress to be a strong and practical woman. She acted promptly, hoping her wealthy father-in-law, who by her own account 'was loath to part with anything', would assist her. At first the crotchety old man, who disliked his daughter-in-law, reluctantly agreed to help, but after the death of his son in September 1704, he withdrew his promise. Elizabeth then offered her most valuable household goods for sale; but as this hurt the pride of 'Father Austen', as she called him, the sale was cancelled and he again agreed to help satisfy his son's creditors. Once more Fate intervened, for John Austen III died in July 1705, after a brief illness that 'seiz'd his brains'. He was buried beside his son in St Margaret's Church, Horsmonden, beneath a massive stone slab carved with the Austen coat of arms.

When his will was read Elizabeth had the mortification of learning that although her eldest son, John Austen V, had been amply provided for, her other six children were only minimally remembered. Undeterred, she took matters into her own hands and by prudent management of the Broadford estate and the sale of her more valuable possessions, by 1708 she had not only paid off most of her husband's debts but was on the lookout for an advantageous situation in a town that would enable her to supervise her younger children's education, there being no school in Horsmonden, '... for I always tho't,' she wrote, 'if they had Learning they might ye better shift for in ye world, with yt small fortune was allotted 'em.'

Luck was with the courageous widow, for when she learned that the schoolhouse in nearby Sevenoaks (she wrote it

'Sen'nock') needed a housekeeper, she let Broadford and took the job on the understanding that her children would have free instruction from the master rather than her receiving a salary. Interestingly, the master turned out to be Elijah Fenton (1683-1730),[18] a minor Augustan poet and excellent classical scholar who was later to assist Alexander Pope with his translation of *The Odyssey*.[19]

By February 1721, when Elizabeth Austen died and was taken back to Tonbridge for burial, she had successfully placed all her surviving younger children in positions to provide for themselves. John Austen V, her eldest son and the young squire of Broadford, with whom she had no concern, had already been sent by his grandfather's executors to Cambridge, where he was admitted as a fellow commoner at Pembroke College.[20]

Francis, her second son, had been apprenticed to a London attorney and later became a successful and wealthy Sevenoaks solicitor. Thomas, the third son, was articled to a London haberdasher but later practised as an apothecary in Tonbridge. Robert, the fifth son, died, unmarried, of smallpox. Stephen, the sixth son, had been apprenticed to a London stationer and later set up as a bookseller and publisher of religious and medical books at the sign of The Angel and Bible in St Paul's Churchyard. The daughter, Elizabeth, married a man named Hooper, presumably the George Hooper who was later a prominent Tonbridge attorney.[21]

William Austen, the fourth son and the grandfather of Jane Austen, merits fuller treatment, but unfortunately little is known concerning him other than the factual information contained in parish registers, legal documents, and on his gravestone in Tonbridge Church.[22] Born at Broadford on 3 February 1701, he received his education at the still flourishing Sevenoaks Grammar School, founded early in the fifteenth century by Sir William Sevenoak, an associate of Sir Richard (Dick) Whittington and his predecessor as Lord Mayor of London in 1418-19.[23] In February 1718 William Austen was articled for a fee of £115 10s. 0d., to William Ellis, a Woolwich surgeon. After completing his apprenticeship, he set up, like his brother Thomas, as a surgeon in Tonbridge, where he practised successfully until his death at the age of thirty-six.

Meanwhile, he had married twice. His first wife (Jane Austen's

grandmother) was Rebecca, widow of Dr William Walter of
Frant, East Sussex. She and Dr Walter were the parents of
William Hampson Walter, the half-brother of Jane Austen's
father and in time the father of Philadelphia, who later recorded
the first known description of Jane Austen as a young girl.

Rebecca (Walter) Austen was a daughter of Sir George
Hampson, 'Doctor of Physic' of the City of Gloucester, where he
was buried in St Michael's Church in September 1724. He was
descended from Henry Hampson, who lived at Brodwell in
Oxfordshire during the reign of Henry VIII, and was also a
grandson three times removed of Sir Robert Hampson (d.
1607),[24] a member of the Merchant Taylors' Company of
London, and an alderman and sheriff of London, who was
knighted by James I at Whitehall in July 1603.[25] Two of Sir
George Hampson's other daughters deserve mention. The first,
Catherine Margaret, married John Cope Freeman I, and later
showed great kindness to William Austen's three orphaned
children. The second, Jane, was the wife of Capel Payne, son,
grandson, and great-grandson of mayors of the City of
Gloucester, which city he also served as town clerk from 1723
until his death in London in 1764. Jane Payne was also a Woman
of the Bedchamber to Princess Augusta of Saxe-Gotha from the
time of the latter's marriage in 1736 to Frederick Louis, Prince of
Wales, until 1767.[26] She was present at the birth of George III in
June 1738.

William and Rebecca Austen were the parents of four children,
all born in Tonbridge. The first, Hampson, a daughter, was born
in 1728 and died in 1730, while the fourth child, Leonora, another
daughter, was born in 1732 and was still living in 1770.[27]
Philadelphia, the second child, played a significant role in the
Austen family during Jane Austen's childhood and young
womanhood. She was born in 1730, went out to India in 1752, and
married there an elderly surgeon, Tysoe Saul Hancock. The
Hancocks subsequently returned to England, and Philadelphia
died in London in 1792. Her only brother, George (Jane Austen's
father), was born on 1 May 1731, and died in Bath in 1805. He and
his sister Philadelphia will be treated at greater length in the next
two chapters.

Shortly after the birth of her daughter Leonora, Rebecca
Austen died on 6 February 1732, at the age of thirty-six. At that

time Jane Austen's father was less than a year old. In May 1736 William Austen married for the second time, his bride, Susannah Kelk, being thirteen years his senior. Earlier biographies of Jane Austen and even the privately printed *Pedigree of Austen* give Susannah's maiden name as Holk, but the original Tonbridge marriage register and the marriage settlement between William Austen and herself entered into in April 1736 agree that her surname was Kelk.[28] The marriage settlement also indicates that both parties were fairly well off; Susannah had property of her own, while William Austen not only owned a substantial home in Tonbridge, but also possessed other property there.

William Austen's second marriage ended abruptly a little over a year later. He died on 7 December 1737, when Jane Austen's father was six years of age. His three surviving children were left as wards of his elder brother, Francis, the prosperous Sevenoaks solicitor. William Austen's widow, who family tradition says was not well disposed towards her step-children, outlived him thirty-one years, dying in 1768. Her will contains no mention of her three step-children. She was buried beside William Austen, his first wife and their infant daughter Hampson, beneath a large gravestone in the north aisle of Tonbridge parish church.[29]

The Rector of Steventon and Deane

THE REVEREND GEORGE AUSTEN, Jane's father, was an excellent example of the best kind of English country clergyman during that period of Anglicanism referred to by the historian Edward Gibbon as 'the fat slumbers of the Church'. Well-educated, particularly in the classics, and endowed with a benevolent disposition enlivened with a quiet sense of humour, he preferred the role of rector of two small Hampshire parishes to the pursuit of the 'fat-goose livings' then so eagerly sought by his more worldly clerical contemporaries. That Jane Austen loved and respected him is evident from the two letters she sent at the time of his death to her elder brother Francis, then serving as captain aboard the *Leopard*. 'Our dear Father has closed his virtuous & happy life, in a death almost as free from suffering as his Children could have wished,' she wrote, adding, 'The loss of such a Parent must be felt, or we should be Brutes.'[1] In her second letter, Jane continued in the same vein. 'His tenderness as a Father, who can do justice to? ... The Serenity of the Corpse is most delightful! — It preserves the sweet, benevolent smile which always distinguished him.'[2]

Twelve years later his son Henry, in the biographical notice he wrote for his sister's posthumously published *Northanger Abbey* and *Persuasion*, recalled his father as having been 'not only a profound scholar, but possessing a most exquisite taste in every species of literature'.[3] In the light of what is known from other sources of Mr Austen's character and accomplishments, it can be said that neither of these tributes was filial exaggeration.

All contemporary accounts indicate that Mr Austen was a tall, well-proportioned, and very good-looking man. His second oldest grand-daughter recalled:

'As a young man I have always understood that he was considered extremely handsome, and it was a beauty which stood by him all his life. At the time when I have the most perfect recollection of him he must have been hard upon

24

seventy, but his hair in its milk-whiteness might have belonged to a much older man. It was very beautiful, with short curls about the ears. His eyes were not large, but of a peculiar and bright hazel. My aunt Jane's were something like them, but none of the children had precisely the same except my uncle Henry.[4]

Mr Austen's manly beauty was enhanced by a gentleness of temperament, highlighted by an eager and sanguine turn of mind tempered with a sense of fairness towards those whom he served as rector. One example will suffice: unlike many litigious Hampshire parsons of his time, in all the years he was rector of Steventon and Deane he never once presented a parishioner before the Consistory Court of the Diocese of Winchester for non-payment of tithes.

Very little is known concerning Mr Austen's early life from the time of his birth in 1731 until 1741 when he became a scholar at Tonbridge School. Family tradition says his fees were paid by Francis Austen, his well-to-do uncle and guardian, who had set up as a solicitor in Sevenoaks with a capital of only £800 and a bundle of quill pens.[5] Tonbridge School had a high reputation in the eighteenth century, which continues to this day. Founded in 1553 by Sir Andrew Judd, a native of Tonbridge, Lord Mayor of London in 1550 and a wealthy member of the Skinners' Company, who had made his fortune in fur-trading with Russia, the school had a later benefactor in his grandson, Sir Thomas Smythe, another wealthy Londoner. Smythe endowed six exhibitions at Tonbridge School, one of which was for boys leaving the school to attend either Oxford or Cambridge to study divinity and afterwards to enter the ministry, to be awarded annually and to last for seven years. In 1753 George Austen was awarded one of these exhibitions.

In his time Tonbridge School occupied a Tudor stone building (no longer in existence) with a high-pitched, dormer-studded roof, and a central open cupola housing the school bell. It was also graced at the south end by a tall decorative chimney on the side of which a large sundial was prominently displayed. The enrolment at that time was between forty and sixty boys, presided over by two masters, a headmaster and his assistant, the latter being referred to as the usher, a post George Austen later filled. All classes, from seven in the morning until five in the evening, were held in a long, high-ceilinged room lit by diamond-paned casements, the headmaster teaching several groups of scholars at one end and the usher instructing additional groups at the other.

As the original school statutes of 1553 still required that before admission all boys should be able 'to Wright competently and to Reade perfectly both in Englishe and latten', George Austen presumably obtained some education elsewhere before becoming a pupil at Tonbridge School. In any event, he acquired an excellent foundation for his subsequent studies at Oxford. Like most anciently endowed grammar schools of that period, Tonbridge School stressed the classics — Latin, rather less Greek, and a little Hebrew if the headmaster knew it — as the necessary preparation for either entering the university or living the life of a cultivated gentleman. If there were any extras, such as French, writing or arithmetic, they could only be acquired after the regular hours by those scholars who could afford them, as no such studies were permitted to trespass on the daily eight-hour classical grind.

On 2 July 1747, aged sixteen, George Austen went up to St John's College, Oxford. At the same time he was awarded the fellowship at St John's that had been assigned by the founder of the College to a scholar from Tonbridge School. Unlike many of the idlers who went up to Oxford with no intention of taking a degree, George applied himself, for he was awarded his Bachelor of Arts degree in 1751. In 1754, one year after receiving a Smythe exhibition, he was made Master of Arts. On March 10th of the same year, two months before his twenty-third birthday, he was ordained deacon in Christ Church Cathedral, Oxford, by Thomas Secker, then Bishop of Oxford, a prelate whose quiet Anglican piety and horror of 'enthusiasm' Mr Austen seems to have shared.

From 1754 until December 1757 or shortly after, George Austen combined his fellowship at St John's College with the duties of perpetual curate of Shipbourne, Kent, and second master (or usher) at his old school at Tonbridge. The headmaster at that time was the Revd James Cawthorne, an Augustan prose writer and versifier, who is remembered in the school annals for his strictness and severity as a flogger. After his death in 1761 the formidable Mr Cawthorne was also responsible for an even more terrifying tradition. Every year on April 15th at midnight his ghost, in clanking chains, was alleged to perambulate the dormitories of the Old School, the anticipation of which must have sent chills of horror up the spine of any sensitive schoolboy.[6]

On 25 May 1755, George, then twenty-four, was ordained priest by Joseph Wilcocks, Bishop of Rochester. Three years later he resumed residence at St John's College, where on 27 March 1758 the college register noted 'George Austen, Fellow, MA, also in Priest's Orders' was elected assistant chaplain of the college. In 1760 he was awarded his Bachelor of Divinity degree, and during the academic year of 1759-60 he served as Junior Proctor of the university, his good looks gaining him the nickname of 'the handsome Proctor'. William Wright of Merton College (1725-85), who was Senior Proctor for the same year, was known as 'Devil Wright', presumably because of his strictness with academic hell-raisers.[7]

Meanwhile plans were being made that resulted in George leaving the architectural splendours of Oxford to take up a new role as rector of Steventon in Hampshire, a small parish 'upon the chalk hills of north Hants, situated in a winding valley about seven miles from Basingstoke'.[8] In 1761, when the living of Steventon fell vacant, its patron, Thomas Knight I of Godmersham, presented it to George, his second cousin. He was instituted to Steventon on 11 November 1761, but it was not until after his marriage in 1764 that he actually took up his duties there, the parish having been served in the interim by yet another Kentish second cousin, the Revd Thomas Bathurst, who had been curate of Steventon since 1754. Bathurst later became the rector of Welwyn, Hertfordshire, where he succeeded the Revd Edward Young, author of the once popular graveyard poem, 'The Complaint: Or Night Thoughts on Life, Death and Immortality'.[9]

No family tradition has survived that records where or when George Austen met his future wife, Cassandra Leigh, but it could easily have been in Oxford, where her father's elder brother, Dr Theophilus Leigh, was Master of Balliol. Presumably the meeting took place some time after 1757-8, when George Austen left Tonbridge and returned to Oxford to prepare for his Bachelor of Divinity degree. In any event, the relationship had developed sufficiently by March 1764 for both parties to sign a marriage contract. Cassandra Leigh, who was then living in Bath, brought to the settlement some leasehold houses in Oxford and the prospective sum of £1,000 she would inherit at the death of her mother. For his part, George Austen pledged certain lands in Tonbridge and one-third of several dwellings complete with out-buildings and adjoining lands in the same town, all of them expectant on the death of his step-mother, Susannah Austen.[10]

The marriage took place on 26 April 1764, in old Walcot Church, Bath, a Gothic structure that was soon afterwards replaced by the present neo-classical building.[11] The couple then set out for Hampshire, their wedding journey being broken only by a day's halt at Andover. But the handsome thirty-three-year-old rector and his sprightly twenty-four-year-old bride did not travel alone, for according to family tradition they were accompanied by a six-year-old boy who linked them with one of the great names in British history.

It will be remembered that Mr Austen's elder sister, Philadelphia, had gone out to India in 1752. There she married Dr Tysoe Saul Hancock, who was a friend of Warren Hastings, later Governor General of India (1773-85). In December 1757 Hastings's first wife gave birth to a son who was baptized George in June 1759. Two years later, after the death of the child's mother, Hastings sent his son back to England under the care of his friend, Francis Sykes. Presumably because of Hastings's close friendship with the Hancocks, the boy was committed to the care of George Austen, who apparently made arrangements for him to be looked after, either at Oxford or elsewhere, until his marriage. In writing of this tradition J. E. Austen-Leigh said:

They [his grandparents] commenced their married life with the charge of a little child, a son of the celebrated Warren Hastings, who had been committed to the care of Mr Austen before his marriage, probably through the influence of his sister, Mrs Hancock, whose husband at that time held some office under Hastings in India. Mr Gleig, in his *Life of Hastings,* [1841] says that his son George, the offspring of his first marriage, was sent to England in 1761 for his education, but that he had never been able to ascertain to whom this precious charge was entrusted, nor what became of him. I am able to state, from family tradition, that he died young, of what was then called putrid sore throat; and that Mrs Austen had become so much attached to him that she always declared that his death had been as great a grief to her as if he had been a child of her own.[12]

Warren Hastings returned to England from India in 1765, at which time he was told that his son had 'died the previous autumn at George Austen's rectory'.[13] 'The news was the first thing Hastings heard on landing in England in 1765, and it left a shadow on his face for years.'[14]

Unfortunately, no evidence in the form of a death notice or burial record for little George Hastings has ever been discovered to substantiate his sad story. As J. E. Austen-Leigh was twenty-nine at the time of the death of his grandmother from whom he and other members of his family had presumably heard the story, there is no reason to doubt it. However, ample contemporary evidence shows that the tragedy had no lasting effect on the cordial relationship that continued to exist between Warren Hastings and Mr Austen and the other members of his family.

Although Mr Austen was the rector of Steventon he and his bride did not begin their married life there. The parsonage, described in a document dated 1696 as 'consisting of two Bays of building, outletted at the West end, and part of the South side over the Cellar',[15] was therefore old in 1764, probably in need of repair and unfit for occupation. The problem apparently was solved temporarily by Mr Austen's renting the unoccupied parsonage at Deane from the rector, the wealthy Revd William Hillman, who preferred to live in style at nearby Ashe Park.[16] This supposition is substantiated by the mention of Mr Austen's improvements of Steventon Rectory in a description of the house written by his grand-daughter, Anna, who grew up there:

> The Rectory House at Steventon had been of the most miserable description, but in the possession of my Grand Father it became a tolerably roomy and convenient habitation. He added, and improved; walled in a good kitchen garden, and planted out the east wind — so that in those times, Steventon came to be considered a very comfortable family residence. It stood in the valley, on the right side of the road leading to Popham Lane, and fronting the north.[17]

This was Jane Austen's birthplace and much-loved home for the first twenty-five years of her life. Unfortunately it was demolished in the 1820s, when it was replaced by a more elegant new rectory (now a private residence) on the opposite hill. Today nothing remains but a nettle-fringed well in the centre of a flinty pasture strewn with broken bricks and bits of red clay roof tiles to remind one of the house which formerly stood there.

Even today Steventon is a quiet, secluded place, but if Mr Austen could return he would still recognize the rolling countryside under the spectacular Hampshire skies, his old grey church on the hill, and the ancient yew-tree in the churchyard. But there are a few other things with which he would be familiar. The ancient bells in the church tower that called his parishioners to prayer are still rung, the church silver he used to administer the Sacrament is still there, and the parish registers dating from 1604, containing many entries in his neat handwriting, are carefully preserved. One of his sermons, with annotations showing he preached it seven times at Deane and eight at Steventon, is owned by a descendant. The text, taken from Psalm 5:9 'For there is no faithfulness in their mouth; their inward part is very wickedness; their throat is an open sepulchre; they flatter with their tongue', leads to the speculation that Mr Austen, ordinarily a tolerant man, had this pulpit blast in readiness when there was a notable falling-off of Christian charity in the Steventon-Deane communities.[18]

Mr Austen's three oldest children, James (1765), George (1766), and Edward (1767), were born while he and his wife lived at Deane. By 1768, however, when Mrs Austen's mother, Jane Leigh, died and was buried at Steventon,[19] the family had moved into the presumably refurbished rectory at Steventon where Mr Austen continued to reside until his retirement to Bath in 1801.

His position in the Steventon community was unusual for a rector of that period. As his Kentish cousins, who owned most of the land in the parish, never lived there, Mr Austen came to be regarded by his parishioners as the local representative of the Knights of Godmersham. This placed him in a much higher social position than was usual for country parsons of that period. His status was additionally strengthened by two other factors. First, Mrs Austen's aristocratic and academic family connections enabled the rector and his family to move in the best social circles of the Steventon area. At the top these included the titled Portsmouths of Hurstbourne, the Boltons of Hackwood, and the Dorchesters of Greywell and later of Kempshott, while the landed gentry included the Portals of Freefolk and Laverstoke, Mr Holder at Ashe Park, the Harwoods at Deane House, the Chutes at The Vyne, the Bramstons at Oakley Hall, and the Bigg-Withers at Manydown Park. Secondly, as a recognized gentleman scholar with highly respectable family connections of his own, George Austen was undoubtedly the best-educated man in the Steventon community, making him the acknowledged authority on spiritual, temporal, and cultural matters and even those of a more trivial nature. This is amusingly illustrated by a family anecdote that tells of a 'neighbouring squire, a man of many acres' who questioned the rector: 'You know all about these sort of things. Do tell us. Is Paris in France, or France in Paris? for my wife has been disputing with me about it.'[20]

In 1773, twelve years after being instituted to Steventon, Mr Austen also became the rector of nearby Deane, the living having been purchased for him 'for this time only' by his wealthy solicitor uncle, Francis Austen of Sevenoaks.[21] At that time, according to the Winchester diocesan records, the Steventon living was valued at £100 a year, and the Deane living at £110. With the greater purchasing power of money at that period, the income from the combined livings, plus the perquisites attached to them in the way of arable glebe lands and tithes, guaranteed Mr Austen a comfortable if not opulent way of life. To prevent the charge of plurality being levelled against him, three of his clerical friends from the neighbouring parishes of Dummer, North Waltham and Worting signed joint letters to the Bishop of Winchester, the Lord High Chancellor of England, and the Archbishop of Canterbury stating that the Steventon and Deane livings adjoined one another and were no more than two miles apart. Those assurances met with success, for in March 1773 Frederick Cornwallis, then Archbishop of Canterbury, signified his approval of the Revd George Austen holding the two small livings in plurality.[22]

Mr Austen supplemented his clerical income by farming, and by taking private pupils into his rectory. His activities as a schoolmaster served a dual purpose, for while he was instructing his paying pupils he also taught his own children at the same time.

Two of his pupils, taken at random, will indicate the social class from which he drew his scholars. The first was John Charles Wallop (1767-1853) of Hurstbourne Park, Hampshire, known as Lord Lymington at the time he was under George Austen's care.[23] Later, when he became the third Earl of Portsmouth, his eccentricities were commented on in one of Jane Austen's letters.[24] Cokayne is more succinct: 'So. long as he was sane, he took no part in politics.'[25] The second pupil was Richard Buller (1776?-1806), later vicar of Colyton, Devon, a son of William Buller, Bishop of Exeter, and a grandson of John Thomas, Bishop of Winchester.[26] These and others from similar backgrounds, together with the Austens' large family, were responsible for the occasional overcrowding of Steventon Rectory that no doubt caused Cassandra and Jane to be sent away at an early age to boarding-schools in Oxford, Southampton, and Reading.

Mr Austen was not a well-to-do man; his combined income never exceeded £600 per annum. But life at Steventon Rectory was comfortable and cultured. As one member of the family later recalled, 'The home conversation was rich in shrewd remarks, bright with playfulness and humour and occasional flashes of wit.'[27] Mrs Austen, a clever woman and a careful housekeeper, her husband, and their bright and handsome children were held in high esteem by their more affluent neighbours. Firm but compassionate parental discipline and the well-documented Austen congeniality created a contented and happy home atmosphere conducive to individual character development.

Leisurely visits to family relations in Kent, Berkshire, Bath, and London were also regularly made, usually at Christmas or during the summer months when pupils had gone home for the holidays. It was after such a visit in 1788 that Mr Austen's niece, Eliza, Comtesse de Feuillide, wrote from London to her cousin, Philadelphia Walter, giving a charming glimpse of her uncle at that time:

> What did you think of my Uncle's looks? I was much pleased with them, and if possible he appeared more amiable than ever to me. What an excellent & pleasing man he is; I love him most sincerely as indeed I do all of the family.[28]

The last five of the Austens' eight children were born at Steventon: Henry Thomas (1771), Cassandra Elizabeth (1773),

Francis William (1774), Jane, known as Jenny during her childhood (1775), and Charles John (1779). With the exception of Jane, each will be dealt with later in separate chapters.

As a farmer, Mr Austen employed a bailiff named John Bond, and it is concerning the latter that the first Lord Brabourne, Mr Austen's great-grandson, tells the following story:

> There is an anecdote extant relating to this worthy which may as well be told here: Mr Austen used to join Mr Digweed (his neighbour at Steventon Manor) in buying twenty or thirty sheep, and that all might be fair, it was their custom to open the pen, and the first half of the sheep which ran out were counted as belonging to the rector. Going down to the fold on one occasion after this process had been gone through, Mr Austen remarked one sheep among his lot larger and finer than the rest. 'Well, John,' he observed to Bond, who was with him, 'I think we have had the best of the luck with Mr Digweed to-day in getting that sheep.' 'Maybe not so much in the luck as you think, sir,' responded the faithful John. 'I see'd her the moment I come in, and set eyes on the sheep, so when we opened the pen I just giv'd her a "huck" with my stick, and out a [she] run.'[29]

Mr Austen lived to see his third son Edward installed as the squire of Godmersham. In a letter written by Jane Austen in October 1798, when she and her parents were returning home from their first visit to Edward at Godmersham, she included a delightful vignette of her father sitting in his room at the Bull and George in Dartford after a meal of beefsteak and boiled chicken, contentedly reading *The Midnight Bell*, a recently published Gothic thriller he had borrowed from a circulating library.[30] It is not recorded what Mr Austen thought of that particular book, but apparently he was as avid a novel reader as the rest of his family. Not only did he encourage his younger daughter's budding and sometimes boisterous literary talents, he also presented her with at least one of the three copy books, now known as *Volume the First*, *Volume the Second*, and *Volume the Third*, in which she set down her juvenile writings. One of these, a miniature comedy called *The Mystery*, is dedicated to her father.[31] This, and Jane Austen's other juvenilia, were apparently written for the general amusement of her family. But once she had begun to write seriously, her father took an even keener delight in her efforts, and when she had completed *First Impressions* he liked it so well he tried to arrange for its publication by the leading publishers, Cadell & Davies, in London. His letter offering to send them the manuscript has fortunately been preserved at St John's College. Although it has been printed many times since it first appeared in J. E. Austen-Leigh's *Memoir*, it has not hitherto been printed as Mr Austen actually wrote it:

Sirs
      I have in my possession a Manuscript Novel, comprised in three Vols. about the length of Miss Burney's *Evelina*. As I am well aware of what consequence it is that a work of this sort should make its' first appearance under a respectable name I apply to you. Shall be much obliged therefore if you will inform me whether you chuse to be concerned in it; what will be the expense of publishing at the Author's risk; & what you will advance for the Property of it, if on a perusal it is approved of?
      Should your answer give me encouragement I will send you the work.
      I am, Sirs, Yr. obt. hble Servt:

Geo Austen[32]

Steventon near Overton
      Hants
1st Novr. 1797

The letter is endorsed 'declined by Return of Post' in a bold clerical hand at the top of the sheet, which must have occasioned bitter disappointment to the young author and her kind father. But the temporary rebuff by Cadell & Davies was posterity's gain, for *First Impressions* was later considerably revised and rewritten and was launched on its triumphant career as *Pride and Prejudice* thirteen years later.
      Until the end of the eighteenth century it seemed likely that Mr Austen would remain rector of Steventon until his death. The rectory, which by that time had become a comfortable home, was constantly being improved. New furniture was bought, the latest books, including Boswell's *Life of Samuel Johnson* and William Cowper's poems, were ordered from Winchester for the rector's

library or for reading aloud to the family in the evenings, while elaborate plans were projected for the rectory grounds. Then, quite suddenly, Mr Austen decided to appoint his eldest son James as his representative at Steventon and to retire with his wife and two daughters to Bath. By then the once fashionable inland spa was being deserted by the aristocracy for newer and more stylish seaside resorts, and was fast becoming the haunt of persons like Mr Austen in search of a comfortable and convenient place in which to end their days.

Nothing has survived to indicate the reasons for George Austen's abrupt decision, but it seems likely that age was one factor. He was sixty-nine, and his wife was sixty-one, ages that were old for that time. Mrs Austen's health was not good, and the efforts to maintain her high standards of housekeeping were becoming increasingly exacting. A series of bad harvests throughout the south of England had also undoubtedly cut deeply into the rector's income. Last, but not least, Cassandra was twenty-six, and Jane was twenty-four. As both of them were still unmarried, their parents may have felt that their matrimonial chances would be better in Bath than in the country neighbourhood in which they had grown up.

The decision was made late in 1800 while both daughters were away from home, Cassandra in Kent, Jane visiting her friend Martha Lloyd at Ibthorp on the other side of Hampshire. When Jane and Martha returned to Steventon together late in December 1800, Mrs Austen greeted them with, 'Well, girls, it is all settled. We have decided to leave Steventon and go to Bath,' whereupon Jane is reported to have fainted from the shock.[33] That she was greatly disturbed by the suddenness of the decision is apparent from a letter written in April 1869 by Jane's niece, Caroline Austen, to her brother, James Edward Austen-Leigh, then engaged in writing the memoir of his aunt. 'My Aunt was very sorry to leave her native home, as I have heard my Mother relate,' she said, adding, 'My Mother who was present said my Aunt was greatly distressed. All things were done in a hurry by Mr Austen.'[34]

The last sentence is significant, for by the late spring of 1801 most of the rectory furnishings, including Mr Austen's library of upward of five hundred volumes and Jane Austen's pianoforte, had been inventoried for sale. After a visit to his son Edward at

Godmersham Mr Austen joined his wife and daughters for a summer holiday at Sidmouth, on the South Devon coast, after which they moved into their first Bath home at 4 Sydney Place. The next year their summer rambles included Dawlish and Teignmouth. Two years later, Mr and Mrs Austen and Jane stayed at Lyme Regis, from where Jane wrote to Cassandra:

> The Ball last night was pleasant, but not full for Thursday. My Father staid very contentedly till half-past-nine (we went a little after eight), and then walked home with James and a lanthorn, though I believe the lanthorn was not lit, as the moon was up, but this lanthorn may sometimes be a great convenience to him. My Mother and I stayed about an hour later.[35]

When the Austens returned to Bath from Lyme Regis they moved from Sydney Place to 27 Green Park Buildings. It was there, on 21 January 1805, that Mr Austen died peacefully after a brief illness at the age of seventy-three.

In her letter of 22 January 1805 to her brother Francis, Jane Austen said:

> 'Everything I trust & believe was done for him that was possible! — It has been very sudden! — within twenty four hours of his death he was walking with only the help of a stick, was even reading!... Except the restlessness & confusion of high Fever, he did not suffer — & he was mercifully spared from knowing that he was about to quit the Objects so beloved, so fondly cherished as his wife & Children ever were.[36]

The Revd George Austen was buried on 26 January 1805 in the crypt of Walcot Church, Bath, just inside the door leading from the graveyard. The gravestone has since been moved to a safer position in the church.[37] His memory was long cherished because of his gentleness, his strong attachment to his family, his scholarship, and his faithful performance of clerical duties. But his real distinction was an early and appreciative perception of Jane Austen's literary gifts.

Friends of Warren Hastings

GEORGE AUSTEN's sister, Mrs Philadelphia Hancock, and her daughter Eliza, Comtesse de Feuillide, later Mrs Henry Austen, were the exotic birds of passage in the otherwise stay-at-home Austen family. Philadelphia, who had lost her parents by the time she was seven, was befriended during her early life by her maternal aunt, Mrs John Cope Freeman, her step-mother having been, according to family tradition, unsympathetic towards her husband's children by his first marriage.[1] Nothing further is known concerning Philadelphia until November 1751, when, at the age of twenty-one, she petitioned the Court of Directors of the East India Company for permission to go to friends at Fort St David, a Company post in India on the Coromandel Coast. A similar petition was made at the same time by a Mary Elliott, presumably one of Philadelphia's friends.[2] The names of the friends at Fort St David that Philadelphia proposed to visit were not given. As she and Mary Elliott were both dowerless spinsters, it is likely they felt their chances of obtaining well-to-do husbands in India, where women of their class were rare, were more favourable. In Philadelphia's case, another speculation is possible. As Francis Austen, her wealthy uncle and guardian, acted over a long period as the English attorney for the man she married shortly after her arrival in India, it could be that she was shipped out to India by her uncle as a prospective bride for his bachelor client, a fairly common practice at that time.[3]

Both petitions were granted in December 1751, but Mary Elliott did not accompany Philadelphia to India, having in the meantime found a husband at home. In 1753, a year after Philadelphia had sailed for India, Mary Elliott married Captain John Buchanan, who had recently transferred from the regular army to the East India Company. After their marriage the Buchanans took passage for Bengal. Captain Buchanan died in the Black Hole of Calcutta in June 1756; his widow became the first wife of Warren Hastings, then a junior grade writer for the East India Company in Bengal.[4]

Meanwhile the *Bombay Castle*, with Philadelphia on board, had sailed for India in January 1752. Four months later, Charles Boddam, a friend of Robert Clive (later Baron Clive of Plassey), wrote from London to his friend, who was then rising to military prominence in India.[5] In announcing the departure of the *Bombay Castle*, Boddam wrote:

> 'There are eleven ladies coming out, viz. Mrs Keene and Mrs Edwards, two young ladies to Mrs Ackell, Miss Eliot [sic] and Miss Austin[sic], Miss Ross, a Scotch lady, and a prodigious fine girl it's said, and Miss Maskelyne, your friend's sister. The others I have not heard the names of, but however I would advise you to guard your heart well against them... these beauties will have a wonderful effect upon you.[6]

Boddam was in error in reporting Mary Elliott as being on board the *Bombay Castle*, but the Miss Maskelyne mentioned by him was Margaret Maskelyne who had gone out to India as Clive's prospective bride and was married to him at Fort St David on 18 February 1753.[7]

Four days later Philadelphia Austen married Tysoe Saul Hancock, a surgeon, 'Esteemed very skillful in that profession', at Cuddalore, a settlement a few miles south of Fort St David.[8] As the bridegroom was twenty years older than the bride (another reason for presuming the marriage had been pre-arranged), and the subsequent marital history of the Hancocks was far from ideal, it is tempting to speculate that the sixteen-year-old Jane Austen had her aunt and uncle in mind when, in 1792, after the death of both parties, she incorporated the following fragment of family history into her unfinished juvenile novel *Catharine or The Bower*:

> The eldest daughter had been obliged to accept the offer of one of her cousins to equip her for the East Indies, and tho' infinitely against her inclinations had been necessitated to embrace the only possibility that was offered to her, of a Maintenance;... Her personal Attractions had gained her a husband as soon as she had arrived at Bengal, and she had been married nearly a twelvemonth. Splendidly, yet unhappily married. United to a Man of double her own age, whose disposition was not amiable, and whose Manners were unpleasing, though his Character was respectable.[9]

Little is known concerning Tysoe Saul Hancock's early life except that he was born in 1711, and, according to his own testimony, had been 'a Coxcomb in my younger Years'.[10] By the late 1740s he was serving as a surgeon's mate for the East India Company in India, at which time he also 'Assisted in the King's Hospital at Cuddalore during the time the Sea and Land Forces were here.' In 1751 he was appointed surgeon at Dovecottah, a settlement about thirty miles south of Fort St David, and in 1752 he successfully treated Robert Clive for wounds received in April of the same year. This act of professional kindness gained him Clive's grateful friendship. One year later Hancock was listed as a surgeon at Fort St David, a post held until early in 1759, when at the instigation of Clive, then Governor of Bengal, he was appointed surgeon at Fort William, Calcutta.[11]

It was then the intimacy between the Hancocks and Warren Hastings and his family began. After serving as surgeon at Fort William for two years, Hancock resigned his post in November 1761 and entered into a mercantile partnership with Hastings, trading in salt, timber, carpets, Bihar opium, and rice for the Madras market. The social ties between the two families also became increasingly close, for when Mary Hastings died in July 1759, soon after the death of her infant daughter Elizabeth, it was presumably Philadelphia Hancock who persuaded Hastings to send his little son George to England to be cared for by her brother, the Revd George Austen. Later, on 22 December 1761, when the Hancocks' only child, Elizabeth, was born in Calcutta, Hastings became her godfather and gave her the name of his own little daughter who had died two years earlier.

The increasing familiarity between Hastings and the Hancocks, the great disparity of age between Hancock and Philadelphia, and the fact that the couple had been married almost nine years before their only child was born, raised all sorts of surmises in the close-knit, gossip-loving Calcutta of that time. These speculations led many to believe the relationship between the lonely and recently widowed Hastings and vivacious Philadelphia Hancock was more than a platonic friendship. The scandal did not surface, however, until Hastings and the Hancocks had returned to England in 1765. Even so, there are no indications in the surviving communications between Philadelphia and her daughter and Hastings that give credence to the story. But there is other undisputed contemporary evidence, to be presented later, to support the Calcutta tittle-tattle which claimed Elizabeth Hancock was the child of Philadelphia by Warren Hastings.

Meanwhile, the Hancocks occupied a prominent position in the Anglo-Indian society of Calcutta, a barbaric combination of transplanted English customs and institutions and oriental lavishness, while their bright and precocious daughter, whose name had now been altered from Elizabeth to Betsy, was described as a 'fine little girl' who took an impish delight in pulling the noses of her elders.[12] As for Philadelphia, there is also a record of her being the unintentional cause of scandal among Bengal's officialdom. This took place in 1763, when Henry Vansittart, who had replaced Clive as Governor of Bengal, took his wife and Philadelphia along when he went in state to confer with an important nawab. This action was a flagrant disregard of native custom and profoundly shocked high-caste Bengalis, for Hindu women of the class of Philadelphia Hancock and Mrs Vansittart never appeared in public.[13]

In the meantime serious trouble was brewing in Bengal between the resentful native princes and the rapacious servants of the East India Company. This eventually erupted in the bloody Bengal War, but before that broke out those whose foresight enabled them to sense the danger hastened to realize their assets and prepare to return to England. Among these were Hastings and Hancock. In December 1764 Hastings resigned his post with the East India Company, after which he joined the Hancocks and their native servants, Peter and Clarinda, and took passage for England on the *Medway*, disembarking in June 1765. It was then that Hastings is said to have learned that his little son George had died the previous autumn at George Austen's rectory.[14]

The Hancocks took a house in London in Norfolk Street, off the Strand, while Hastings finally settled close by in Essex Street. Meanwhile, Robert Clive, who had been raised to the Irish peerage as Baron Clive of Plassey, had been sent out to India in 1764 by the East India Company as governor and commander-in-chief of Bengal to right the disorders there. Shortly after Hastings and the Hancocks arrived home from India he wrote to Lady Clive, who was then living in England:

In no circumstances whatever keep company with Mrs Hancock for it is beyond a doubt that she abandoned herself to Mr Hastings, indeed, I would rather you had no acquaintance with the ladies who have been in India, they stand in such little esteem in England that their company cannot be of credit to Lady Clive.[15]

Clive's letter is dated 24 August and 29 September 1765 and is preserved in the Powis Collection. In commenting on it, Mark Bence-Jones says, 'These lines, though still legible, have been crossed out, almost certainly by Margaret [Lady Clive], who wished to preserve Philadelphia's good name, while knowing already that her child was rumoured to be by Warren Hastings.'[16]

As a dutiful wife, Lady Clive obeyed her husband's injunction to avoid Philadelphia Hancock, for it is a matter of record that she rebuffed Philadelphia's offers to renew their acquaintance in London. It is almost impossible today to discover all the facts in this case, but it is apparent from the surviving evidence that the scandal was agitated by Jenny Kelsall, a cousin of Lady Clive, whose husband, Sir Henry Strachey, was Clive's secretary. After his return to India in 1769, Hancock wrote to Philadelphia in London in November 1773:

You ought not, I think, [to] have hesitated to tell Mrs. Strachey that her Behavior to you while in India, which plainly proved her contempt of you, gave her no right to expect any favor from you. I am much mistaken if Lady Clive's most extraordinary Coolness be not owing to the Pride of that Woman. Surely I did enough for her when I saved her Life — her return for which was basest Ingratitude to you....[17]

Whether this slur on Philadelphia's good name or the question of the legitimacy of her child ever reached the ears of Jane Austen or other members of her family cannot now be definitely known. If it did, there must have been agreement among them that silence was better than angry refutation.

Tysoe Saul Hancock's dream of retiring in comfort in England did not materialize. Four years after his homecoming in 1765 he found it necessary to return alone to Bengal to attempt to recoup his fortunes. He was followed shortly afterwards by Warren Hastings, who had been appointed second-in-command at

Madras by the East India Company. It is perhaps significant that before Hastings embarked he left a substantial sum with Philadelphia to relieve her from financial embarrassment until she could receive remittances from her husband. Hancock's first letter from Calcutta, written in November 1769, is the beginning of a series now preserved in the British Library. The letters show a tired, lonely, and 'very infirm Old Man', who was already ill on his arrival in Bengal, where he discovered that a famine had wiped out a third of the population. Although Hancock was successful in securing an appointment as a supernumerary surgeon at Fort William, he was hampered from further advancement by an order forbidding his promotion. This forced him to resume the 'private practice of physic' which he loathed, but which guaranteed him a livelihood.[18] His dreams of increasing his fortunes in another way were also blocked because of his inability to obtain a licence to trade privately under the East India Company's protection.

Despite the gloomy tone of most of Hancock's letters to Philadelphia, they preserve a touching record of a foolishly fond old man whose primary concern was that his child, or the child he believed he had fathered, should be given every advantage to enable her to become a cultivated woman of the world. It is from Hancock's querulous admonishments concerning Betsy's cultural and practical progress and her heedless acceptance of her advantages that one begins to perceive for the first time the initial development of the self-willed woman who later played such an important role in the affairs of Jane Austen and her family.

Meanwhile Philadelphia, who was having a difficult time making ends meet on a very limited income, must have been hard-pressed to fulfil her husband's demands that Betsy be provided with an expensive Kirkman harpsichord and first-rate music masters; that she must be indulged with a small but elegant horse (although Hancock forbade her to ride to hounds as he considered it an 'indecent amusement for ladies'): and was to be well-grounded in calligraphy and arithmetic in addition to all the extra accomplishments then deemed necessary for a young lady of quality. At the same time, Philadelphia tried to make her husband's lot bearable with presents of Hollands gin, the latest London newspapers, embroidered waistcoats (which he refused to wear), a portrait of Betsy (which he criticized for being a poor likeness), and religious books (which he informed her with blunt rudeness he had 'neither the Time nor Inclination to read'). For his part, Hancock sent home presents of attar of roses, silver coins and gold mohurs 'quite new from the mint', bolts of fine muslin and more practical sheets and shifts, usually accompanied by the plea, 'Pray endeavour to keep Betsy's Recollection of me alive. I fear she will only remember me by the name of a Father.'[19]

It was a trying time emotionally as well as financially for Philadelphia, and there is evidence that she had to turn to her brother George Austen for occasional loans.[20] But she made the best of it by devoting most of her time to pampering her daughter, and by regular visits to Hampshire where she assisted Jane Austen's mother with her frequent pregnancies. On another occasion, when she was staying with her half-brother, William Hampson Walter, in Kent, her visit was considerably enlivened when one of his young sons became so infatuated with the already flirtatious Betsy that, as the latter recalled, 'he made verses on me in which he compared me to Venus & I know not what other Divinity, & played off fireworks in the cellar in honour of my charms'.[21]

By late 1771, when Betsy was ten, Philadelphia requested her husband to allow her to bring her daughter to Calcutta. Unfortunately Philadelphia's letter making this proposal is no longer extant, but Hancock's reply, written in September 1772, is quite emphatic in his refusal:

> I will now give you my opinion concerning Betsy's coming to India, — You know very well that no girl, tho' but fourteen years old, can arrive in India without attracting the notice of every Coxcomb in the Place, of whom there is very great plenty at Calcutta with very good persons & no other recommendation. You yourself know how impossible it is for a young girl to avoid being attached to a young handsome man whose address is agreeable to her. Debauchery under the polite name of gallantry is the reigning vice of the settlement.[22]

Shortly before Hancock wrote this letter Warren Hastings had been appointed Governor of Bengal by the East India Company. When he moved from Madras to Calcutta he resumed his former intimacy with Hancock, whom he discovered to be in such poor health that it was obvious he could do little to provide for his family in England; whereupon Hastings did something for

Philadelphia and Betsy to remove them from certain want should Hancock die penniless. Hastings took his old partner into his confidence, for in December 1772 Hancock wrote to Philadelphia:

> A few days ago Mr Hastings under the polite term of making his goddaughter a present made over to me a Respondentia bond for 40,000 rupees to be paid in China. I have given directions for the amount, which will be about £5,000 to be immediately remitted home to my attorneys... Tell Betsy only that her godfather has made her a great present, but not the particulars: let her write a proper letter on the occasion.[23]

Later, Hastings increased the gift to £10,000 to benefit both Philadelphia and Betsy, for in March 1775 Hancock wrote to Philadelphia:

> The enclosed paper will sufficiently shew the intentions of it, but I think it proper to explain to you that it is in lieu of what the Donor gave me in the name of Betsy... The interest of this money will produce to you while you shall live nearly £400 per annum; & the whole, should she marry, be a large fortune to Betsy after your death.[24]

After instructing Philadelphia to appoint her brother George Austen and Hastings's brother-in-law, John Woodman, as trustees for the gift, Hancock added pathetically: 'As you and the child are now provided for, I may venture to tell you that I am not well enough to write a long letter...'

Considered as a strictly friendly gesture, the settlement of £10,000 on Philadelphia Hancock and her daughter can easily be attributed to Hastings's generosity and high regard for his old commercial partner and his family. When regarded in the light of Clive's emphatic statement that Philadelphia had 'abandoned herself to Mr Hastings', however, it raises the question whether that was Hastings's way of repaying Philadelphia for her more than sympathetic response during his time of emotional need, as well as providing for the child resulting from the liaison.

In December 1774, a few months before he had notified Philadelphia of Hastings's gift, Hancock made his will, naming Hastings as one of his executors. One of his bequests is interesting as it seemingly reflects his rejection of the gossip concerning Philadelphia and Hastings:

> To my daughter Elizabeth I bequeath the miniature picture of her mother painted by Smart and set in a ring with diamonds around it which I request she will never part with as I intend it to remind her of her mother's virtues as well as of her person.[25]

Hancock died in Calcutta in November 1775 at the age of sixty-four, but the news of his death did not reach his wife in London until the following June. Fortunately Jane Austen's parents were staying with her when the bad news arrived. Later that month John Woodman wrote to Hastings:

> Since my letter to you on the 11th instant, Mrs Hancock has received yours confirming to her the death of Mr Hancock ... I am sorry to find Mr Hancock's affairs are in so bad a situation: all his effects will not more than clear his debts here.[26]

Hancock's lonely death in faraway India enabled his widow to carry out a plan she had considered for some time — that of taking Betsy to the Continent to complete her education and perhaps also to find her a suitable husband. It was also a good move for economic reasons: the £400 annual income from the trust Hastings had settled on her and her fifteen-year-old daughter enabled them to live more comfortably on the Continent, where the cost of living was cheaper than in England.

Philadelphia and Betsy, accompanied by their servant Clarinda, left England in 1777, living at first in Germany and Flanders. In 1778 they were in Brussels, but by the end of 1779 they had arrived in Paris, where, according to Betsy's airy letters to her cousin Philadelphia Walter in England, they moved in very genteel society.[27] By that time Betsy had modified her name again to the more fashionable one of Eliza, which she continued to use until her death. Her graphically descriptive but egotistical letters to Philadelphia Walter reveal a colourful, self-assured, young social butterfly whose superficiality was fortunately tempered with genuine family affection, particularly towards her mother and her uncle, Jane Austen's father.

It was for her uncle that she sat for a miniature in 1780, shortly after becoming a minor luminary of the elegant world of Paris and Versailles.[28] The small oval portrait depicts a self-confident young woman with piquant features and large dark eyes, wearing a fashionably low-cut white dress and a blue ribbon casually threaded through her upswept powdered hair. The vivacious portrait also bears out another characterization of Eliza as being 'a clever woman, and highly accomplished, after the French rather than the English mode'.[29] By the autumn of 1781, however, Eliza had other things to think of beside posing for miniatures for relations in England. She had become engaged to Jean Gabriel Capotte, Comte de Feuillide, a Captain of Dragoons in the Queen's regiment and a man ten years older than herself. The news was received by Jane Austen's father with mixed emotions as he feared the marriage would cause Eliza and her mother to give up their friends, their country, and even their religion.[30] It is therefore not surprising that he and John Woodman refused to comply when Philadelphia requested they relinquish their trusteeship of Warren Hastings's gift and transfer the money to Eliza and her husband for reinvestment in the French funds. This scheme disturbed George Austen so badly that he declared Eliza's fashionable new friends seemed 'already desirous of draining the mother of every shilling she has'.[31]

Meanwhile, Eliza rhapsodized to Philadelphia Walter concerning her husband:

It is too little to say he loves, since he literally adores me, ... & making my inclinations the guide of all his actions, the whole study of his life seems to be to contribute to the happiness of mine.[32]

While this temporary euphoria lasted Eliza entered whole-heartedly into the diversions of a society headed for revolution. Besides being able to turn a deft epistolary phrase, Eliza was also a skilful performer on the harpsichord and harp ('the latter is at present the fashionable instrument', she assured Philadelphia Walter), a talented and vivacious amateur actress, and a keen observer of the foibles of her acquaintances. It is therefore a pity her letters of that period to her Steventon relations have not been preserved, for if they were anything like those she wrote to Philadelphia Walter, they must have been a gold-mine of raw material for Jane Austen, whose first attempts at authorship began about that time.

It was presumably not before 1786, however, that eleven-year-old Jane met her fashionable cousin in person, at which time Eliza conceivably presented Jane with the set of Arnaud Berquin's *L'ami des enfans*, now in the Houghton Library at Harvard University.[33] This speculation is supported by the fact that volume five of the set not only contains Jane Austen's signature and the date 18 December 1786, but is also inscribed 'Pour dear Jane Austen' in another hand, supposedly Eliza's. As Eliza is known to have paid several extended visits to Steventon before the removal of Jane Austen and her parents to Bath in 1801, it is surmised that she also helped her talented young cousin to perfect her knowledge of French, introduced her to Italian, encouraged her musical abilities, and familiarized her with at least some of the fashionable French literature of the period. In reciprocation, after Jane Austen had completed *Love and Freindship* on 13 June 1790 she copied it into one of her notebooks, known as *Volume the Second*, with the dedication: 'To Madame La Comtesse De Feuillide This Novel is inscribed by Her obliged Humble Servant The Author.'[34]

Eliza and her mother had returned to England early in June 1786, as one of her letters, written in May of that year from France, stated she intended to spend a few days in London and then go on to Steventon.[35] But Eliza's plan to visit Hampshire during the summer months did not materialize, for having been in the last stages of pregnancy when she left France, she gave birth to her child in London on 25 June 1786. The Comte, who for some reason had been detained in France, had desired that the child be born in England. Unfortunately, the baby, a boy christened Hastings in honour of Warren Hastings, grew up mentally and physically handicapped.

Eliza had taken a house in Orchard Street in London, and had, according to her own description, become the 'greatest rake imaginable'.[36] This is supported not only by her own letters, but also by those of Philadelphia Walter, who frequently stayed with her. Eliza liked nothing better than having a good time, particularly if there were plenty of beaux in attendance. While her mother cared for little Hastings at home, Eliza drove around London in a 'coach with a coronet', attended Drawing Rooms at court, danced until dawn at Almack's and private balls given by the nobility, enjoyed the latest plays and operas as a guest in Warren Hastings's box at the theatre, and even took Philadelphia

Walter to Westminster Hall during the impeachment trial of
Hastings where they sat for hours on hard benches listening to
the oratory of Sheridan, Burke, and Charles James Fox.[37]

Christmas 1787 found Eliza at Steventon where her talents as
an amateur actress automatically made her the star in the holiday
theatricals arranged by her cousins, James and Henry Austen.
Both cousins, who were handsome young men, had already met
with Eliza's flirtatious approval, while they in turn were
completely captivated by her sophisticated gaiety. Eliza even
tried to persuade Philadelphia Walter to be one of the Steventon
acting party, but was turned down by her somewhat prim cousin,
who said: 'I should not have the courage to act a part, nor do I
wish to attain it'.[38] Philadelphia's refusal did not trouble Eliza
long for she was soon off to visit Warren Hastings and his second
wife Marion at Beaumont Lodge near Windsor. Later she
dropped in on her cousins James and Henry Austen at St John's
College, Oxford, and they drove over to Blenheim, where Eliza
was delighted with the park and exterior of the mansion, but
found 'the furniture very old fashioned & very shabby...'[39]

Eliza and her mother went to France late in 1788, but the
following year they were planning a return to England. This
apparently took place after the fall of the Bastille in July, for Eliza,
who reported that her nerves were 'exceedingly disordered' by
the violent turn of events, was still in Paris in February.[40] Eliza's
return to England with her mother and child late in 1789 or early
the next year was the beginning of a period of personal
tribulation. The Comte, 'a strong *Aristocrate* or Royalist in his
heart', was lending his support to the French princes of the blood
who had gathered at Turin to plot the overthrow of the
revolutionary government in Paris.[41] Her mother was in the first
stages of breast cancer, and her son was beginning to show signs of
abnormality. When the Comte finally joined her in London, he
found Eliza's mother near death.

Later, in October 1791, Philadelphia Walter wrote to her
brother James:

> Poor Eliza must be left at last friendless & alone. The gay and
> dissipated life she has long had so plentiful a share of has not
> ensur'd her friends among the worthy: on the contrary many
> who otherwise have regarded her have blamed her conduct and

will now resign her acquaintance. I always felt concerned and pitied her thoughtlessness. I have frequently looked forward to the approaching awful period, and regretted the manner of her life, & the mistaken results of my poor aunt's intended, well-meant kindness: she will soon feel the loss & her want of domestic knowledge.[42]

Philadelphia Hancock died in London on 26 February 1792, after which the Comte took Eliza to Bath. As she found little solace there they returned to London, where the Comte was notified that if he did not return to France immediately he would be considered an *émigré* and his property would be confiscated.

Not long after his return to Paris Eliza's husband found himself in serious trouble with the revolutionary government. In 1793 the Marquise de Marboeuf was accused of conspiring against the republic, one of the chief charges against her being that on her estate near Meaux she had planted arable land with lucerne, sainfoin and clover rather than edible crops, with the object of producing a famine. The Marquise was arrested and imprisoned in the Conciergerie in Paris. To defend herself she published a memorial of her case, stating she was not guilty of the accusation, and adding that even if she had been she had a right to do what she liked with her own land. The reply did not please her accusers, and it became obvious that unless she could enlist the help of someone in authority her plea would fall on deaf ears. At that point, the Comte de Feuillide, a friend of the Marquise, tried to help her. But when he attempted to bribe one of the secretaries of the Committee of Safety to destroy the evidence and to use his influence to secure the release of the Marquise, the man betrayed him to the Committee and he was arrested. The Marquise was tried and was condemned to death. Shortly afterwards the Comte de Feuillide was also tried on the charge of bribery and suborning witnesses. When the Committee chose to believe the evidence against him, he also received the death sentence on 22 February 1794 and was sent to the guillotine the same day. The record of the trial reveals he was forty-three at the time of his death; that he had contracted considerable debts between 1784 and 1793 in his own name as well as that of his wife, 'Dame Elizabeth Hancock', and that one of the witnesses who gave evidence against him at his trial was 'la citoyenne Grandville, l'ancienne maîtresse de Feuillide'.[43]

It is not known where Eliza was staying when the news of her husband's death reached her. Judging from her strong attachment to her uncle George Austen, however, it is reasonable to suppose that sooner or later she sought the comfort of his sympathetic family at Steventon. The horror that had overtaken the Comte de Feuillide during the Reign of Terror also had a profound effect on the passionately English eighteen-year-old Jane Austen. From then on she heartily detested the French. It was an antipathy she never overcame, for in September 1816, in a letter to Cassandra, she mentioned that the second son of her good friend Mrs Lefroy of Ashe Rectory had just returned from a trip across the Channel: 'He is come back from France, thinking of the French as one could wish, disappointed in everything.'[44]

Eliza did not long mourn her guillotined husband; her surviving letters reveal only too plainly that she thoroughly enjoyed the role of flirtatious merry widow. Her conduct at that time was also a matter of great concern for Jane Austen's parents, as they were aware she was dallying with the affections of their susceptible sons, James and Henry, while casting about for richer or more eligible matrimonial prospects.

The Leigh heritage

LEIGH

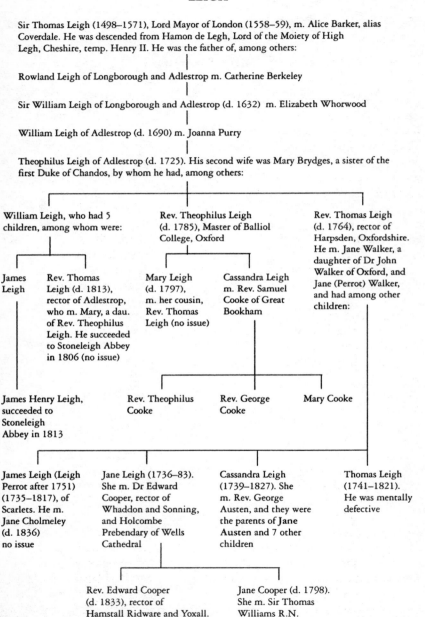

Sir Thomas Leigh (1498–1571), Lord Mayor of London (1558–59), m. Alice Barker, alias Coverdale. He was descended from Hamon de Legh, Lord of the Moiety of High Legh, Cheshire, temp. Henry II. He was the father of, among others:

Rowland Leigh of Longborough and Adlestrop m. Catherine Berkeley

Sir William Leigh of Longborough and Adlestrop (d. 1632) m. Elizabeth Whorwood

William Leigh of Adlestrop (d. 1690) m. Joanna Purry

Theophilus Leigh of Adlestrop (d. 1725). His second wife was Mary Brydges, a sister of the first Duke of Chandos, by whom he had, among others:

William Leigh, who had 5 children, among whom were:

Rev. Theophilus Leigh (d. 1785), Master of Balliol College, Oxford

Rev. Thomas Leigh (d. 1764), rector of Harpsden, Oxfordshire. He m. Jane Walker, a daughter of Dr John Walker of Oxford, and Jane (Perrot) Walker, and had among other children:

James Leigh

Rev. Thomas Leigh (d. 1813), rector of Adlestrop, who m. Mary, a dau. of Rev. Theophilus Leigh. He succeeded to Stoneleigh Abbey in 1806 (no issue)

Mary Leigh (d. 1797), m. her cousin, Rev. Thomas Leigh (no issue)

Cassandra Leigh m. Rev. Samuel Cooke of Great Bookham

James Henry Leigh, succeeded to Stoneleigh Abbey in 1813

Rev. Theophilus Cooke

Rev. George Cooke

Mary Cooke

James Leigh (Leigh Perrot after 1751) (1735–1817), of Scarlets. He m. Jane Cholmeley (d. 1836) no issue

Jane Leigh (1736–83). She m. Dr Edward Cooper, rector of Whaddon and Sonning, and Holcombe Prebendary of Wells Cathedral

Cassandra Leigh (1739–1827). She m. Rev. George Austen, and they were the parents of Jane Austen and 7 other children

Thomas Leigh (1741–1821). He was mentally defective

Rev. Edward Cooper (d. 1833), rector of Hamstall Ridware and Yoxall. He m. Caroline Lybe Powys

Jane Cooper (d. 1798). She m. Sir Thomas Williams R.N.

The aristocratic Leighs

THE LEIGHS of Cheshire, from whom Jane Austen was descended on the maternal side, were a much more aristocratic and colourful family than the somewhat staid Austens of Kent. Their long lineage extending back in English history to Hamon de Legh, Lord of the Moiety of High Legh in Cheshire at the time of Henry II, need not detain us further than to mention that Sir Thomas Leigh (1498-1571), Jane Austen's most important maternal ancestor (her grandfather six times removed), was descended from that line.[1] Sir Thomas was also the common ancestor of some of the most important people in English history.[2] Whether Jane Austen was aware of her kinship with many of the more notable figures of her time cannot now be definitely known. As detailed accounts of the Leigh family and its ramifications were available in all the contemporary published peerages, and as Mrs Austen was proud of her family background, it is more than likely that Jane knew of at least some of these exalted relationships.

Born during the reign of Henry VII, Thomas Leigh, who was descended from several ancestors who had distinguished themselves at Crécy and Agincourt,[3] was a son of Roger Leigh of Wellington, Shropshire, and a younger brother of William Leigh, a gentleman usher to Henry VIII. Thomas came at an early age to London where he was articled to Sir Thomas Seymer, a member of the powerful Mercers' Company. After serving his apprenticeship he was admitted as a freeman of the Mercers' Company in 1526.[4] Ten years later the poor but well-born boy who had come to London to make his fortune was appointed a Justice of the Peace for his native Shropshire.

Young Leigh's business acumen had been noticed by Sir Rowland Hill, a wealthy member of the Mercers' Company who, in 1549, is said to have been the first Protestant to serve as Lord Mayor of London.[5] Leigh was employed by Sir Rowland as his 'factor beyond sea'.[6] His performance was so satisfactory that Sir Rowland gave him in marriage his favourite niece, Alice, daughter of John Barker, *alias* Coverall, of Wolverton, Shropshire. Later, at his death, Sir Rowland left her the greater part of his property. Dame Alice Leigh outlived her husband thirty-two years, dying in January 1603 at Stoneleigh Abbey, the Warwickshire home of her second son, Sir Thomas Leigh II, 'having seen her children's children to the fourth generation'.[7] Leigh was Master of the Mercers' Company in 1554, 1558 and 1564, an alderman and sheriff of London, and was elected Lord Mayor on 28 October 1558.[8] When Queen Mary Tudor died less than a month later, Leigh, as Lord Mayor, lost no time in having Elizabeth proclaimed queen 'at the Crosse in Cheape, and other places of the citye'[9] in the presence of large crowds of nobles and citizens.

Holinshed's *Chronicles* furnish two colourful vignettes of Leigh's participation in the activities preceding and following the coronation that ushered in Elizabeth's forty-four-year reign. On 12 January 1559, when Elizabeth 'remooued from hir palace of Westminster by water vnto the tower of London', she was accompanied on the Thames by a flotilla of gaily bedecked craft led by the Lord Mayor's barge equipped with cannon 'shooting off lustilie as they went, with great and pleasant melodie of instruments, which plaied in most sweet and heauenlie manner'.[10] Later, at the coronation banquet in Westminster Hall on 15 January 1559, Leigh, who acted as 'Butler to that high feast', again played a prominent role. Holinshed recorded:

> Now after this, at the serving vp of the wafers, the lord maior of London went to the cupboord, and filling a cup of gold with ipocrasse, bare it to the queene: and kneeling before hir took the assaie, and she reciuing it of him, and drinking of it, gaue the cup with the couer vnto the said lord maior for his fee, which cup and couer weied sixteene ounces Troie weight.[11]

Leigh's loyalty and the pains he took in his official capacity to add splendour to the coronation festivities were rewarded shortly afterwards when Elizabeth knighted him during his mayoralty. Sir Thomas died twelve years later on 17 November 1571 and was buried in the Mercers' Chapel. The handsome monument erected to his memory by his widow was destroyed during the Great Fire of London in 1666. Fortunately the rhymed epitaph was copied down before its destruction:

Sir Thomas Leigh bi civil life
All offices did beare,
  Which in this City worshipfull
  Or honourable were:
Whom as God blessed with great wealth,
So losses did he feele:
Yet never chang'd he constant minde,
Tho' Fortune turn'd her wheele.
  Learning he lov'd and helpt the poore,
  To them that knew him deere;
For whom his Lady and loving wife
This Tomb hath builded here.[12]

Interestingly, Jane Austen's famous Elizabethan ancestor is still remembered in London over four centuries after his death by a magnificent silver-gilt cup (not the one presented to him by Queen Elizabeth at her coronation banquet) which he bequeathed to the Mercers' Company, and which is still used at the election of new wardens. Known as the 'Leigh Cup', it bears the hallmark for 1499-1500, and is, with the exception of the Anathema cup at Pembroke College, Cambridge, the earliest surviving hanap or covered cup bearing an English hallmark.[13] In leaving the cup to the Mercers' Company, Sir Thomas Leigh described it this way in his will:

I give and bequeath to my loveing brethren, the Company of Mercers, one faire cupp, or standing cupp of silver, all guilt, garnished with maidenheads, roses and flaggins [flagons] with a cover of the like work, enameled blew, as the boddy of the cupp is, with posies therein graven, of letters guilt and a maiden in the knopp with a unicorne fawning on her lap, and the same cupp I give them, to use it at the chooseing of the Wardens of the Company, if they shall thinke it soe good.

True to Sir Thomas Leigh's wishes, the following inscription was incorporated in the elaborate decoration: TO ELECT — THE MASTER — OF THE — MERCERIE — HITHER AM — I SENT — AND BY — SIR THOMAS LEIGH — FOR THE — SAME — ENTENT.[14]
Sir Thomas and Dame Alice Leigh were the parents of three sons, Rowland Leigh of Longborough and Adlestrop, Glou-

cestershire, from whom Jane Austen was descended; Sir Thomas Leigh II of Stoneleigh Abbey, Warwickshire; and Sir William Leigh of Newnham Regis, Warwickshire; and four daughters, Mary, Alice, Katherine, and Winifred Leigh.[15]

Sir Thomas Leigh II of Stoneleigh, ancestor of the Lords Leigh of the first creation, had two daughters whose husbands played prominent roles in English history. Katherine, the eldest, was the wife of Robert Catesby, one of the principal conspirators in the Gunpowder Plot.[16] Alice, a younger daughter, married Sir Robert Dudley, the son of Robert Dudley, Earl of Leicester, Queen Elizabeth's favourite. The younger Dudley deserted his wife and frisked off to the Continent in 1605 in the company of his mistress, the beautiful Elizabeth Southwell, who disguised herself as his page. Many years later, Dudley's deserted wife, the former Alice Leigh, was created Duchess Dudley in her own right by Charles I. She is buried in a magnificent tomb at Stoneleigh.[17]

Her father, Sir Thomas Leigh II, was also the grandfather of Sir Thomas Leigh III, of whom Jane Austen, an ardent admirer of the Stuarts, would have approved. He was created Baron Leigh of Stoneleigh in July 1643 by Charles I in recognition of his loyalty to the royal cause:

> Before the King had set up his Standard at Nottingham, he march'd to *Coventry*, but finding the Gates shut against him, and no Summons could prevail with the Mayor and Magistrates to open them, he went the same night to *Stoneley*, the house of Sir *Thomas Leigh*, where, as my Lord *Clarendon* observes, he was well received.[18]

Later, as a punishment for his loyalty to the King, Sir Thomas was required to pay £4,895 to the Cromwellian government in order to retain his estates.

Sir William Leigh, the youngest son of Sir Thomas and Dame Alice Leigh, was the grandfather of Sir Francis Leigh, Earl of Chichester, another loyal cavalier. His descendants included William Pitt the Elder, the first Earl of Chatham; his son, William Pitt the Younger, who was Prime Minister of Great Britain for much of Jane Austen's lifetime; and Lady Hester Stanhope, the celebrated Oriental traveller and eccentric.[19]

Winifred Leigh, the youngest daughter of Sir Thomas and Dame Alice Leigh, had equally distinguished descendants. She married Alderman Sir George Bond, Lord Mayor of London at the time of the Spanish Armada. One of their daughters, Rosa Bond, married William Hale of King's Walden, Hertfordshire, from whom William Lamb, second Viscount Melbourne, Queen Victoria's first Prime Minister, was descended. Genealogical purists might object to this statement, for it was common gossip that the first Lady Melbourne was the mother of William Lamb, second Viscount Melbourne, by George Wyndham, third Earl of Egremont. However, so long as William Lamb is listed in the standard peerages as the legitimate son of Sir Peniston Lamb, first Viscount Melbourne, it seems only fair to be charitable as far as his lady, the former Elizabeth Milbanke, is concerned.[20]

The descendants of Dionysia Bond, another daughter of Sir George Bond and the former Winifred Leigh, were equally celebrated. Dionysia married Sir Henry Winston, and their daughter Sarah became the wife of John Churchill of Wootton Glanville. Their son, Sir Winston Churchill, married Elizabeth Drake, and they in turn were the parents of John Churchill, the first Duke of Marlborough, from whom Sir Winston Churchill (1874-1965) was descended.[21]

Rowland Leigh of Longborough and Adlestrop, the eldest son of Sir Thomas and Dame Alice Leigh and the ancestor of Jane Austen as well as the present Lords Leigh of the second creation, was content to live the quiet life of a Gloucestershire country squire while his brothers and younger sister were hob-nobbing with the mighty. His second wife, from whom Jane Austen was descended, was Catherine Berkeley, a daughter of Sir Richard Berkeley of Stoke Giffard, Gloucester,[22] a member of a cadet branch of the well-known family of the same name that had held Berkeley Castle in Gloucestershire since the eleventh century. Their son and heir was Sir William Leigh (c. 1585-1632), who was knighted in 1624. He married Elizabeth, a daughter of Sir William Whorwood of Sandwell Castle, Staffordshire. She outlived her husband for thirty-four years, during which time her house at Longborough, according to the Leigh family chronicle, 'proved a staunch asylum to every friend of the royal cause'.[23] Sir William and his wife are buried beneath a handsome stone canopied tomb in Longborough Church that includes their life-sized effigies dressed in the elaborate costumes of their period.

Sir William was succeeded by his eldest son, William Leigh

(1604-90), who took up his residence at nearby Adlestrop, where he laid out extensive pleasure gardens 'ornamented with a canal, fountain and several alcoves, and expensive showy summer houses, one decorated with historic painting'.[24] Unfortunately these were all swept away by Humphrey Repton, the fashionable 'improver', during Jane Austen's lifetime.[25] As communications between the Leighs of Adlestrop and the Steventon Austens were fairly frequent when these alterations were taking place, it is interesting to speculate that the idea of employing Repton at Sotherton, Mr Rushworth's fine estate in *Mansfield Park*, originated in Jane Austen's indignation over similar 'improvements' to William Leigh's pleasant, old-fashioned garden at Adlestrop.

William Leigh's marriage to Joanna Pury, a daughter of Thomas Pury of the City of Gloucester, is a romantic episode that deserves mention. As High Sheriff of Gloucester, William Leigh was required to collect the hated Ship Money tax imposed by Charles I that enabled him to run the country without summoning Parliament. When the Royalist cause was defeated William Leigh was arrested by his enemies, his estates were confiscated, and he was thrown into Gloucester Gaol, the governor of which was Thomas Pury. When Joanna 'heard of and pitied Mr Leigh's sufferings', the two lovers planned and effected a private marriage. According to tradition, Pury was not long in forgiving them, and because of his influence with the Cromwellian government Leigh 'was pardoned in consideration of the merits of the wife's family', and his estates were restored to him. The marriage was obviously one of affection, for Leigh always began his letters to his wife with 'My dere Harte', and it is further recorded that they lived for many years at Adlestrop as 'patterns of conjugal happiness and greatly respected in their vicinage'.[26]

Joanna Leigh is also remembered in the family chronicle by a charming anecdote no doubt well known to Jane Austen. In her youth, Joanna and her sisters, staunch Royalists despite their father's Parliamentary leanings, had a lady's maid named Anne Clarges who later rose in the world and married General George Monck who played an important role in the restoration of Charles II in 1660. One source suggests Monck's changeover from the Cromwellian to the Stuart side was frequently 'quickened with a curtain lecture' by his wife,[27] who had been imbued earlier with strong royalist principles by the ladies of the Pury family.

After the restoration of Charles II and the elevation of General Monck to the Dukedom of Albemarle, Joanna Leigh, who was staying at Oxford, drove to London in her 'cumbrous old chariot' drawn by 'four heavy plough horses' to pay a courtesy call on the new Duchess. The family chronicle relates:

When Mrs Leigh first attended her Grace's circle, she [the Duchess] exhibited an uncommon mark of polite humility. Somewhat hurried on her first entrance, Mrs Leigh could not unpin the long train of her gown, which was indispensable on those occasions. The court ladies enjoyed the country lady's embarrassment (for then they were quite a different species of beings) upon which her Grace stepping forward cried, 'Suffer me, my good friend, to adjust the train. You know formerly it was my business to pin it up.'[28]

William and Joanna Leigh were the parents of Theophilus Leigh of Adlestrop (*c.* 1643-1725), Jane Austen's great-grandfather, whose eccentricities were no doubt remembered in the Steventon rectory circle. Theophilus was recalled by the family chronicler as an excellent though strict parent who liked to sit by the fire in a great chair, wearing a high fur morning cap, deep in the study of 'judicial Astrology'.[29] He was also remembered as a very polite and accomplished man who had received a liberal education and had travelled on the Continent before settling down as the squire of Adlestrop. Although he was not a member of the Court of Charles II, 'he was much acquainted with many of those gay people who surrounded that joyous monarch', imbibed much of their style, and to the day of his death retained the long cravat and the large black wig fashionable at the time of the Merry Monarch.

'He had the low bow (even to adoration) for his superiors and for the ladies;' the family chronicle relates, 'he had the running bow, the collected bow, the blowing out of the cheeks, the sweep of the chin over the cravat, which, distinguishing the sovereign, was imitated by the *then* people of *ton*.'[30] A good horseman with a well-stocked stable of Turkish or Arabian grey Galloways, he was also in the habit of riding out to visit his neighbours 'in great parade, ornamented with a broad belt or hanger'.[31] Theophilus, who was a staunch champion of the Stuarts, never reconciled himself to the Glorious Revolution of 1688, and to the end of his days refused to acknowledge George I as his sovereign. The family chronicle continues:

> His dinners were the same every day in each week, allowing for seasons, and his sons often took care to ride from Oxford to meet the Thursday's boiled rump. Till after they had taken their Bachelor's degree they always continued their custom of rising as soon as they had dined and forming a row in the Dining Parlour, till desired to sit down and drink Church and King.[32]

— the king in this instance being James II, and after his death the Old Pretender.

Theophilus Leigh was married twice. His second wife (Jane Austen's great-grandmother) was the Hon. Mary Brydges. They were married in November 1689 in the Chapel of Henry VII in Westminster Abbey, the bride being twenty-two years younger than her husband.[33] Mary Brydges was the eldest daughter of Sir James Brydges (1642-1714), eighth Lord Chandos of Sudeley, at one time British Ambassador to Turkey.[34] Her mother was Elizabeth Barnard (1642-1719), a daughter of Sir Henry Barnard, a rich London Turkey merchant. Mary Brydges was also the sister of James Brydges, the first Duke of Chandos, 'the principal profiteer out of the War of Spanish Succession... who had paid the accounts as Paymaster-General to the Forces of Marlborough's overseas armies and kept a good deal of the change.'[35] It was this ostentatious brother of Mary Leigh whose magnificence of living at Cannons, his splendid baroque mansion near London, gained him the double-edged nickname of 'princely' Chandos. He was also remembered in Jane Austen's mother's family as the husband of Cassandra Willoughby,[36] the second of his three wives, whose Christian name was a favourite for generations of the Leigh family, including not only Jane Austen's mother but also her sister.

Mary (Brydges) Leigh was also directly descended from Sir John Brydges (*c.* 1490-1556), first Baron Chandos, a member of an ancient family who was Lieutenant of the Tower of London at the time of the accession of Queen Mary Tudor.[37] He took an active part in the suppression of Wyatt's Rebellion, and on 12

February 1554 attended Lady Jane Grey on the scaffold. At that time she presented him with her prayer book (now preserved in the British Library) in which she had written him a personal message:

> Forasmutche as you have desired so simple a woman to wrighte in so worthy a booke, gode Mayster Lieuftenante, therefore, I shalle as a friende desyre you, and as a Christian require you, to call uppon God, to encline youre harte to his lawes, to quicken you in his waye, and not to take the worde of trewethe utterlye oute of your mouthe. Lyve stylle to dye, that by deathe you may purchase eternall life; and remember howe the ende of Mathusael, whoe as we reade in the scriptures, was the longeste liver that was of a manne, died at the laste. For, as the Preacher sayeth, there is a tyme to be borne, and a tyme to dye; and the daye of death is better than the day of our birthe. Youres as the Lord Knoweth as a frende, Jane Duddeley.[38]

Fourteen years after the marriage of Theophilus Leigh and Mary Brydges, during which time she bore him twelve children, her mother made this entry in her family register:

> My most dear daughter Leigh departed this life within one hour after she was safe brought to bed of her daughter Ann, the aforesaid, the 13th of June 1703 & was buried the 14th, at night, in their burying place at Adlestrop, being 37 years & four months wanting four days old. She left six sons and five daughters living.[39]

Only two of the sons are important in the Jane Austen story. The first was Dr Theophilus Leigh (1693-1785), Master of Balliol College, Oxford, for more than half a century, and also Vice Chancellor of Oxford University. His dry wit, a characteristic of the Leighs, was shared by his great-niece Jane Austen. The second was the Revd Thomas Leigh (1696-1764), rector of Harpsden, Oxfordshire, and Jane Austen's grandfather.

Dr Theophilus Leigh, who was praised by a contemporary as 'a little tiny man with a huge bagge full of sense in his head and many packets of good humor in his pockets',[40] was also called that 'famous Wight yclep'd Pimp Leigh'[41] by one of his detractors. But derogatory criticism did not seem to trouble him, for he went about his way until his death at the age of ninety-two, enlivening the dulness of the university of his time with dubious puns and scholarly jests that were relished for generations in Jane Austen's family. Dr Leigh's reputation for wit was not confined to Oxford. On one occasion Mrs Thrale sent a query concerning him to Dr Samuel Johnson. The mistress of Streatham Park referred to Dr Leigh in her letter as 'Dr Lee', but there can be no doubt that she meant the witty Theophilus. 'Are you acquainted with Dr Lee, the Master of Balliol College,' Mrs Thrale asked, 'and are you not delighted with his gaiety of manners and youthful vivacity, now that he is eighty-six years of age? I never heard a more perfect or excellent pun than his, when some one told him how, in a late dispute among the Privy Councillors, the Lord Chancellor struck the table with such violence that he split it. "No, no, no," replied the Master; "I can hardly persuade myself that he *split* the *table*, though I believe he *divided* the *Board*." '[42]

On another occasion when Leigh was visiting a notoriously un-bookish Oxford friend, he was asked to inspect a room overlooking the busy Bath Road. When the man flung open the door and announced 'This, Doctor, I call my study,' a quick glance showed Leigh that the room was conspicuous for its lack of books of any kind. Turning to his host, Leigh quipped, 'And very well named too, sir, for you know Pope tells us, "The proper *study* of mankind is *Man*." '[43] Even the approach of death did not alter Dr Leigh's ability to 'shoot folly as it flies', for upon being informed three days before he died that an old friend had lately been married, having recovered from a long illness by eating eggs, and that the wits said he had been egged on to matrimony, the incorrigible old punster observed, 'Then may the yoke sit easy on him'.[44]

The Revd Thomas Leigh, Jane Austen's maternal grandfather, was of a more tranquil nature than his colourful elder brother. 'He was one of the most contented, quiet, sweet-tempered, generous, cheerful men I ever knew, and his wife was his counterpart,' the chronicler of the Leigh family recorded. 'The spirit of the pugnacious Theophilus dwelt not in him; nor that eternal love of company which distinguished the other brothers, yet he was by no means unsocial.'[45] Born at Adlestrop in December 1696, Thomas Leigh went up to Christ Church, Oxford, at the early age of sixteen, at which time he was nicknamed 'Chick Leigh' because of his youthful appearance.[46]

Two years later he was elected a Fellow of All Souls College, Oxford, where he received his Bachelor of Arts degree in 1716 and his Master of Arts degree in 1720. He was also made a Bachelor of Divinity in 1741, but that was almost ten years after he had accepted the living of Harpsden. He remained rector there until his death in January 1764 in Bath, where he had gone to seek treatment for the gout. In 1731, the year he became rector of Harpsden, he married Jane Walker (1704-68), a daughter of Dr John Walker, an Oxford physician, who had married Jane Perrot (d. 1709), a connection that later was to prove valuable to two of Jane Austen's brothers.

Jane Perrot was a grand-daughter of James Perrot, gentleman, of Northleigh, Oxfordshire (1607-87), who married Anne Dale, a daughter of George Dale, doctor-of-law, of Somerset, whose wife, before her marriage, was Mary Leach. She in turn was a daughter of William Leach and Anne, a daughter of John Bridgeman and Mary White. Mary White was a sister of Sir Thomas White (1492-1567), Lord Mayor of London in 1553 and the founder of St John's College, Oxford.[47] It was Sir Thomas White of whom it was said, 'whithersoever he went, left the finger-marks of his charity behind him'.[48]

At the time St John's was founded in the middle years of the sixteenth century, Sir Thomas White specified that any youth in the generations coming after him who could prove descent from his family would be entitled to a Founder's Kin scholarship at the college. A little over two hundred years later, when Jane Austen's eldest brother James was ready to go up to Oxford in 1779, he produced a carefully worked out pedigree that established his right to a Founder's Kin scholarship at St John's College through Sir Thomas White's sister, Mary (White) Bridgeman, his grandmother seven times removed. This pedigree is still preserved in the College archives. Later, in 1788, Henry Austen was also awarded a Founder's Kin scholarship on the basis of the same pedigree.[49]

Little is known concerning Dr John Walker, Jane Leigh's father, except that he was responsible for the demolition of a famous Oxford medieval landmark:

> On Friday last was pull'd down the famous Postern Gate in Oxford, call'd the Turl Gate commonly (being a Corruption for Therold Gate), wch was done by the means of one Dr

Walker, a Physician, who lives by it, and pretends that 'twas a Detrimt to his House.[50]

Of Jane Perrot, Dr Walker's wife, there is more to tell. A daughter of James Perrot (1652-1724) of the Middle Temple, London, and Northleigh in Oxfordshire, and his wife, Anne Dawtry, she was directly descended from Robert Perrot (d. 1550), Bachelor of Music and organist at Magdalen College, Oxford, and a member of an ancient Pembrokeshire family, and Alice, a daughter of Robert Gardiner of Sunningwell, Berkshire.[51] Although Robert Perrot is reputed to have composed a good deal of liturgical music before the Reformation, none of his compositions has survived. Like Dr John Walker of Oxford, however, he seems to have had a passion for demolishing medieval buildings. Upon the dissolution of the monasteries under Henry VIII he purchased Rewley Abbey near Oxford, had it torn down, and sold the materials for building purposes in Oxford. Robert Perrot had also at one time been Principal of Trinity Hall, Oxford, a religious house before the dissolution, at which time it was converted into an inn. Later, Perrot obtained a lease of the house and chapel from the municipality of Oxford, demolished them, and 'in the same place built a barn, a stable, and a hog stie'.[52]

The Revd Thomas Leigh, Jane Austen's grandfather, was buried in the graveyard of Walcot Church, Bath, on 24 January 1764. His widow died on 29 August 1768, and was buried at Steventon.[53] Thomas and Jane Leigh were the parents of six children, all born at Harpsden, only four of whom are concerned in Jane Austen's family history: James, (later James Leigh Perrot) (1735-1817); Jane (1736-83); Cassandra (1739-1827), Jane Austen's mother; and Thomas (1747-1821). The other two, Anne (1734-8), and Mary (1737), died young.

Of Thomas Leigh, Mrs Austen's youngest brother, little is known except that he grew up mentally deficient. He did not live at home but was cared for outside the family. One of the few surviving references to Thomas in the Austen family records is a mention of him as 'our unfortunate uncle' made in a letter written in May 1822 by Charles, Jane's youngest brother.[54] Thomas Leigh was twenty-eight when Jane Austen was born; he outlived her, dying at the age of seventy-four in December 1821.

Jane Leigh was the beauty of the family. In 1768 she married Edward Cooper (1727-92), a well-to-do Anglican clergyman, of

Southcote, near Reading, who was vicar of Sonning, Berkshire, rector of Whaddon, near Bath, and Holcombe Prebendary of Wells. They were the parents of two children, Jane Austen's only first cousins on the maternal side: Edward Cooper (1770-1833), a well-known evangelical preacher and rector of Hamstall Ridware and Yoxall in Staffordshire; and Jane (1771-98), a school companion of Jane and Cassandra Austen and a frequent visitor to Steventon, where she was married in December 1792 to Captain Thomas Williams of the Navy. She was killed in a carriage accident on the Isle of Wight in August 1798. Jane Austen liked her and dedicated two of her juvenilia, *Henry and Eliza*,[55] and *A Collection of Letters*,[56] to her. Jane did not approve of her cousin Edward Cooper's sermons, however, and criticized them as being too full of 'Regeneration & Conversion ... with the addition of his zeal in the cause of the Bible Society.'[57]

The Rector's sprack-witted wife

JANE AUSTEN was singularly fortunate in her intellectual heritage. From her scholarly father she received elegance of mind, serene rationality, objectivity, and discerning appreciation of the niceties of style. From her clever mother she derived lively wit, ironic humour, and an accurate perception of character. The combination, enlivened by her own genius, was a powerful one.

According to her grand-daughter Anna, Mrs Austen was:

> A little, slight woman, with fine, well-cut features, large grey eyes, and good eyebrows, but without any brightness of complexion. She was amusingly particular about people's noses, having a very aristocratic one herself, which she had the pleasure of transmitting to a good many of her children. . . . She was a quick-witted woman with plenty of sparkle and spirit in her talk, who could write an excellent letter, either in prose or verse, making no pretence to poetry but being simply playful common sense in rhyme.[1]

J. E. Austen-Leigh remembered his grandmother thus:

> In Mrs Austen also was to be found the germ of much of the ability which was concentrated in Jane, but of which others of her children had a share. She united strong common sense with a lively imagination, and often expressed herself, both in writing and conversation, with epigrammatic force and point.[2]

Mrs Austen herself attributed her cleverness to 'my own Sprack wit', a brisk Old English country phrase denoting a lively perception of the characters and foibles of others.[3] She was not exaggerating when she claimed to possess it.

Born in the rectory at Harpsden, Cassandra Leigh was baptized by her father on 26 September 1739 (16 September, old style), in his church dedicated to St Margaret of Antioch in Pisidia.[4]

Even at the age of six Jane Austen's mother had already achieved recognition for her cleverness. In 1745 when her witty uncle, Theophilus Leigh, was visiting her parents he wrote home praising his niece Cassandra for having delighted him by playing the lead in an extemporary nursery charade. At the same time, Dr Leigh added that Cassandra was already 'the poet of the family' and had entertained him with several 'smart pieces'.[5]

Nothing survives to indicate the extent of Cassandra Leigh's education. As she grew up to be a notable housewife (as well as an accomplished needlewoman, a skill she passed on to her daughter Jane), it is certain she was well instructed in domestic accomplishments when she was a girl. Surviving examples of her letters and other writings also show she wrote a clear, assured hand, while the fact that she learned early to express herself in stately but playful prose is demonstrated in the following letter, written some years before her own marriage, to a gentleman, a near connection and an old neighbour, but not a relation:

> Permit me dear Mr P. — , to appear in the list of your congratulatory friends, for not one of them I am certain can feel more real joy on the occasion than myself. In any instance of your good fortune I should have rejoiced, but I am infinitely happy to know you the rector of F — , as I well remember to have heard you wish for that appellation, at a time when there was little probability of our living to see the day. May every wish of your heart meet with the same success, may every blessing attend you, for no one more deserves to be blessed; and as the greatest felicity on earth, may you soon be happy in the possession of some fair one, who must be one of the very best of her sex or she will not merit the good fortune that awaits her. If her heart be as full of love and tenderness toward you as mine is of esteem and friendship, you will have no cause to complain, but will find yourself as completely happy in that respect as you are sincerely wished in every other, by your very affectionate and infinitely obliged, Cassandra Leigh.[6]

According to family tradition, apart from what she learned in boarding-schools, Jane Austen's education was received from her well-informed father. Her eldest brother James, who was himself an excellent classical scholar and a minor author, is also reported to have exerted considerable influence in directing his precocious sister's reading and the forming of her style.[7] With the above letter as evidence, however, it is apparent that Mrs Austen, who has hitherto been omitted from the list of those who contributed to Jane Austen's cultural development, was not only capable of turning a felicitous phrase, but undoubtedly took an active part in the early intellectual — as well as the domestic — instruction of her talented younger daughter.

Although it is not certain where Cassandra Leigh first met George Austen, she is known to have visited the Steventon area some time between 1761, when her future husband was presented to the living, and 1764, the year of their marriage. In his description of Steventon J. E. Austen-Leigh wrote:

> Of this somewhat tame country, Steventon, from the fall of the ground, and the abundance of its timber, is certainly one of the prettiest spots; yet one cannot be surprised that, when Jane's mother, a little before her marriage, was shown the scenery of her future home, she should have thought it unattractive, compared with the broad river, the rich valley, and the noble hills which she had been accustomed to behold at her native home near Henley-upon-Thames.[8]

At the time of her marriage Cassandra Leigh was living with her parents in Bath. Two months after her father's death in January 1764 she was married to George Austen in old Walcot Church. The parish register reads:

> Geo Austen Bachelor of the Parish of Steventon, County of Hampshire to Cassandra Leigh, Spinster. Married by licence this 26 April by me — Thos Powys Minister in the presence of James Leigh Perrot and Jane Leigh.[9]

When the couple set out for Steventon the bride wore a fashionable scarlet riding habit that after years of use was finally converted into a hunting outfit for her fifth son.

Mrs Austen bore eight children in fourteen years, the first three at Deane, and the other five at Steventon. Following the custom of that time, all were weaned early and were then entrusted to reputable cottagers by whom they were cared for until they were deemed sufficiently trained to be brought back home again. This does not mean they were neglected by their parents:

> The infant was daily visited by one or both of its parents, and frequently brought to them at the parsonage, but the cottage was its home, and must have remained so till it was old enough to run about and talk; for I know that one of them, in after life,

used to speak of his foster mother as 'Movie', the name by which he had called her in his infancy.[10]

Some time after the birth of their third son, Edward, in 1767, the Austens moved from their temporary home at Deane to Steventon rectory. Family tradition says that when the move was made, the rough cart track from Deane to Steventon was in such poor condition that Mrs Austen, who was not well, made the short journey perched on a feather bed placed upon other soft articles of household furniture in the wagon to lessen the jolts caused by deep ruts along the way.[11]

At Steventon rectory Mrs Austen's careful management and love of neatness complemented her husband's work in the garden and orchard by turning the interior into a comfortable country home. Catherine Hubback, a daughter of Sir Francis Austen, in an account of his childhood, described it thus:

> The parsonage consisted of three rooms in front on the ground floor, the best parlour, the common parlour, and the kitchen; behind there were Mr Austen's study, the back kitchen and the stairs; above them were seven bedrooms and three attics. The rooms were low-pitched but not otherwise bad, and compared with the usual style of such buildings it might be considered a very good house.[12]

Anna Lefroy's description of the rectory, in which she grew up, provides further details:

> The Dining, or common sitting room looked to the front, & was lighted by two casement windows; on the same side, the principal door of the house opened into a parlour of smaller size. Visitors it may be presumed were few and rare; but not a whit the less welcome would they have been to my Grand Mother on account of their finding her seated in this very entrance parlour, busily engaged with her needle, in making or repairing.[13]

J. E. Austen-Leigh, who also grew up there, recalled:

> North of the house, the road from Deane to Popham Lane ran at a sufficient distance from the front to allow a carriage drive, through turf and trees. On the south side the ground rose gently, and was occupied by one of those old-fashioned

gardens in which vegetables and flowers are combined, flanked
and protected on the east by one of the thatched mud walls
common in that country, and overshadowed by fine elms.
Along the upper or southern side of this garden, ran a terrace
of the finest turf, which must have been in the writer's
thoughts when she described Catherine Morland's childish
delight in 'rolling down the green slope at the back of the
house'.[14]

This was Mrs Austen's domestic domain, and from all accounts
she presided over it with efficient dignity. But Mrs Austen was no
rarified clergyman's lady who sat on a cushion and sewed a fine
seam. She was a busy, plain-spoken country gentlewoman, loving
all rural things. Her surviving letters give ample evidence of her
forthrightness. In a letter to her sister-in-law, Mrs Walter,
written from Steventon in 1773, she said her sister, Jane Cooper,
had 'not been breeding' lately, an expression having the true
Georgian ring. Mrs Austen's description of her barnyard in the
same letter is also another example. of her eighteenth-century
directness of speech. 'I have got a nice dairy fitted up, and am now
worth a bull and six cows, and you would laugh to see them; for
they are not much bigger than Jack-asses. . . .'[15]

During the early part of his married life Mr Austen took in
private pupils to augment his income. This meant added
responsibility for his wife, but she seems to have handled the
situation with grace and humour. This is illustrated by a spirited
piece of doggerel she wrote concerning the weathercock that
crowned the maypole in the rectory grounds, the 'scrooping
sound' of which greatly annoyed two of Mr Austen's pupils.
When they appealed to Mrs Austen to help them bring the
matter to her husband's attention she dashed off 'The humble
petition of R. Buller and William Goodenough':

Dear Sir: We beseech and entreat and request
You'd remove a sad nuisance that breaks our night's rest.
That creaking old weathercock o'er our heads
Will scarcely permit us to sleep in our beds.
It whines and it groans and makes such a noise
That it greatly disturbs two unfortunate boys
Who hope you will not be displeased when they say
If they don't sleep by night, they can't study by day.

But if you will kindly grant their petition
And they sleep all night long without intermission
They promise to study hard every day
And moreover as bounden in duty will pray etc, etc.[16]

Mrs Austen was thirty-six when Jane was born on 16 December 1775. Four years later she gave birth to her youngest child, Charles John. After that, to use the word she undoubtedly would have employed, her breeding days were over. In announcing the birth of Jane to his sister-in-law, Susanna Walter, on 17 December 1775, Mr Austen wrote:

> You have doubtless been for some time in expectation of hearing from Hampshire, and perhaps wondered a little we were in our old age grown such bad reckoners but so it was, for Cassey certainly expected to have been brought to bed a month ago: however last night the time came, and without a great deal of warning, everything was soon happily over.... Your sister thank God is pure well after it, and sends her love to you and my brother, not forgetting James and Philly.[17]

During the earlier part of her married life Mrs Austen was a loving helpmate to her husband, a firm but kindly mother to her children, and a highly regarded matron in the Steventon community. Her love of cards and good company also made her an excellent chaperone when her daughters first began to attend dances at Basingstoke or the more exclusive private balls given by the neighbouring nobility and gentry. Like the rest of her family, she was a great novel reader, a taste that provided her and the family circle with plenty of light reading matter. She also greatly enjoyed the lively amateur theatricals that were an important highlight of the annual Christmas festivities at Steventon rectory for several years, while her skill with rhyme made her an excellent charade writer, a favourite pastime with the Austens. Mrs Austen even enjoyed an occasional jaunt to London, and while there, according to a letter written many years later to her grand-daughter, Anna Lefroy, she described the 'pleasure of a particular sort' that she had derived from at least three visits to Westminster Abbey.[18] In the main, however, Mrs Austen did not like London, and in writing to her sister-in-law Mrs Walter in August 1770 after leaving London for Steventon, she said, ' 'tis a sad place, I would not live in it on any account: one has not time to do one's duty either to God or man.'[19]

Mrs Austen was in her forties when her talented younger daughter first began to write, and one of Jane's earliest parodies of the contemporary fiction then being read and laughed at around the rectory fireside was a rollicking novelette called *Amelia Webster* that was dedicated to her mother.[20] Apparently Mrs Austen was pleased and amused, and remembering her own early scribbling proclivities she made no effort to curb her daughter's literary jokes.

During the midsummer months when pupils went home on holiday, Mrs Austen also liked to pay long visits with her husband and her two daughters to their relations. On one of these excursions to Seale in the Kentish Weald in July 1788, her sharp-eyed half-niece, Philadelphia Walter, recorded:

> My aunt has lost several fore-teeth which makes her look old: my uncle is quite white-haired, but looks vastly well: all in high spirits & disposed to be pleased with each other...[21]

All of which confirms the family tradition that the well-known Austen family solidarity was sometimes a bit too much for an outsider, even for one as closely related as Philadelphia Walter. We have it on the authority of J. E. Austen-Leigh:

> There was so much that was agreeable and attractive in this family party that its members may be excused if they were inclined to live somewhat too exclusively within it. They might see in each other much to love and esteem, and something to admire. The family talk had abundance of spirit and vivacity, and was never troubled by disagreements even in little matters, for it was not their habit to dispute or argue with each other: above all, there was strong family affection and firm union, never to be broken but by death.[22]

By the 1790s, when Mrs Austen was nearing sixty, she seems temporarily to have lost her robust zest for life and to have developed a tendency towards hypochondria. Her sons had left home and as her husband had given up taking private pupils by that time, the remote Hampshire rectory that had once overflowed with youthful family merriment must have suddenly seemed a lonely place. Both Cassandra and Jane were well aware of their mother's increasing tendency to play the *malade imaginaire*, and Jane's surviving letters of the period contain many references to Mrs Austen's real or imagined ailments, indicating she was not completely taken in by her mother's complaints. In December 1798 Jane wrote to Cassandra: 'My mother continues hearty, her appetite & nights are very good, but her Bowels are still not entirely settled, & she sometimes complains of an Asthma, a Dropsy, Water in her Chest & a Liver Disorder,'[23] a tongue-in-cheek catalogue which invites the speculation that Mrs Austen's desire for sympathy sometimes led her to broaden the sphere of her ailments.

Nevertheless, as a dutiful daughter (for Jane Austen was reared to observe the Fifth Commandment), she cheerfully doled out her mother's 'twelve drops of laudanum' as a composer,[24] and went about her household duties, while her father read aloud of an evening to his dozing wife from Cowper's poems, a recent purchase for the rectory library. Then, late in 1800, Mr Austen decided quite suddenly to retire, a decision in which his wife readily concurred. That Jane disapproved of the plan is well known, but by January 1801 she had more or less reconciled herself to the situation. In a letter to Cassandra, she made the best of a bad situation by reporting:

> My Mother looks forward with as much certainty as you can do to our keeping two Maids — my father is the only one not in the secret. — We plan having a steady Cook, & a young giddy Housemaid, with a sedate, middle aged Man, who is to undertake the double office of Husband to the former & sweetheart to the latter. — No Children of course to be allowed on either side.[25]

The same letter also contains a sly and perhaps a trifle envious commentary on the marital felicity of the still happily married rector and his wife. 'My father & mother wisely aware of the difficulty of finding in all Bath such a bed as their own, have resolved on taking it with them.'[26]

After having been the mistress of Steventon rectory for thirty years, Mrs Austen handed the keys over to Mary Austen, her strong-willed and rather grasping daughter-in-law (James's wife) in May 1801, and, accompanied by Jane, set out for Bath. 'Our journey here was perfectly free from accident or event; we changed horses at the end of every stage, and paid at almost every turnpike,' Jane reported in mock solemnity to Cassandra. 'We had charming weather, hardly any dust, and were exceedingly agreeable, as we did not speak above once in three miles.'[27] Mrs Austen celebrated her move from the parsonage to Bath by buying a new bonnet.[28] Then, after she and Jane had been joined by her husband and Cassandra, they spent a quiet holiday at Sidmouth before moving into their first Bath home at 4 Sydney Place, where they continued to live until the autumn of 1804, when they moved to 27 Green Park Buildings nearer the centre of the city.

It was presumably at some time during this period that Mrs Austen and her husband sat for an unidentified Bath artist to make the two silhouettes of themselves which are now in Jane Austen's House in Chawton. Mr Austen is depicted as an elderly gentleman with a sensitive profile and little duck tails of hair curling up from the collar of his greatcoat. Mrs Austen's profile, however, is a much better performance, for the silhouettist, who was perhaps better at depicting women than men, caught the sprightly 'sprack-witted' humour of her profile, dominated by a great beak of a nose, and enhanced by a fashionable ribbon-trimmed cap held in place by a wide lace band under her double chin.

It was also during the years the Austens lived at 4 Sydney Place that Mrs Austen suffered a serious bout of illness. Once she had recovered, to live another twenty years or so, her old spirit of fun revived at the same time and she celebrated the event by writing a 'Dialogue between Death and Mrs A,' a witty set of impromptu verses proving her hand had not lost its cunning:

Says Death, 'I've been trying these three weeks and more
To seize an old Madam here at Number Four.
Yet I still try in vain, tho's she's turned of three score;
    To what is my ill success owing?'

'I'll tell you, old Fellow, if you cannot guess,
To what you're indebted for your ill success —
To the prayers of my husband, whose love I possess,
To the care of my daughters, whom Heaven will bless,
    To the skill and attention of Bowen.'[29]

The Bowen mentioned in the last line of Mrs Austen's poem was Dr William Bowen (1761-1815), whose memorial tablet and the hundreds of others like it in Bath Abbey were responsible for the waggish epigram: 'These walls, so full of monuments and bust, / Show how Bath waters serve to lay the dust.'[30]

At Mr Austen's death in January 1805 Mrs Austen and her two daughters were left with an income of only £210 a year, but this was soon raised to £460 by an annual contribution of £100 from her son Edward, and £50 apiece each year from James, Henry and Francis. This enabled the Austen ladies to live in prudently quiet comfort.[31] Although at first Mrs Austen was reluctant to leave Bath because her gouty brother, James Leigh Perrot, lived there most of the year, she eventually changed her mind, and one year later she and her daughters had left Bath for good. Their departure coincided with the transfer of Stoneleigh Abbey from the family of the Lords Leigh of the first creation to Mrs Austen's branch of the Leigh family. As they were staying at that time with their cousin, the Revd Thomas Leigh, the rector of Adlestrop, who eventually succeeded to the Leigh estates in Warwickshire, they accompanied him to Stoneleigh. His solicitor had urged him to take immediate possession, fearing there might be other claimants. The visit was a memorable one for Mrs Austen, who sent a minute description of the great Georgian country house beside the Avon to Mary Austen at Steventon. Mrs Austen's letter also contains a clue revealing that, like most of her family, she continued to enjoy a good novel. 'Behind the smaller drawing Room is the state Bed Chamber,' she wrote, 'with a high dark crimson Velvet Bed: an *alarming* apartment, just fit for a Heroine....'[32]

Shortly after her stay at Stoneleigh Mrs Austen settled in Southampton, where she and her daughters and their friend Martha Lloyd, who had recently lost her mother, joined forces with Captain Francis Austen and his bride. The party rented a large, old-fashioned house in Castle Square, described as having 'a pleasant garden, bounded on one side by the old city walls', the top of which 'was sufficiently wide to afford a pleasant walk, with an extensive view, easily accessible to ladies by steps.'[33] Mrs Austen's landlord, the second Marquis of Lansdowne, lived nearby in a whimsical Strawberry Hill sham Gothic structure he had erected on the site of the old keep of Southampton Castle which had witnessed the embarkation of Henry V before the Battle of Agincourt. The building and its occupants made a great impression on J. E. Austen-Leigh, who frequently visited his grandmother there when he was a child:

> At that time Castle Square was occupied by a fantastic edifice, too large for the space in which it stood, though too small to accord with its castellated style, erected by the second Marquis of Lansdowne.... The Marchioness had a light phaeton, drawn by six, and sometimes by eight little ponies, each pair decreasing in size, and becoming lighter in colour, through all the grades of dark brown, light brown, bay, and chestnut, as it was placed farther away from the carriage. The two leading pairs were managed by two boyish postilions, the two pairs nearest to the carriage were driven in hand. It was a delight to me to look down from the window and see this fairy equipage put together; for the premises of this castle were so contracted that the whole process went on in the little space that remained of the open square. Like other fairy works, however, it all proved evanescent. Not only carriage and ponies, but castle itself, soon vanished away, 'like the baseless fabric of a vision'. On the death of the Marquis in 1809, the castle was pulled down.[34]

Jane Austen, being more of a realist than her romantically-minded nephew, recorded a more practical detail concerning the fitting up of their Southampton home. She wrote to Cassandra:

> Our Dressing-Table is constructing on the spot, out of a large Kitchen Table belonging to the House, for doing which we have the permission of Mr Husket Lord Lansdown's [sic] Painter, — domestic Painter I shd call him, for he lives in the Castle. Domestic Chaplains have given way to this more necessary office, & I suppose whenever the Walls want no touching up, he is employed about my Lady's face.[35]

Mrs Austen's stay in Southampton was a pleasant contrast to the family's five-year residence in what Jane Austen later referred to in *Persuasion* as 'the white glare of Bath', but by 1809 she had moved with her daughters and Martha Lloyd to Chawton, where her wealthy son Edward had provided the house that is now known as Jane Austen's House. In recalling her grandmother's Chawton home, Caroline Austen wrote:

> Everything indoors and *out* was well kept — the house was well furnished, and it was altogether a comfortable and ladylike establishment, tho' I believe the means which supported it, were but small.... In the time of my childhood, it was a cheerful house — my Uncles, one or another, frequently coming for a few days, and they were all pleasant in their own family.[36]

By the time of the move from Southampton to Chawton, Mrs Austen was seventy, and, to quote Caroline Austen further, she 'had suffered herself to be superseded by her daughters' and had 'ceased even to sit at the head of the table'.[37] But Mrs Austen was far from idle, for according to one of Anna Lefroy's daughters,

> ...she found plenty of occupation for herself in gardening and needlework. The former was, with her, no idle pastime, no mere cutting of roses and tying up of flowers. She dug up her own potatoes, and I have no doubt she planted them, for the kitchen garden was as much her delight as the flower borders, and I have heard my mother say that when at work, she wore a green round frock like a day-labourer's.[38]

Mrs Austen had also retained her knack for scribbling sprightly verses, and when Martha Lloyd began to compile a household book, she contributed 'A Receipt for a Pudding' which shows she still knew her way around the kitchen:

> If the vicar you treat,
> You must give him to eat,
> A pudding to his affection,
> And to make his repast,
> By the canon of taste,
> Be the present receipt your direction.
>
> First take 2 lbs of bread,
> Be the crumb only weigh'd,
> For the crust the good housewife refuses.
> The proportions you'll guess
> May be made more or less
> To the size the family chuses.

Then its sweetness to make;
Some currants you take
And sugar, of each half a pound
Be not butter forgot.
And the quantity sought
Must the same with your currants be found.

Cloves and mace you will want,
With rose water I grant,
And more savoury things if well chosen.
Then to bind each ingredient,
You'll find it expedient,
Of eggs to put in half a dozen.

Some milk, don't refuse it,
But boiled ere you use it,
A proper hint for its maker.
And the whole when complete,
In a pan clean and neat
With care recommend to the baker.

In praise of this pudding,
I vouch it a good one,
Or should you suspect a fond word,
To every guest,
Perhaps it is best
Two puddings should smoke on the board.

Two puddings! — yet — no,
For if one will do
The other comes in out of season;
And these lines but obey,
Nor can anyone say,
That this pudding's without rhyme or reason.[39]

After moving to Chawton Mrs Austen settled into the routine of resigned but cheerfully philosophic old age, marred only occasionally by bouts of her earlier hypochondria. In June 1812, in the company of Jane Austen, she paid her last visit to Steventon. After that she never spent a night away from home again.[40] But even if the daily routine at Chawton was staid, there was an undercurrent of excitement there, for Jane Austen was busily writing again, and after years of disappointment and frustration at not being able to find a publisher the tide had begun to turn. Her novels began to appear regularly three years after the family moved from Southampton to Chawton.

Sense and Sensibility came out in 1811, followed by *Pride and Prejudice* in 1813, and it is a matter of record that Mrs Austen thought highly of the final version of what had begun as *First Impressions* in October 1796 at Steventon. When *Mansfield Park* appeared in 1814 Mrs Austen did not like it as well as *Pride and Prejudice*.[41] She thought Fanny Price insipid, but enjoyed Mrs Norris. Despite her criticism, however, Mrs Austen was proud of Jane's published efforts, for on Christmas Day 1814, she wrote to her grand-daughter, Anna Lefroy: 'I have just finished *Waverley*, which has afforded me more entertainment than any modern production (Aunt Jane's excepted)...'[42] Later, when *Emma* came out in 1816 Mrs Austen thought it more entertaining than *Mansfield Park*, but not so humorous as *Pride and Prejudice*. 'No characters equal to Ly Catherine & Mr Collins', was her verdict.[43]

After the publication of *Emma*, Jane Austen's health began to deteriorate rapidly, but despite encroaching illness her consideration for her mother was still thoughtful. According to Caroline Austen,

> In my later visits to Chawton Cottage, I remember Aunt Jane used often to lie down after dinner — My Grandmother herself was frequently on the sofa — sometimes in the afternoon, sometimes in the evening, at no fixed period of the day, — She had not bad health for her age, and she worked often for hours in the garden, and naturally wanted rest afterwards — There was only one sofa in the room — and Aunt Jane laid upon 3 chairs which she arranged for herself — I think she had a pillow, but it never looked comfortable — She called it *her* sofa, and even when the *other* was unoccupied, *she* never took it — It seemed understood that she preferred the chairs — I wondered and wondered — for the real sofa was frequently vacant, and *still* she laid in this comfortless manner — I often asked her how she *could* like the chairs best — and I suppose I worried her into telling me the reason of her choice — which was, that if she ever used the sofa, Grandmama would be

leaving it for her, and would not lie down, as she did now, when she felt inclined —[44]

A good deal of malicious nonsense has been written concerning this sofa incident, most of it suggesting Mrs Austen was a selfish, self-centred woman who placed her own comfort and well-being over the needs of her critically ill daughter. To begin with, the gravity of Jane's illness was not realized, but the truth of the matter is that Jane Austen, being a well-bred gentlewoman with consideration and respect for her mother, thirty-six years older than herself, was merely obeying the elemental code of manners that is the basis of any civilized family loyalty.

In March 1817, on the death of Mrs Austen's wealthy and childless brother, James Leigh Perrot, she discovered she was not mentioned in his will. It was a bitter disappointment, for even a small legacy would have made her old age more comfortable. But Mrs Austen endured the slight, for the more pressing concern of Jane's illness was then uppermost in her mind. Before going to Winchester for better medical treatment, Jane wrote to her friend Anne Sharpe: 'I have not mentioned my dear Mother; she suffered much for me when I was at the worst, but is tolerably well.'[45]

After Jane's death in July 1817 Mrs Austen wrote:

I am certainly in great affliction. I trust God will support me. I was not prepared for the blow, for though it in a manner hung over us, I had reason to think it at a distance, and was not quite without hope that she might in part recover. I had a letter from Cassandra this morning; she bears her sorrow as a Christian should.[46]

Mrs Austen outlived Jane for ten years, during which time she was cared for by Cassandra and Martha Lloyd. In recalling her last years, J. E. Austen-Leigh wrote:

She lived, like many of her family, to an advanced age. During the last years of her life she endured continual pain, not only patiently but with characteristic cheerfulness. She once said to me, 'Ah, my dear, you find me just where you left me — on the sofa. I sometimes think that God Almighty must have forgotten me; but I dare say He will come for me in His own good time.'[47]

Mrs Austen died on 18 January 1827, in her eighty-eighth year. She is buried in the churchyard of St Nicholas' Church, Chawton. As a lover of all country things, she would be happy to know that cowslips still bloom each spring around her grave.

Mrs Leigh Perrot stands accused

JAMES LEIGH and his wife were Jane Austen's closest and most important maternal relations. Born in Harpsden in 1735, James Leigh added Perrot to his name in 1751 when under the provision of the will of his great-uncle, Thomas Perrot, he inherited the bulk of the latter's property at Northleigh, Oxfordshire. In 1764 he married Jane Cholmeley, a member of an old Lincolnshire family. He called her Jenny, and she addressed him as Perrot. It was to this childless couple that Jane Austen always referred as 'my Uncle' and 'my Aunt' in her letters.

Around the time of his marriage Perrot demolished the family home at Northleigh, sold the land to the Duke of Marlborough, and built Scarlets, a handsome house at Hare Hatch on the Bath Road, midway between Maidenhead and Reading.[1] There, according to his widow's recollections, they lived in style, 'dining with thirty families'[2] and had, among other close neighbours, Richard Lovell Edgeworth, the father of the novelist Maria Edgeworth; Thomas Day, the author of the once popular children's moral tale, *Sandford and Merton;* and the lawyer Joseph Hill, a friend of the poet William Cowper.

According to J. E. Austen-Leigh, Perrot was 'a man of considerable power, with much of the wit of his uncle, the Master of Balliol [Dr Theophilus Leigh], and wrote clever epigrams and riddles, some of which, though without his name, found their way into print.'[3] To judge from family tradition and passages in Jane Austen's letters, his wife was a formidable and opinionated woman whose wealth enabled her to exert considerable influence over her poorer relations. Like many wealthy people, Mrs Leigh Perrot dearly loved a bargain, and it was this weakness that led her to patronize a cheap shop in Bath where she was apparently victimized by unprincipled employees. In describing herself on one occasion, Mrs Leigh Perrot said, 'I cannot dissemble with anyone ... if I am angry all must know it — if I am miserable I cannot hide it.'[4] Her surviving letters reveal a forceful personality, enlivened with a mordant sense of humour. Even

Jane Austen, who did not like her, admitted she could be obliging
if the occasion or her own sense of propriety demanded kindness.
Moreover, when trouble overtook her, she faced the ordeal with
dignity and fortitude. Mrs Leigh Perrot's misfortune also
involved Jane Austen in scandal by association, the closest she
ever came to the real thing in her lifetime.

Some time after 1770, when Perrot began to suffer from gout
and rheumatism, the couple took a house at 1 Paragon Buildings
in Bath, where they spent a large part of every year from then on
in order that Perrot might benefit from drinking the medicinal
waters. Jane Austen visited her uncle and aunt at Paragon
Buildings when she was in Bath in 1797 and 1799, at which time
Perrot, who was fond of his niece, presented her with several
handsomely bound literary works that are still preserved.[5]
Shortly after Jane's return to Steventon in 1799, Mrs Leigh
Perrot was arrested on a seemingly trumped up charge of theft,
and since the value of the article alleged to have been stolen was
more than one shilling, the charge came within the category of
grand larceny.

Mrs Leigh Perrot's troubles began on 7 August 1799 when she
went to buy some black lace at a shop in Bath Street kept by a
Miss Elizabeth Gregory. The shop had formerly been operated
by Miss Gregory's brother-in-law, William Smith, whose name
was still over the door. Smith had absconded and had been
declared a bankrupt, at which time the court had appointed
William Gye, a Bath printer of questionable reputation, and a
man named Lacon Lamb, as trustees for Smith's creditors. Gye
and Lamb had turned over the shop to Miss Gregory, who had
agreed to pay for the stock in hand. Miss Gregory was assisted by
a shopman named Charles Filby, who, according to his own
testimony taken later, had been living with Miss Gregory for six
months. This bit of scandal gives point to Mrs Leigh Perrot's
reference to the couple in one of her letters as *'my pretty pair of
lovers'*.[6] Filby was an unsavoury character who in London had
twice been declared a bankrupt. Also working in the shop was an
apprentice named Sarah Raines. That Mrs Leigh Perrot had been
a long-standing customer was also brought out later at the trial.

On August 7 Mrs Leigh Perrot only looked at lace, for Miss
Gregory told her she was expecting a new supply from London.
She therefore decided to return later in order to have the

advantage of a better selection. Presumably the plot to trap Mrs Leigh Perrot was laid after she had left the shop on August 7 by Miss Gregory and her two employees, for it was later proved that they had attempted to blackmail other customers by including in their parcels items other than their purchases — the same trick played on Mrs Leigh Perrot. These earlier attempts had failed, however, when the customers promptly returned the extra items before blackmail threats could be made. As the wife of a well known and wealthy Bath resident, who conceivably would do anything to preserve his wife's good name, Mrs Leigh Perrot was a perfect target.

On the afternoon of August 8, 1799 Mrs Leigh Perrot called again at the shop and asked if the fresh supply of lace had arrived from London. When Miss Gregory told her it had not, she bought a length of black lace for £1 9s. from the stock in hand and paid for it with a £5 note. Filby took the black lace to the back of the shop to wrap it up, at which time he presumably included an extra card of white lace with Mrs Leigh Perrot's purchase. Later, he maintained that when he delivered the parcel and the change to Mrs Leigh Perrot, he saw her take up a card of white lace from a box on the counter and hide it under her cloak. Even so, Filby said nothing about it at the time, and Mrs Leigh Perrot left the shop to seek her husband, who usually drank the medicinal waters at that hour.

Meanwhile, Filby told Miss Gregory of the theft, and when the latter saw the Leigh Perrots pass her shop on the opposite side of the street, she ran out and accosted Mrs Leigh Perrot, saying, 'Pray, madam, have not you a card of white lace as well as of black,' to which Mrs Leigh Perrot replied, 'No, I have not a bit of white lace about me.' Miss Gregory then asked to examine the parcel, and when it was opened the incriminating card of white lace was found wrapped up with Mrs Leigh Perrot's regular purchase. At that point Mrs Leigh Perrot is reputed to have 'trembled very much, looked very red, and appeared much frightened',[7] at the same time insisting a mistake had been made. Whereupon Miss Gregory declared, ' 'Tis no such thing! 'tis no such thing! — You stole it!' After that she took the card of white lace and returned to her shop and the Leigh Perrots walked on. Shortly afterwards Filby ran after the couple and asked Mrs Leigh Perrot to identify herself. Perrot, who by then was obviously annoyed, informed the shopman he lived at 1 Paragon Buildings and his name was on the brass plate on his door.

Filby then went to Paragon Buildings and jotted down the name. But instead of returning to the shop, he went instead, according to his sworn testimony taken later, to Gye's printing premises.[8] That was significant, for Gye, as one of the trustees in bankruptcy for Smith obviously had an interest in Miss Gregory's shop. It was subsequently shown that the shop was in financial difficulties, thereby providing the motive for the blackmail plot against Mrs Leigh Perrot. Gye was also accused later by several anonymous Bath letter-writers, who obviously knew a great deal concerning his shady reputation, of being the 'chief plotter' in the attempt to blackmail Perrot into paying a large sum of money to prevent his wife's prosecution. One writer even reported that the blackmail plot 'was planned put in execution and insisted on by that notorious Villain',[9] and that the card of lace was kept at the printer's house the night after Mrs Leigh Perrot supposedly took it from Miss Gregory's shop.

In the meantime, the Leigh Perrots returned home and nothing further was heard of the incident until five nights later when they came in from an evening party and found an anonymous letter addressed to 'Mrs Leigh Perrot, Lace Dealer'. It read:

> Your many visiting Acquaintance, before they again admit you into their houses, will think it right to know how you came by the piece of Lace stolen from Bath St:, a few days ago. Your husband is said to be privy to it![10]

In the interim Miss Gregory and Filby, apparently at Gye's urging, had tried to lay information against Mrs Leigh Perrot at the Town Hall. As the magistrates were busily engaged in dealing with several companies of drunken and disorderly militia who were then passing through Bath, it was not until August 14, and after Miss Gregory and Filby had again been closeted with Gye, that they succeeded in securing a warrant.

A constable was then sent with a summons for Mrs Leigh Perrot's immediate appearance before the magistrates. Upon its receipt, she and her husband set out for the Town Hall. The mayor and the magistrates, all well-acquainted with the couple, were apologetic. With the sworn evidence before them, however, they could only do their duty, and Mrs Leigh Perrot was sent to

the County Gaol at Ilchester to await trial at the Spring Assizes
for the County of Somerset to be held at Taunton the following
March. Mrs Leigh Perrot was accused of stealing lace to the value
of twenty shillings from Miss Gregory's shop. This being a theft
of the value of more than twelvepence was a felony at that time,
and the punishment upon conviction was death or transportation.

Mrs Leigh Perrot was fortunate in her jailer, a man named
Edward Scadding, who owed his appointment as Governor of
Ilchester Gaol to the influence of the father of one of her friends.[11]
Because she could afford to pay for the few concessions Scadding
could legally offer, Mrs Leigh Perrot was spared the humiliation
of having to wear the coarse brown-and-yellow striped prison
garb. Also, instead of having to sleep on straw in a cheerless
woman felon's cell, she and her husband, who remained at her side
throughout her imprisonment, lived with Scadding and his wife
and their numerous children in his own house. Scadding even
accompanied the Leigh Perrots to London in an unsuccessful
attempt to obtain an order from a Judge of the King's Bench to
release his prisoner until the time of her trial.

For gentlefolk like the Leigh Perrots, accustomed to every
comfort, the long wait in the jailkeeper's sordid house was a
nightmare. This was made plain by Mrs Leigh Perrot in a letter to
her cousin, Mountague Cholmeley, dated 10 November 1799:

> ... the *Dining Room* I was to consider my own whenever I
> chose to be alone — and so it was till Fires began; but this
> Room joins to a Room where the Children all lie, and not
> Bedlam itself can be half so noisy, besides which, as not one
> particule [*sic*] of Smoke goes up the Chimney, except you leave
> the door or window open, I leave you to judge of the Comfort I
> can enjoy in such a Room. ... My dearest Perrot with his sweet
> composure adds to my Philosophy; to be sure he bids fair to
> have his patience tried in every way he can. Cleanliness has ever
> been his greatest delight and yet he sees the greasy toast laid by
> the dirty Children on his Knees, and feels the small Beer trickle
> down his sleeves on its way across the table unmoved. ... *Mrs
> Scadding's Knife well licked to clean it from fried onions,* helps
> me now and then — you may believe how the Mess I am helped
> to is disposed of — here are *two dogs and three Cats* always *full
> as hungry* as myself.[12]

As if this was not bad enough, Perrot had a severe attack of gout, but his wife hesitated to call in the *'Medical Man of Ilchester'* as 'his *trades* are *Apothecary, Surgeon, Coal dealer, Brick and Tile Maker*, &c, which seemed to bespeak his being good at none'.[13] But these troubles did not prevent Perrot from arranging for his wife's defence by hiring some of the most able members of the Bar in London.

Meanwhile the news of Mrs Leigh Perrot's arrest and imprisonment must have caused consternation among the Austens at Steventon, but the details of the reaction of Jane or other members of her family have not survived. There is no evidence, however, to support the assertions made by some of Jane Austen's biographers that the absence of any member of her immediate family, either at Ilchester or at the trial at Taunton, caused long-standing ill-will between the two families. If anything, the contrary is true, for in a letter addressed to Mrs Leigh Perrot by one of her Cholmeley relatives, it is evident that early in her sister-in-law's imprisonment Mrs Austen had offered to send 'one, or both of her Daughters' to their aunt 'to continue with you during your stay in that vile Place'. But Mrs Leigh Perrot had turned down the offer because she could not procure accommodation in Scadding's house for 'those Elegant young Women', and it would have been unthinkable for them to be 'Inmates in a Prison'.[14]

Also, in another letter written by Mrs Leigh Perrot before her trial to her cousin Mountague Cholmeley, she emphatically stated:

My dear Affectionate Sister Austen, tho' in a state of health not equal to *trials* of any kind, has been with the greatest difficulty kept from me. In a letter from her a few days ago I had the pain to hear of her Valuable Son *James* having had his Horse fall with him by which his leg was broken. This is a loss indeed because he had been a perfect Son to me in Affection and his firm Friendship all through this trying Business had taught me to look to him and his wife (a Relation of Lord Craven's well bred and sensible) to have come to us at the Assizes. *Now* I can neither ask Mother or Wife to leave him nor could I accept the Offer of my Nieces — to have two Young Creatures gazed at in a public Court would cut one to the very heart.[15]

Finally, after her acquittal, in a letter written to Cholmeley in April 1800 Mrs Leigh Perrot said, '... my dear and Affectionate Sister Austen is impatient for our getting into Hampshire, but I cannot go just yet'.[16] With this evidence in mind, it is obvious Mrs Leigh Perrot was perfectly sincere when she used the endearing terms she employed to describe her Steventon relations and their efforts to help her in her time of trouble. If there was any rancour later between her and her Austen kin, it was probably caused by her justified indignation over the £10,000 loss her husband sustained when his nephew Henry Austen was declared a bankrupt in 1816.

Mrs Leigh Perrot's trial, presided over by Sir Soulden Lawrence, a Judge of the King's Bench, was held in the Great Hall of Taunton Castle on Saturday, 29 March 1800. The case had attracted a great deal of attention, and by early morning it was estimated that over two thousand persons, including 'many elegantly dressed women',[17] had occupied every available place 'and were almost pressed to death and suffocated with heat, merely for the satisfaction of seeing the Criminal Court from a distance'.[18] The fashionable *Lady's Magazine* had a reporter and an artist on hand. While the latter was busily sketching the prisoner for the engraving that later embellished the account of her trial in the April issue, the reporter noted that Mrs Leigh Perrot, who appeared very pale and emaciated, was dressed in 'a very light lead-colour pelisse, a muslin handkerchief on her neck, with a cambric cravat. Her hair of dark brown, curled on her forehead; a small black bonnet, round which was a purple ribband, and over it a black lace veil, which was thrown up over her head.'[19]

After the indictment had been read and Mrs Leigh Perrot had pleaded Not Guilty, the jury was sworn in. The counsel for the prosecution then summoned its three witnesses, Miss Gregory, Filby and Sarah Raines. By that time, having been baulked in their attempt at blackmail, the trio had concocted such a well-tailored story that it appeared at first as though their mutually corroborative evidence would result in Mrs Leigh Perrot's conviction. But they had not reckoned with the able counsel for the defence, and when Mrs Leigh Perrot's lawyers had completed cross-examining the witnesses it was shown Filby had perjured himself under oath.

After the cross-examination was completed, Mr Justice Lawrence told Mrs Leigh Perrot it was her turn to speak in her own defence. By then she had become extremely agitated, and in an attempt to address the court her voice failed her so frequently the judge asked one of her counsel to sit by her and repeat what she said. As the printed accounts of Mrs Leigh Perrot's statement published after her acquittal do not agree with her own copy included in a letter to her cousin Mountague Cholmeley, the latter will be quoted here as it was probably copied from the original statement prepared by her counsel:

My Lord and Gentlemen of the Jury,
I am told that my Counsel cannot be permitted to address to you any remarks on my Case. The circumstances of it do not render it necessary to detain you long, but as my Counsel are prevented I cannot (altho' nearly unequal to the speaking in such an Assembly) help taking advantage of this Opportunity. Placed in a Situation in every respect the most Enviable — blessed with a Tender and most Affectionate Husband who is ever anxious to indulge my Wants and anticipate my Wishes and whose Supply of Money is so ample as to leave me rich even after every desire is gratified what inducement could I have to commit this offence? Depraved indeed must have been my Mind if with these Comforts I could have been tempted to this Crime. You will hear from my Noble and highly respectable Friends what has been my conduct, and what has been, and still is their opinion of me. Can you think it possible they have been so many years deceived? Is it possible that at this time of Life my disposition should so suddenly change and that I should foolishly hazard the well earned reputation of a whole Life by such Conduct, or endanger the Peace of Mind of a Husband for whom I would willingly lay down that Life?

At that point Mrs Leigh Perrot's voice faltered, and her husband, who had until then borne up under the indignity of the situation, placed his handkerchief over his face and wept violently, an emotion that was shared by many of those present. Once she had regained her composure, Mrs Leigh Perrot continued:

You have heard their Evidence. I shall not, nor indeed can I make any comments on it: I leave that where I am satisfied it will be used with Justice and Mercy. I will only ask you whether to be found opposite to the Shop within the space of a little more than half an hour, and with the Lace in my Hand is like the conduct of a Guilty Person. My Oath is on this occasion inadmissible: but I most solemnly assure you and call on that God whom we all acknowledge and adore, to reward or punish me as I now speak true or false and to witness my Assertion, that I did not take the White Lace knowingly from Smith's Shop, nor had I any reason to suspect or believe that the same was in my Parcel when Accosted by my Prosecutrix.[20]

When Mrs Leigh Perrot had finished speaking, her counsel then called three witnesses in her behalf, one of whom, a London pawnbroker, showed that Filby had perjured himself under oath. The others testified that extra items besides their regular purchases had been included in their parcels at Miss Gregory's shop. They were followed by eleven friends of Mrs Leigh Perrot, all of the highest social and clerical standing, who attested to her good character. A Mrs Winstone, stated testily: '. . . if she had not been of that opinion she should not have appeared in the public situation she was now standing in.'[21] Three Bath tradesmen were then called, all of whom gave evidence of the prisoner's integrity. With that the counsel for the defence rested.

Mr Justice Lawrence then summed up the evidence in a fifty-five-minute address to the jury. Although the testimony as given by the three witnesses for the prosecution had been initially incriminating, it had been damaged by contradictions brought out by counsel for the defence in cross-examination, particularly of Filby. Then, after calling the jury's attention to the additional incriminating evidence given against Miss Gregory and her associates by the witnesses for the defence, the Judge emphasized that Mrs Leigh Perrot's 'returning and passing by Miss Gregory's shop, with the parcel containing the lace in her hand, so soon after she had left it, when it was proved by the witness Filby that sufficient time had elapsed for her to have gone home and concealed it', did not appear to be the conduct of a guilty person.[22]

The case was then turned over to the jury, and after a brief consultation, it brought in a verdict of Not Guilty. In reporting the reaction to the verdict, the *Lady's Magazine* said, 'The trial lasted seven hours and the scene at the acquittal was extremely affecting. The agitation and embraces of Mr and Mrs Perrot may be more easily conceived than described.'

The long ordeal for the Leigh Perrots was over and Mrs Leigh Perrot's name was cleared. But family tradition says that had she been found guilty and condemned to death, a sentence that undoubtedly would have been commuted to transportation to Botany Bay, her loyal husband had arranged to sell his property and accompany her.

Instead of going to Scarlets, their country home in Berkshire, the Leigh Perrots returned triumphantly to Bath, where, according to one of Mrs Leigh Perrot's letters, '. . . my whole time has been taken up in *kissing* and crying',[23] so numerous were the callers who came to congratulate her. Later, in another letter, she also wrote, 'To be sure (as a kind Friend told me) I stand some chance of being killed by Popularity — tho' I have escaped from Villainy.'[24] But her best comment is a good example of her own mordant wit. 'Lace,' she wrote cryptically, 'is not necessary to my happiness.'[25]

It is uncertain if Mrs Leigh Perrot and her husband accepted the Austens' invitation to relax at Steventon after her acquittal, but there is a hint in one of Jane Austen's letters, written in November 1800, that they did, and even a suggestion they brought along presents for the family. In describing a ball at Hurstbourne Park she had attended the night before the letter was written, Jane said, 'I wore my aunt's gown & a handkerchief, & my hair at least was tidy . . .'[26]

This vague clue serves to introduce the question of why Jane Austen disliked her aunt, for references to Mrs Leigh Perrot in her letters are usually uncomplimentary. The obvious explanation is the difference of age and disposition. Mrs Leigh Perrot was a dominating and opinionated matron of fifty-six, while Jane was a vivacious and satirically irreverent young woman just approaching her twenty-fifth birthday. The animosity on Jane's side — for there are no indications in her own or her aunt's existing letters that the feeling was reciprocated — could also have stemmed from the fact that Mrs Leigh Perrot, being securely married, might have felt, and perhaps openly expressed her fears, that Jane's mocking cleverness was a hindrance in attracting an eligible husband. These are merely suggestions, but the unmistakable fact remains that in her surviving letters Jane

Austen never missed an opportunity to call attention to the absurdity of Mrs Leigh Perrot's thoughts and actions. That she could be gracious under socially acceptable circumstances was true, and Jane, to her credit, never failed to acknowledge these actions. But as an economically secure woman, which Jane was not, with all of the advantages a congenial marriage could bestow, Mrs Leigh Perrot had a high regard for herself and expected her opinions, as well as her frequent real or imaginary ailments, to be taken seriously. Also, having been born into that sphere of society she referred to as 'the best company',[27] she expected the deference of those who were unfortunately not so well placed economically or socially as herself.

Five years after his wife's acquittal, Perrot, who was already a rich man, came into even greater wealth. In 1786, when Edward, the last of the Lords Leigh of the first creation, died childless and insane, Stoneleigh Abbey, his home in Warwickshire, had passed to his sister, the Honourable Mary Leigh. When she died in July 1806 the estate reverted to the nearest male descendants of Rowland Leigh of Longborough and Adlestrop, Jane Austen's ancestor. There were three legal claimants: Thomas Leigh, rector of Adlestrop; his nephew James Henry Leigh of Adlestrop House, and James Leigh Perrot.[28] The settlement of the estate was a complicated one, but when a final agreement was reached the Stoneleigh estates went first to the Revd Thomas Leigh. When he died in 1813, Stoneleigh Abbey would have been inherited by James Leigh Perrot, had the latter not agreed beforehand to a monetary settlement. In November 1808 he relinquished all rights of inheritance to Stoneleigh to James Henry Leigh for a consideration of £20,000 secured by a mortgage on the Stoneleigh estate, a personal bond for £4,000 from James Henry Leigh, and a yearly allowance of £2,000 for himself, to continue to his wife if she survived him. It was a fortunate arrangement for although Perrot survived the settlement for only nine years his widow reaped the benefit for a further nineteen years.

Perrot's good fortune naturally raised Mrs Austen's hopes that her brother would do something for her in the way of an annuity to supplement her small income. But she was disappointed, for the benefit that she had hoped for went instead to her eldest son, James, the rector of Steventon, who by that time was living comfortably on £1,100 a year. James was rewarded by his uncle and aunt because they approved of a conscientious refusal he had made of a Berkshire living. Their approval and its reward of an additional windfall of £100 a year were followed by the hope that James and his wife would see a good deal more of their benefactors in the future, a turn of events that caused Jane Austen to write angrily, 'My Expectations for my Mother do not rise with this Event.'[29]

An even greater shock was in store for Mrs Austen. Although she was unaware of it at the time, when her brother made his will in March 1811 he made no mention of her. Instead, he left everything to his wife, and placed Scarlets and his Bath property and a considerable sum of money at her free disposal. He also left a large sum, subject to his wife's life interest, to his nephew and executor, James Austen, and £1,000 apiece to each of Mrs Austen's children who survived his wife.[30] These arrangements were not known until March 1817, when Perrot died at Scarlets, at which time Jane Austen was entering the last stages of her fatal illness.

In a letter to her brother Charles in April 1817, Jane wrote:

A few days ago my complaint appeared removed, but I am ashamed to say that the shock of my Uncle's will brought on a relapse, & I was so ill on friday & thought myself so likely to be worse that I could not but press for Cassandra's returning with Frank after the Funeral last night, which she of course did. . . . I am the only one of the Legatees who has been so silly, but a weak Body must excuse weak Nerves. My Mother has born the forgetfulness of her extremely well; — her expectations for herself were never beyond the extreme of moderation, & she thinks with you that my Uncle always looked forward to surviving her.[31]

After Perrot's death, Mrs Leigh Perrot seems to have turned gradually to some of the members of her husband's family for comfort, and although she never once allowed any of them to influence her right to make her own decisions, she was not the tight-fisted ogress many of Jane Austen's biographers have painted her. After all, she was not a blood relation of either the Austens or the Leighs, and therefore was under no obligation to be generous to any of her husband's kin who were either openly or overtly resentful of her wealth or the way she and her husband had spent, or hoarded, it. It is also a matter of record that she was very generous to members of her own family who were not so fortunate as herself. It was quite natural for her husband to make a will in her favour, for not only did he love her, a fact his surviving letters prove, but he undoubtedly felt that guaranteeing her financial independence was a small compensation for the ordeal she had undergone when she endured the rigours of imprisonment and social embarrassment at the time of her trial.

Mrs Leigh Perrot did in fact provide annuities that enabled some of the Austens to live in relative comfort until the final division of the estate after her death. For instance, in 1820, she settled £100 a year on Jane Austen's mother to compensate for the loss in income she had sustained on the death of her eldest son James in 1819.[32] At the same time she settled £300 a year on his son, James Edward, who later became her principal heir. That he chose in 1824 to become an Anglican priest like his father and grandfather angered his benefactress, who wanted him to be a smart young man of the world, and for a time she threatened to do nothing for him in the future. But the grim old mistress of Scarlets relented in 1828 when he married Emma Smith, a well-connected young lady. Not only did Mrs Leigh Perrot increase his yearly allowance to £600, she assigned the £100-a-year allowance that had been drawn by Mrs Austen until her death in 1827, to his mother, Mary Austen, of whom, contrary to Jane Austen's assertions, she was not particularly fond.[33] When the young couple's first child, a boy, was christened Cholmeley after Mrs Leigh Perrot's maiden name, thenceforth there was nothing too good for the great-nephew who had once written to his father, 'I am very sorry and certainly surprised at this last notion of Mrs L. Perrot, but I have long thought too meanly of her, to be much astonished at any fresh instance of want of feeling or of hypocrisy.'[34]

Towards the end of her life Mrs Leigh Perrot even paid a belated tribute to the genius of the niece who had been so critical of her. In a letter to her great-nephew, written from Scarlets when she was eighty-four, she said,

> We have quite a summer's day — I have been enjoying my garden, & creeping about, notwithstanding my cold — You I daresay are as happily engaged — I have been reading *Emma* a

second time, but I still cannot like it so well as poor Jane's other novels. Excepting Mr Knightly & Jane Fairfax, I do not think any of the characters *good*. Frank Churchill is quite insufferable. I believe *I* should not have married him, had I been Jane. Emma is a vain meddling woman. I am sick of Miss Bates. *Pride & Prejudice* is the novel for me. Your *Emma* is a very different character, or I am much mistaken...[35]

Mrs Leigh Perrot died at her 'beloved Scarlets' in November 1836 at the age of ninety-two. Her great-nephew then took the name of Austen-Leigh and not only inherited what would have come to his father under the provision of Perrot's will, but also became the master of Scarlets with enough money to provide between £500 and £600 a year for its maintenance. At the same time Mrs Leigh Perrot also remembered her own family with legacies amounting to £27,000. She was buried beside her husband in the churchyard at Wargrave, and a memorial to her was erected inside the church by her great-nephew. The original church was burned down in 1917 by suffragettes but Mrs Leigh Perrot's memorial tablet survived the fire. It reads as follows:

> Jane, Daughter Of Robert Cholmeley
> Esq. And Widow Of James Leigh Perrot
> Esq. Died At Scarlets In This Parish
>   Nov. 13th 1836 Aged 92
> In Humble Hope That Through The Merits
> Of Her Redeemer She Shall Rejoin In
> Heaven, Him Who Had Been The Object
> Of Her Constant And Undiminished
> Affection Upon Earth Through Fifty
> Years Of Wedlock And Twenty Years Of
>   Widowhood.[36]

The Hampshire-born Austens

James
the poet of the family

JANE AUSTEN's eldest brother James, who is credited by family tradition with having had a large share in directing her early reading and forming her taste, was the first of the Hampshire-born Austens. He was privately baptized at Deane on 13 February 1765. (It was Mr Austen's habit to baptize his children as soon after birth as possible.) Known in the family as Jemmy during his childhood, James was also the scholar of the family; he was remembered by his mother, who outlived him eight years, for his 'Classical Knowledge, Literary Taste and the power of Elegant Composition.'[1] Tall like his father, his personality was an unequal blending of sociability and brooding melancholy, the latter predominating as he grew older. His surviving writings, particularly his introspective but biographically revealing poems, show him to have been deeply religious, a lover of natural scenery, and a person of wide reading.[2] His second wife, a more positive person than himself, dominated him completely, much to Jane Austen's regret. But the poems he dedicated to her indicate he loved her, even if he was aware of her manipulation of himself and others, a situation he accepted with quiet resignation.

From his earliest years James was educated at home by his father. When he was fourteen he went up to Oxford as a scholar at St John's College. As a direct descendant on his mother's side of a sister of Sir Thomas White, the founder of the college, he was eligible for a Founder's Kin scholarship.[3] James's early days at university also provided his family with another anecdote concerning his witty great-uncle, Dr Theophilus Leigh, the Master of Balliol. 'When my father went to Oxford he was honoured with an invitation to dine with this dignified cousin,' J. E. Austen-Leigh recalled. 'Being a raw undergraduate, unaccustomed to the habits of the University, he was about to take off his gown, as if it were a great coat, when the old man, then considerably turned eighty, said, with a grim smile, "Young man, you need not strip, we are not going to fight." '4

Before going to Oxford, James had become a close friend of Fulwar Craven Fowle, a son of the Revd Thomas Fowle, vicar of Kintbury, Berkshire. By then James had begun to try his hand at poetry, and his earliest-known verses, written when he was fifteen, celebrated their joint rambles through the Berkshire countryside. About the same time James also joined the ranks of the countless imitators of Gray's famous 'Elegy' by composing a threnody of his own. None of these early poetic efforts is remarkable, but they do reveal a sincere, if stilted, appreciation of natural beauty.[5] James's muse was also invoked for a livelier purpose in 1782, when the first of a series of amateur theatricals took place at Steventon. As the budding poet of the family, he was called on to provide the prologues and epilogues for these performances. Tradition says the plays were presented in the rectory dining-parlour during the winter, while the rector's barn was used as a makeshift theatre during milder weather.

James's theatrical verses give a good idea of the type of plays performed at Steventon between 1782 and 1790. According to family tradition, James's younger brother, Henry, and his coquettish cousin, Eliza, Comtesse de Feuillide, revived play-acting at Steventon after Eliza's husband was guillotined in Paris in 1794, the outcome being that Henry became Eliza's second husband. The tradition is questionable, however, for the movements of both Henry and Eliza during that period are well-documented and no mention of theatricals at Steventon between 1794 and 1797 occurs. There are also no surviving prologues or epilogues by James or any other member of his family for plays supposedly presented there or at any other place during that time. Nor is there mention of amateur theatricals of any description at Steventon in Jane Austen's surviving letters for the period in question.

In 1782, the first play for which James Austen provided a prologue and epilogue was *Matilda* by Dr Thomas Francklin, a bombastic tragedy that offered three of Mr Austen's pupils an opportunity as the principal male actors to rant in highly ornate blank verse. It is not known who played the two equally florid female roles of Matilda and Bertha, but it is likely they were acted by two of the younger pupils with unbroken voices,. James's prologue and epilogue revealed a greater sophistication than his earlier poetic efforts had shown. His curtain-raiser for *Matilda* was spoken by his fifteen-year-old brother Edward, while the epilogue, beginning with the rousing line, 'Halloo! Good Gentlefolks! What none asleep!' was delivered by Thomas Fowle.[6]

James took his Bachelor of Arts degree in 1783. The following year amateur theatricals were resumed at Steventon with Sheridan's *The Rivals*, a more ambitious production than the one given two years earlier. Again James provided a prologue and epilogue, the first being spoken by his handsome thirteen-year-old brother Henry, while the epilogue was delivered by an unidentified actor who had played the part of Bob Acres.[7]

In 1785, when James was twenty, he fell in love with Lady Catherine Powlett, a daughter of the sixth Duke of Bolton of Hackwood Park. To her he wrote a flowery sonnet in which he renounced 'the charms of Paphos' blooming grove' for the pleasure of seeing his latter-day Venus walk on Hampshire soil. Five other sonnets, four of them dedicated individually to the four seasons, and the other written 'on leaving Oxford in the Evening of May 14th 1785', also date from the same period. They indicate James had at least learned the mechanics of constructing a sonnet, even if the contents were routine.[8]

In 1786 the cultural horizons of the Steventon area were widened when the recently married poet and antiquarian bibliographer Samuel Egerton Brydges rented the vacant rectory at Deane in order to be near his sister Anne, wife of the Revd George Lefroy, rector of the neighbouring parish of Ashe.[9] With him came a younger sister, Charlotte Brydges, whose charms soon caused James to forget his former attachment to Lady Catherine Powlett. Not only did he address Charlotte in a set of ardent verses, he followed these with an equally passionate sonnet ending with the lines: 'Teach me not then to bear a load of pain, / But teach me Sweet Enchantress how to die.'[10]

At some time between 1786 and 1787 James visited France, and he may have stayed with his cousin-by-marriage, the Comte de Feuillide. The Comtesse, James's only first cousin on his father's side of the family, was already in England, having crossed the Channel with her mother early in 1786 in order that the child she was carrying might be born on English soil. James was back in England by mid-November 1787, when the Comtesse reported his return in a letter to her cousin Philadelphia Walter.[11] As the Comte's estates were in the south-western part of France,[12] it is possible James accompanied him there, and that he made a short excursion across the border to Pamplona in Spain for the annual running of the bulls during the Fiesta de San Fermin (6-14 July). This conjecture is based on hypothetical evidence to be found in a prologue for *The Tragedy of Tom Thumb*, written by James a year after he returned to England; it contains a possible eye-witness account of the event.[13] As the same prologue also includes a vivid description of winter sports in Holland, James may have visited the Netherlands during his Continental rambles.

On 19 December 1787 James Austen, a 'Fellow of St John's College, Oxon', with four other Oxford men was ordained deacon in St David's Cathedral, Wales.[14] At the same time he was busy writing a prologue and epilogue for the play scheduled for performance at Steventon during the Christmas holidays. Earlier in September of the same year when Eliza de Feuillide was staying at Tunbridge Wells, she had asked that the comedies *Which is the Man* by Mrs Hannah Cowley, and *Bon Ton, or, High Life Above Stairs* by David Garrick, be presented at the Tunbridge Wells theatre.[15] These plays were also intended for performance at Steventon at Christmas, but in fact the play presented there on 26-28 December 1787 was *The Wonder: A Woman Keeps a Secret*, a lively comedy by Susannah Centlivre.[16]

James's prologue, tracing the history of Christmas customs in England from feudal times to his own, is one of his best. His epilogue, 'spoken by a Lady in the character of Violante', is a saucy declaration of independence of 'Creation's fairest part' from the dominion of 'Creation's mighty Lords'. As Eliza de Feuillide had descended on Steventon that Christmas like a Parisian bird of paradise and had, according to family tradition, openly flirted with both James and his younger brother Henry, it is apparent that James's epilogue was tailored to her specifications. Also, considering her predilection to coquetry, it is easy to imagine she delivered the provocative lines with considerable *brio*. The precocious twelve-year-old Jane Austen would certainly have been an interested spectator of the intrigues that accompanied the highly-charged rehearsals and performances of *The Wonder*.

James also wrote three other prologues for plays performed at

Steventon during the early part of 1788. For the first, David Garrick's adaptation of John Fletcher's comedy *The Chances,* he provided a satirical commentary on contemporary parental permissiveness. For the second, the title of which has not been preserved, being referred to only as 'a private Theatrical Exhibition at Steventon', he included scathing pen portraits of politicians, courtiers, and fortune-hunters. In his third, the curtain-raiser for *The Tragedy of Tom Thumb,* which was either Henry Fielding's original play or a later adaptation by Kane O'Hara, James treated his audience to a lively comparison of the manners of France, Spain, Holland, and his native England, including a description of English field sports, and a spirited poetical account of a cricket match.[17]

In 1788, the year his younger brother Henry went up to Oxford, James received his Master of Arts degree. He was licensed in July of the same year to his first curacy — Stoke Charity, near Steventon. Meanwhile, Eliza de Feuillide, who was still flirting with her two Austen cousins, wrote to Philadelphia Walter in August 1788:

> I am but just returned from an excursion into Berkshire, during which we made some little stay in Oxford. My cousin James met us there, & as well as his brother was so good as to take the trouble of showing us the lions. We visited several of the colleges, the museum etc & were very elegantly entertained by our gallant relation at St John's, where I was mighty taken with the garden & longed to be a *Fellow* that I might walk in it every day, besides I was delighted with the black gown & thought the square cap mighty becoming.[18]

In May 1789, James's intention to offer himself for priesting was published in Stoke Charity Church. He was ordained on 7 June 1789 in Oxford. His ordination as deacon and priest and Henry's matriculation at Oxford took place between 1787 and 1790, the period assigned to Jane Austen's earliest literary efforts. In view of the continual theatrical productions at Steventon during these years it was only natural Jane would try her hand at short dramatic sketches. One of these, *The Visit, a Comedy in Two Acts,* was dedicated to James, the wording of his sister's mock dedication being of interest as it either preserves the titles of two of her own juvenile efforts that have not survived, or two plays by James no longer in existence. After the preamble, the dedication reads:

> The following Drama, which I humbly recommend to your Protection & Patronage, tho' inferior to those celebrated Comedies called 'The School for Jealousy' & 'The travelled Man', will I hope afford some amusement to so respectable a *Curate* as yourself; which was the end in view when it was first composed by your Humble Servant the Author.[19]

James's only published prose works also date from this period. A few months before his ordination to the priesthood, with the help of his brother Henry and a few other Oxford friends he founded a weekly periodical called *The Loiterer,* one of many imitations of *The Spectator* and *The Rambler.* The publication, which ran for sixty numbers, first appeared in January 1789 and continued until March 1790, at which time the names of the contributors and the issues they had written were revealed. The paper took as its motto 'Speak of us as we are', and originally set out to give 'a rough but not entirely inaccurate Sketch of the Characters, the Manners, and the Amusements at Oxford at the close of the eighteenth century'. This policy was later found to be too limiting. When it was abandoned the essays covered a wider variety of cultural, topical, and amusing subjects. In later life, James is reported to have spoken disparagingly of *The Loiterer,*[20] but his criticism was unjust. The essays are not only well written, they also constitute a revealing microcosm of the conservative stratum of English society to which he and his family and the other contributors belonged. As the greater number of the essays were written by either James or Henry Austen, they also serve as a cultural barometer of the intellectual climate at Steventon rectory. Many reflect the amusement of the Austens, all keen novel-readers, at the then popular school of exaggerated sentimental fiction that Jane burlesqued so effectively in her juvenilia.

A careful reading of *The Loiterer* also reveals source material used by Jane in her early and even in her more mature writings. Moreover, there is also the tantalizing possibility that she was the author of a spirited epistle, over the mocking signature of 'Sophia Sentiment', that appeared in the ninth issue of the paper, published when she was thirteen and already fully capable of writing the letter in question. The certainty of its authorship cannot now be determined, but a highly plausible attribution to Jane has been made by Sir Zachary Cope in a fascinating bit of literary detection.[21] Any perceptive reader of *The Loiterer* will immediately recognize the similarities of style between Jane Austen's juvenilia and many of the contributions made by her two brothers.

It is worth noting that after the last number of *The Loiterer* was published the subscribers were provided with title pages, lists of errata, and tables of contents, making it possible to bind up the loose issues into two handy volumes.

The last two plays known to have been presented at Steventon were *The Sultan, or a Peep into the Seraglio,* a comedy by Isaac Bickerstaffe, and James Townley's farce, *High Life Below Stairs.*[22] No prologue or epilogue for the latter exists among James's surviving writings, but the witty afterpiece he provided for Bickerstaffe's comedy bears the date of January 1790, and states it was 'spoken by Miss Cooper as Roxalana'.[23] It is also known from a letter of Eliza de Feuillide that Henry Austen played the leading role of the Sultan in the same performance.[24]

About this time James Austen became the curate at Overton, Hampshire, and in September 1791 he was inducted as vicar of Sherborne St John in the same county. In February 1792 he also became vicar of Cubbington and curate of Hunningham, both in Warwickshire, though he never resided in either of these parishes. At Overton James met Anne Mathew, whom he married at Laverstoke in March 1792. The bride was a daughter of General Edward Mathew of Laverstoke House, later of Clanville Lodge, Hampshire, a former Governer of Grenada and Commander-in-Chief in the British West Indies, and Lady Jane Mathew, a daughter of Peregrine Bertie, second Duke of Ancaster. Family tradition says the young couple began their married life on an annual income of £300, of which £100 was an allowance made by General Mathew. Out of this income, James, who had been a keen rider in his younger days, kept a pack of harriers for himself, and a closed carriage for his wife.

Anne Austen, who was endowed like the other women of her family with 'large dark eyes, & a good deal of nose',[25] was the mother of Jane Anna Elizabeth, the Anna of Jane Austen's letters, who was born at Laverstoke in April 1793. Meanwhile

James had become his father's curate at Deane, and he and his wife and child moved into the rectory where he had been born. Anne Austen, who was sickly and older than her husband, did not long survive the move and died in May 1795. There is a handsome marble memorial to her in Steventon Church on which the Austen and Mathew arms are impaled.

Free to remarry, James began to look around for a second wife, and the earliest of Jane Austen's surviving letters report his regular attendance at local balls, his improvement in dancing, and, on one occasion, his 'cutting up the turkey last night with great perseverance'.[26] Meanwhile his cousin Eliza de Feuillide had fled to England with her mother and child to escape the turmoil of the French Revolution. After her mother's death in 1792 and the guillotining of her husband in February 1794, Eliza spent a great deal of time at Steventon, only a mile from Deane where James was living. At that time, according to family tradition, James began to court his vivacious cousin in earnest, but Eliza was reluctant to renounce the pleasures of fashionable society for the role of a country parson's wife. In the meantime, while casting about for a more exalted match, she made James miserable by her dalliance.

This is made clear by a flippantly oblique reference to the state of affairs in one of Eliza's letters written in December 1796 to her cousin Philadelphia Walter:

> I am glad to find you have made up your mind to visiting the Rectory, but at the same time, and in spite of all your conjectures & belief, I do assert that Preliminaries are so far from settled that I do not believe the parties will ever come together, not however that they have quarrelled, but one of them cannot bring her mind to give up dear Liberty, & yet dearer flirtation — After a few months stay in the country she sometimes thinks it possible to undertake sober matrimony, but a few weeks stay in London convince her how little the state suits her taste — Lord S —— 's card has this moment been brought me which I think very ominous considering I was talking of matrimony, but it does not signify, I shall certainly escape both peer & parson.[27]

Weary of being treated so cavalierly, James turned his attentions elsewhere and after a period of hesitation between

Mary Harrison of Andover and Mary Lloyd of Ibthrop, a lifelong friend, he settled on the latter. They were married at Hurstbourne Tarrant, Hampshire, in January 1797.

Mrs Austen's letter to Mary Lloyd, written at the time of her engagement to James, with its carefully underlined words, is still extant and reads in part:

> Had the Election been mine, you, my dear Mary, are the person I should have chosen for *James's Wife, Anna's Mother,* and *my Daughter,* being as certain, as I can be of anything in this uncertain world, that you will greatly increase and promote the happiness of each of the three.[28]

In the light of subsequent events, Mrs Austen's predictions were over-confident, for Mary, whom Jane had liked when she was a girl, grew up to be a formidable woman. One of her granddaughters described her as:

> a person of strong and original character, whose sayings often amused her friends. In manner she was downright, at times perhaps brusque, and though this did not affect the strong love her own children bore her, it may have occasionally been felt by her step-daughter, who grew up to be a handsome, clever, and high-spirited girl.[29]

This guarded pen portrait was later given a few extra unflattering touches by Mrs Bellas, a daughter of Anna Lefroy, the 'handsome, clever, and high-spirited girl' in question. Mrs Bellas recorded that Eliza de Feuillide (then Mrs Henry Austen) was distinctly hurt when her advances to her niece Anna, whom she had invited to London, were rebuffed by Mary Austen, who could never forget that her husband had once fallen under Eliza's spell. Mrs Bellas added further that Mary Austen continued to the end of her life to disparage Eliza, who, in Mrs Bellas's opinion, was the more amiable of the two.[30]

James's choice of Mary Lloyd, a young woman of very decided opinions, whose face had been dreadfully scarred by smallpox,[31] is not altogether strange. A careful study of his character makes it plain that, although possessing many estimable qualities, he was the least positive of Jane Austen's brothers, and evidently had difficulty in disengaging himself from the close-knit family circle. Even after he married Mary Lloyd, he spent so much time with his family at Steventon that she complained bitterly of his absences from home, particularly before the birth at Deane in November 1798 of her first child, James Edward.[32] Time eventually favoured Mary Austen, however, for after the birth of her son, whose well-being became an obsession with his doting father, James came to be more and more under her sway. Clever enough to persuade James that her decisions were always in the best interests of the family, it was not long before her domination over him was complete. But she did not reckon with the vigilant awareness of her perceptive sister-in-law, and the telling touches concerning her self-importance and grasping ways that occur throughout Jane Austen's letters add up to a rather unattractive character.

Although James became his father's deputy at Steventon when the latter retired and moved to Bath in 1801, he did not become rector of Steventon until after his father's death in January 1805. By that time Mary Austen had everything under control. In 1805 she gave birth to her only daughter, Caroline Mary Craven, whose reminiscences of Jane Austen written in 1867 provide valuable firsthand information concerning her famous aunt.

In a birthday poem he dedicated to her the year he became rector of Steventon Mary was eulogized by her infatuated husband as 'Anxious and earnest to fulfill / The claims of Mother, Friend and Wife...'[33] But another side of James's nature was revealed by his sister Jane in a letter she wrote to Cassandra in February 1807, after he had returned home from a visit to his mother at Southampton:

> I am sorry & angry that his Visits should not give one more pleasure; the company of so good & so clever a Man ought to be gratifying in itself; — but his Chat seems all forced, his Opinions on many points too much copied from his Wife's, & his time here is spent I think in walking about the House & banging the doors, or ringing the bell for a glass of water.[34]

This unflattering description not only shows a dull, restless middle-aged man, but also betrays the disappointment of a devoted sister at the change that had come over the brother whose earlier and more cheerful conduct had made him a delightful companion and mentor. When Jane wrote this letter, James's alienation from his relations was an accomplished fact. From then on until the time of his death twelve years later, he became increasingly preoccupied with his immediate family and his duties as rector of Steventon, while a brooding melancholy seems to have become his prevailing state of mind, relieved only occasionally by brief flashes of his earlier cheerfulness.

His surviving poems, of which more than fifty remain, reveal he was obsessively devoted to his son and daughter by Mary; there is not a single line among them concerning his elder daughter Anna. Reliable family tradition, strengthened by evidence in Jane's letters, indicates that Anna and her step-mother were not compatible — an uneasy situation not relieved until Anna's marriage and removal from Steventon five years before her father's death.

From 1811 to 1813 James was busily invoking his own muse. Most of his poems of that period are rigidly didactic, but there is one among them in which the playfulness of his early prologues and epilogues flashed up again like a bright flame from dying embers. The poem, dated 1812, was a tongue-in-cheek defence of his daughter Caroline's cat after it had been accused by the rectory cook of spoiling the dough she had prepared for making bread:

Tyger's Letter to Caroline

Ever honoured Mistress mine,
Condescend to read a line
Written by my little paws,
And defend poor Tyger's cause.
　Wicked Harriet has said
Tyger heavy made the bread;
Believe her not; 'tis all a lie,
Harriet spoilt the bread, not I.
Very true it is, I know,
I slept a little on the dough;
But surely that would do no harm;
No, no, 'twas Betsey up at Farm
Sent her down some shocking barm.
　Or else Harriet had been drinking,
Or upon her sweet heart thinking,
And did not knead the dough enough,
And when she found her bread was tough

Laid it on Tyger in a huff.
Tell her a shame it is that she
Should lay her careless faults on me,
And that I'll make her rue the day
If she again the same should say.
For, should I see a hundred mice
Eating up her tartlets nice,
I will not interrupt their fun,
I will not catch a single one.
Hence forth for me, both rat & mouse
Shall unmolested haunt the house,
Shall run about where e'er they please
And nibble bread & meat & cheese.
    Nay more, when Harriet goes to bed
The mice shall frisk about her head,
And when she tries her eyes to close
A rat shall bite her by the nose.
Besides, I'll tell you what I'll do,
Close at her door all night I'll mew
And such a dismal wailing keep
She shall not get a wink of sleep,
Shall lose her rest, & health, & fat
Because she blamed a harmless cat.[35]

This charming poem, and one other in the same vein, an 'Address to Tyger on stealing the steak reserved for the author's lunch',[36] were the last spirited rhymes James ever wrote. From then on, his verses became increasingly introverted. During the last six years of his life his health declined, and as early as 1813 Jane Austen noted his diet had been restricted to bread, meat, and water.[37] When his wealthy uncle James Leigh Perrot died early in 1817, James served as his executor, but he was disappointed to be named only as the reversionary heir in the will, his uncle having left everything to his wife for her lifetime. As she did not die until 1836, seventeen years after his own death, James never reaped any personal benefits from the bequest.

    When *Mansfield Park* was published James characteristically echoed his wife's criticisms of the novel. Mary Austen was 'very much pleased. Enjoyed Mrs Norris particularly, & the scene at Portsmouth. Thought Henry Crawford's going off with Mrs

Rushworth very natural.' James opined, 'a warm admirer of it in general. — Delighted with the Portsmouth Scene.'[38] Later, when *Emma* came out, Jane reported, 'Mr & Mrs J.A. — did not like it so well as either of the 3 others. Language different from the others; not so easy to read.'[39]

When it became necessary to take Jane Austen to Winchester for medical treatment for what is now believed to have been Addison's disease, the move was made in the Steventon rectory carriage. In commenting on the loan of the vehicle in a letter to her friend Anne Sharpe, Jane wrote:

> Now, that is the sort of thing which Mrs J. Austen does in the kindest manner! — But still she is in the main *not* a liberal-minded Woman, & as to this reversionary Property's amending that part of her Character, expect it not my dear Anne, — too late, too late in the day....[40]

Although Jane's condition improved briefly when she first went to Winchester, she soon suffered a relapse. James was unwell himself, but he rode over frequently from Steventon to be with her. Presumably he was at Jane's bedside when she 'made a point of receiving the sacrament before excessive bodily weakness might have rendered her perception unequal to her wishes'.[41] That James was alarmed by her condition is apparent from an undated letter written to his son at Oxford shortly before Jane's death:

> My dear Edward, — I grieve to write what you will grieve to read: but I must tell you that we can no longer flatter ourselves with the least hope of having your dear valuable Aunt Jane restored to us. The symptoms which returned after the first four or five days at Winchester have never been subdued and Mr Lyford has candidly told us that her case is desperate. I need not say what a melancholy gloom it has cast over us all. Your grandmamma has suffered much; but her affliction can be nothing to Cassandra's. She will indeed need to be pitied. It is some consolation to know that our poor invalid has hitherto felt no very severe pain, which is rather an extraordinary circumstance in her complaint. I saw her on Tuesday and found her much altered but comparatively cheerful. She is well aware of her situation. Your mother has been there since Tuesday and returns not till all is over, how long that may be

we cannot say. Lyford said he saw no signs of immediate
dissolution but added that with such a pulse — 120 — it was
impossible for any person to last long. And indeed we cannot
wish it — an easy departure from this to a better world is all we
can pray for. I am going to Winchester again to-morrow. You
may depend upon early information when any change takes
place and should prepare yourself for what the next letter *may*
announce. Mrs Heathcote is the greatest possible comfort to
them all. . . .

> Your affectionate father,
> J. Austen[42]

It will be noted that Mary Austen had come over from
Steventon to help Cassandra with the nursing. According to
Mary's daughter Caroline, Jane, who believed herself dying some
time before her actual death occurred, 'thanked her for being
there, and said, "You have always been a kind sister to me,
Mary." '[43] As for James, although he was at his sister's bedside the
day before she died, he was too unwell to attend her funeral in
Winchester Cathedral six days later. At that time he was
represented by his son, 'the youngest of the mourners', who had
come from Oxford for the occasion.[44]

Shortly afterwards James Austen wrote a poem lamenting Jane
Austen's untimely death. Up to the present, this poem has been
mistakenly thought to be a description of Winchester Cathedral.
From line 23, however, the poem is James's heartfelt, if somewhat
stilted, lament for his beloved and gifted sister.

> Venta, within thy sacred Fane
> Rests many a chief in battle slain,
> And many a Statesman great & wise
> Beneath thy hallowed pavement lies:
> Tracing thy venerable Pile
> Thy Gothic Choir & Pillar'd Aisle,
> Frequent we tread the vaulted grave
> Where sleep the Learned & the Brave;
> High on the Screen on either hand
> Old Saxon Monarch's coffins stand,
> Below, beneath his sable stone
> Lies the Conqueror's haughty son:

Immured within the Chapel wall
Sleep mitred Priest & Cardinal;
And honor'd Wickham lies reclined
In Gothic tracery enshrined.

But sure since William's purer taste
Old Walkelyn's heavier style effaced
O'er the plain roof the fret work spread
And formed the Arch with lancet head;
Ne'er did this venerable Fane
More beauty, sense & worth contain
Than when upon a Sister's bier
Her Brothers dropt the bitter tear.

In her (rare union) were combined
A fair form & a fairer mind;
Hers, Fancy quick & clear good sense
And wit which never gave offence;
A Heart as warm as ever beat,
A Temper, even, calm & sweet:
Though quick & keen her mental eye
Poor Nature's foibles to descry
And seemed for ever on the watch,
Some traits of ridicule to catch,
Yet not a word she ever pen'd
Which hurt the feelings of a friend,
And not one line she ever wrote
Which dying she would wish to blot;
But to her family alone
Her real, genuine worth was known.
Yes, they whose lot it was to prove
Her Sisterly, her filial love,
They saw her ready still to share
The labours of domestic care,
As if *their* prejudice to shame
Who, jealous of fair female fame,
Maintain that literary taste
In womans mind is much misplaced,
Inflames their vanity & pride,
And draws from useful works aside.

Such wert thou Sister! while below
In this mixt Scene of joy & woe
To have thee with us it was given,
A special kind behest of Heaven.

What now thou art we cannot tell:
Nor where the just made perfect dwell
Know we as yet. To us denied
To draw that parting veil aside
Which 'twixt two different worlds outspread
Divides the Living from the Dead.
But yet with all humility,
The change we trust was gain for thee.
For oh! If so much genuine worth
In its imperfect state on Earth
So fair & so attractive proved,
By all around admired & loved,
Who then the change dare calculate
Attendant on that happy state,
When by the Body unconfined
All Sense, Intelligence & Mind
By Seraphs borne through realms of light
(While Angels gladden at the sight)
The Aetherial Spirit wings its way
To regions of Eternal day.[45]

James, who survived his sister only a little more than two years, spent his last days in paraphrasing three of the more melancholy Psalms into heroic couplets.[46] His son came home from Oxford to be with him during his last illness and was present when he died on 13 December 1819. He was buried in a brick-lined grave in Steventon churchyard and was later commemorated by a handsome Gothic Revival tablet that includes a long poetical tribute by his son, in the chancel of Steventon Church.[47]

Mary Austen died of an apoplectic seizure at Speen, Berkshire, in August 1843. She was buried 'at Steventon where a vacant brick grave at the side of my father's has been waiting nearly 24 years for its tenant.'[48]

George
the unfortunate brother

GEORGE will always be an enigma. Although he lived to the age of seventy-two, dying one year after Queen Victoria ascended the throne, his family was so reticent that very little is known about him. No mention is made of George in J. E. Austen-Leigh's *Memoir*, but his grandson has stated that George 'grew up weak in intellect, and did not die till 1838'.[1]

George was privately baptized on 26 August 1766 at his father's rectory at Deane. He was named after his father and was a godson of Tysoe Saul Hancock, whose wife Philadelphia was Mr Austen's older sister.[2] Like all the Austen children, George was weaned early, after which he was placed in the care of a responsible neighbouring cottager with whom he would ordinarily have remained until he was deemed sufficiently trained to rejoin his parents at the rectory. But George was different from his healthier brothers and sisters, and never was a regular member of the family circle either at Deane or at Steventon.

In July 1770 his father wrote to his sister-in-law, Susanna Walter: 'I am much obliged to you for your kind wish of George's improvement. God knows only how far it will come to pass, but from the best judgement I can form at present, we must not be too sanguine on this head; be it as it may, we have this comfort, he cannot be a bad or a wicked child.'[3] In December of the same year Mrs Austen wrote to Susanna: 'My poor little George is come to see me to-day, he seems pretty well, tho' he had a fit lately; it was near a twelvemonth since he had one before, so was in hopes they had left him, but must not flatter myself so now.'[4] Two years later, in September 1772, Tysoe Saul Hancock wrote from Calcutta to his wife Philadelphia in London:

That my brother & sister Austen are well, I heartily rejoice, but I cannot say that the News of the violently rapid increase of their family gives me so much pleasure; especially when I consider the case of my godson who must be provided for without the least hopes of his being able to assist himself.[5]

Nothing further is known concerning George until July 1788, when Philadelphia Walter, commenting in a letter to her brother James on Hastings, the handicapped son of her cousin, Eliza de Feuillide, said,

> Madame de F. and my aunt are returned to London. Poor little Hastings has had another fit; we all fear very much his faculties are hurt; many people say he has the appearance of a weak head: that his eyes are particular is very certain: our fears are of his being like poor George Austen. He has every symptom of good health, but cannot yet use his feet in the least, nor yet talk, tho' he makes a great noise continually.[6]

Unlike Hastings de Feuillide, who was kept at home until his death in 1801, George Austen was placed in the care of some kind local family, where he could be visited by members of his own family. His case was similar to that of his mother's younger brother, Thomas Leigh, who was never normal and was cared for outside the family circle.

That George may have been deaf among other things, and that Jane possibly communicated with her brother by means of sign language is suggested by a reference in a letter written in December 1808 by Jane Austen to Cassandra at Godmersham:

> We spent Friday evening with our friends at the boarding house and our curiosity was gratified by the sight of their fellow-inmates, Mrs Drew and Miss Hook, Mr Wynne and Mr Fitzhugh; the latter is brother to Mrs Lance, and very much the gentleman. He has lived in that house more than twenty years, and poor man! is so totally deaf that they say he could not hear a cannon, were it fired close to him; having no cannon at hand to make the experiment, I took it for granted, and talked to him a little with my fingers, which was funny enough. I recommended him to read Corinna.[7]

At the death of Mrs Austen in 1827, the South Sea Annuities she owned were sold and the money divided into five parts among Cassandra, Henry, Francis and Charles Austen, and Edward Knight. Edward allocated his share 'for the use of my brother

George, being his full share of the £3,350 Old South Sea Annuities'.[8]

George died of dropsy at Monk Sherborne, Hampshire, on 17 January 1838 at the age of seventy-two. The scanty information on the death certificate (where he was described as a 'gentleman') was furnished by a man named George Cullum who was in attendance at the time of George's death. He was buried five days later in an unmarked grave in the churchyard of All Saints' Church, Monk Sherborne.[9]

The place of his death is interesting as it is near Sherborne St John, Hampshire, where the Revd James Austen, George's elder brother, was vicar from 1791 until his death in 1819. As both Sherborne St John and Monk Sherborne are only a few miles to the north-east of Steventon, it is possible that James Austen was responsible for the welfare of his mentally retarded brother until his own death in 1819 made it necessary for some other member of the Austen family to assume the obligation.[10]

Edward
the squire of Godmersham

EDWARD AUSTEN (Knight after 1812), the third of the Hampshire-born Austens, was one of those fortunate individuals who, according to the old saying, was born with a silver spoon in his mouth. A compactly built man with dark, deep-set eyes like those of his favourite sister Cassandra, he was remembered as 'not only a very amiable man, kind and indulgent to all connected with him, but possessed also a spirit of fun and liveliness, which made him especially delightful to all young people.'[1] His mother characterized him as a practical man of business, whose clear head, active mind, and sound judgment were tempered by a good disposition. When he died in 1852, at the age of eighty-five, a report in the local paper read:

> We have now lost almost the last of that school of country gentlemen, of which England has been so proud, and they will hereafter exist only in memory and in books. Living in a period when the Continent of Europe was not so accessible as it is in the present day, and, therefore, much less frequented — when London seasons and town residences did not rob May and June of the owners of the soil, and take them from the matchless beauties of nature to the costly productions of art and the follies of the day — this bygone school spent the greater portion of each year upon their estates, famed for field sports, hospitality and dispensing charity to all in need. Mr Knight, though nearly the last, was a worthy specimen of this generation.[2]

Edward was privately baptized at Deane on 7 October 1767. The year of his birth is usually given as 1768, but this is incorrect. Not only is the year recorded plainly as 1767 in the Deane baptismal register, it was the only baptism performed that year. It has also been erroneously reported that Edward was adopted *as a child* by his distant cousin, Thomas Knight II of Godmersham,

118

Kent, and Chawton Manor, Hampshire. That he was adopted is true, but it was definitely not during his early childhood. The Revd George Austen, Edward's father, was presented to the Steventon living in 1761 by Thomas Knight I, who had married Jane Monke, George Austen's second cousin. They were the parents of Edward's benefactor, Thomas Knight II who retired as Member of Parliament for Kent in 1780; he devoted the remainder of his life to enlarging and beautifying Godmersham, and to enjoying the leisurely social life of East Kent where it was jocularly remarked 'they were all first cousins'.[3] In 1779, at the age of forty-three, when Edward was already twelve, Thomas Knight II married Catherine Knatchbull, the daughter of the Revd Dr Wadham Knatchbull, Prebendary of Durham and vicar of Chilham and Molash in Kent. As he had every reason to expect his twenty-six-year-old bride would present him with not only an heir but other children as well, it is fanciful to imagine he would at that time even have considered adopting a twelve-year-old distant cousin in far-off Hampshire, much less making him his heir.

Although the adoption did eventually take place, it was the outcome of a gradual deeper acquaintance. In any event, it could not have happened before 1783, when a commemorative group silhouette depicting George Austen presenting his son Edward to the Knights and another lady, presumably Mrs Knight's mother, was painted by William Wellings, a fashionable London artist, to celebrate the occasion. By then, Edward was sixteen and could hardly have qualified as a child. It is also a matter of record that it was Catherine Knight, who by that time had apparently given up hope of having children of her own, who was responsible for bringing Edward to the favourable attention of her husband. Family tradition is silent concerning exactly when and where she first became acquainted with Jane Austen's sweet-tempered but manly elder brother. In a letter addressed to him in 1797, however, after the adoption had long since taken place, she wrote, 'From the time that my partiality for you induced Mr Knight to treat you as our adopted child I have felt for you the tenderness of a Mother....'[4]

In 1848 James Austen's daughter Caroline questioned her uncle Henry at some length concerning Edward's adoption. He was seventy-seven at that time, and could not remember the exact date of the invitation to his brother to go to Godmersham, evidently antedating it considerably in his mind:

He was very clear as to the purport of the discourse which he heard between his Father & Mother on the morning when they received a letter from Godmersham, begging that little Edward might spend his Holidays there.... My grandfather was *not* disposed to consent to Mr Knight's request. With the single eye of a Teacher, he looked only at one point, which was, that if Edward went away to Godmersham for so many weeks he would get behind in the Latin Grammar. My grandmother seems to have used no arguments, and to have suggested no expectations; she merely said, 'I think, my dear, you had better oblige your cousins, and let the child go'; and so he went, and at the end of the Holidays he came back, as much Edward Austen as before. But after this, the Summer Holidays, at the least were spent with the Knights, he being still left to his Father's tuition. Uncle Henry could not say when it was announced in the family that *one* son was adopted elsewhere — it was, in time, understood so to be; and he supposed that his Parents and the Knights came to an early understanding on the subject.[5]

Edward, who was called Neddy by his family during his childhood, was still under his father's tuition as late as 1782. In that year, when he was fifteen, he spoke the prologue to Dr Thomas Francklin's tragedy *Matilda* which his elder brother James had written for an amateur performance of the play at Steventon. That was the year before the commemorative silhouette was painted. It is therefore safe to assume Edward Austen was adopted as a teen-ager rather than as a child. To quote Caroline Austen further,

Edward Austen was more and more at Godmersham and less at Steventon, but I do not know *when* he was entirely transferred from his Father's house to some other place of education, and to Godmersham as a home, or whether he ever *did* go to any sort of school before he was finished off in Germany.[6]

As far as is known, Edward never attended any other school. Since he was placed by good fortune in the position of being the eventual owner of large estates, his adoptive father saw to it he was properly trained at home to fulfil the duties of a country gentleman. Meanwhile, he was sent on the Grand Tour between 1786 and 1788. In his case, this included a year spent at Dresden, where he received marked attention at court. The tour was extended to Italy, at least as far south as Rome. Many years later when his two eldest sons, Edward and George, had also spent some time in Dresden, and had, like their father, received courtesies from the reigning family, there was an exchange of letters and presents between Prince Maximilian of Saxony and 'Edward Knight *ci-devant* Austen'.[7]

Reared in the congenial and cheerful atmosphere of his own family at Steventon, and having the added advantage of the cultivated country-house society he encountered in Kent, Edward developed into a personable young man. Already known for the sweetness of his disposition, his keen sense of humour, and his obliging and considerate ways, he was also, like most of the Austens, blessed with good looks. This is apparent from his full-length portrait painted in Rome when he was twenty-one. The portrait, now at Jane Austen's House in Chawton, depicts a handsome, florid-faced young man with powdered hair, leaning against a large tree. Dressed in a well-fitting green coat fastened with large round metal buttons, he also wears a white waistcoat, an elaborate gold fob watch, pale yellow breeches, white silk stockings, and black leather pumps set off with enormous silver buckles. To certify that the sitter had actually visited the scenes of antiquity, the artist included a fragment of a broken marble frieze in the foreground, a Corinthian capital among the weeds to the right, and a ruined circular temple in the background. The composition is a pleasing permanent souvenir of Edward's continental travels.

Meanwhile, Edward's good fortune had placed him in a position to make a good marriage. He chose Elizabeth Bridges, a daughter of Sir Brook Bridges of Goodnestone Park near Wingham, Kent. In announcing the engagement, Lady Fanny Bridges, Elizabeth's mother, wrote in March 1791 to a member of the family in London:

> We have for some time observed a great attachment between Mr Austin [*sic*] (Mr Knight's Relation) and our dear Elizth; and Mr Knight has, in the handsomest manner, declared his entire approbation of it; but as they are both very young, he wish'd it not to take place immediately, and as it will not suit him to give up much at present, their Income will be small, and they must be contented to live in the Country, which I think

will be no hardship to either party, as they have no high Ideas, and it is a greater satisfaction to us than if she was to be thrown upon the world in a higher sphere, young and inexperienced as she is. He is a very sensible, amiable young man, and I trust and hope there is every prospect of Happiness to all parties in their union.[8]

That Edward was quite smitten with his intended is apparent from a letter written from London in June 1791 by his cousin, Eliza de Feuillide, to Philadelphia Walter:

He is now preparing to visit the Lakes with Mr & Mrs K. & a large party, as I understood, no less than twelve in number, but his beloved alas! is not to bless him with her presence on this occasion. I asked him how he would be able to exist; which enquiry he answered with that calm smile of resignation which his sex generally wears under the circumstances of this nature.[9]

Later, in November of the same year, Eliza wrote to Philadelphia: 'Edward A I believe will also in another month or two take unto himself a spouse. He showed me the lady's picture which is that of a very pretty woman.'[10] The picture was presumably the still extant miniature of Elizabeth Bridges by Richard Cosway, the most fashionable miniaturist of his time. If so, it shows that Elizabeth Bridges was indeed quite lovely. Edward, then twenty-four, and his eighteen-year-old bride were married two days after Christmas in 1791 and went to live at Rowling, a small Georgian house near Goodnestone, which is still standing. Here the first three of their eleven children were born.

Edward was the first of the Hampshire-born Austens to wed, his marriage being followed by that of his eldest brother James to Anne Mathew in March 1792. One year later, Jane Austen, who was then sixteen, dedicated *The Three Sisters*, one of her rollicking juvenile burlesques, to Edward.[11] Although it had no actual bearing on the events leading up to his marriage or that of his brother, when read today with these events in mind it is tempting to speculate that Jane's mischievous satire on matrimonial scheming was a skit on the pre-nuptial plans which had occupied the centre of the conversational stage at Steventon for some time, to which Jane added a few telling observations of her own.

Thomas Knight II died in October 1794, leaving his estates in Kent and Hampshire to his widow for life, after which they were to be inherited by Edward. The will also provided that in case of a failure of Edward's issue, they were to go to his brothers in succession. This never took place, for his wife bore him six sons and five daughters before her death at the age of thirty-five, thereby ensuring the retention of the property in Edward's immediate family. Mrs Knight continued to live in the great house at Godmersham, but by 1797 she began to realize she was unequal to the task of maintaining the vast estates left by her husband.

As a practical woman, she made plans to turn over the Kent and Hampshire properties to Edward and to retire on an annual income of £2,000 to a smaller house known as The White Friars that she had purchased in Canterbury. The plan was at first rejected by her adopted son, who wrote,

> I am confident we should never be happy at Godmersham whilst you were living at a smaller and less comfortable House — or in reflecting that you had quitted your own favorite Mansion, where I have so often heard you say your whole Happiness was center'd, and had retired to a residence and style of Living to which you have been ever unaccustomed, and this to enrich us.[12]

But Mrs Knight, whose stately, yet sensible, epistolary style confirms the tradition that she was 'a very superior woman, with a good understanding and highly cultivated mind', was not to be thwarted. She replied:

> If anything were wanting, my dearest Edward, to confirm my resolution concerning the plan I propose executing, your Letter would have that effect; it is impossible for any person to express their gratitude and affection in terms more pleasing than you have chosen, and from the bottom of my heart I believe you to be perfectly sincere when you assure me that your happiness is best secured by seeing me in the full enjoyment of every thing that can contribute to my ease and comfort, and that happiness, my dear Edward, will be yours by acceding to my wishes.... Many circumstances attached to large landed Possessions, highly gratifying to a Man, are entirely lost on me at present; but when I see you in the enjoyment of them, I shall, if possible, feel my gratitude to my beloved Husband redoubled, for having placed in my hands

the power of bestowing happiness on one so very dear to me.[13]

Godmersham, which became Edward's home soon after Mrs Knight's removal to The White Friars and remained in his family until it was sold by his son and heir in 1872, is still one of the finest houses of East Kent. Situated $8\frac{1}{2}$ miles south-east of Canterbury on the Ashford road, it occupies a commanding position in the valley of the Stour in a landscaped park below beautifully wooded downland. Built of rose-coloured brick with stone facings, the centre portion, which has been described as 'a country gentleman's house executed with great fastidiousness',[14] was begun in 1732 by Thomas Knight I. Later improvements, including the flanking wings, were added by his son, while Edward is also said to have 'greatly improved the house inside and out' during his ownership. The earliest known account of Godmersham describes it as

> a modern building of a centre and two wings; one of which, the Eastern, contains a most excellent library; in the centre are some good apartments, particularly on the back front, which command exceeding delightful prospects of the hill and pleasure grounds.[15]

This account makes no mention of the two interior architectural glories of Godmersham, the great two-storey formal hall paved with black and white marble, and the adjoining drawing-room. Both are decorated with superb stucco work and richly carved, white-painted woodwork in the style of William Kent. The hall, presided over by a scowling bust of the Emperor Caracalla from a broken pediment over the splendid white marble chimney-piece, is also notable for a handsome decorative frieze incorporating profile medallions of Roman emperors, and three shields displaying the coats of arms of Monke, May quartered with Brodnax, and Brodnax.[16] The adjoining drawing-room is even more richly decorated with stucco swags of musical instruments and an equally handsome frieze incorporating female masks, scallop shells, and acanthus scrolls. It was in this apartment the Knight family portraits hung during the years Jane Austen was a fairly frequent visitor at Godmersham. As her brother's guest, Jane not only revelled in the carefree and comfortable hospitality she enjoyed in his home, referring to it as living '*a la* Godmersham',[17] but also utilized the unique opportunities afforded by her visits to observe the manners as well as the peculiarities of her hospitable brother's guests, thereby providing herself with raw material for her novels.

Once Edward was installed as squire of Godmersham, he was visited by his parents and two sisters during the autumn of 1798. As far as is known, this was Jane Austen's first stay there. It is unfortunate that both sisters were present at the same time as it deprived posterity of an exchange of letters that might have given details of what happened during that particular visit. Once Jane and her parents had returned to Steventon, leaving Cassandra behind, her letters began again. From them we learn that Edward, like his hypochondriac mother, had begun to complain of stomach disorders, faintness, and nerves, eliciting Jane's comment, 'Poor Edward! It is very hard that he, who has everything else in the world that he can wish for, should not have good health too.'[18] But Edward's real or imaginary complaints had one beneficial result. When his doctor ordered him to Bath to drink the waters he went in style in the Godmersham coach, taking with him his wife, his mother, his younger sister, and his two oldest children. Jane's chatty letters to Cassandra, who remained behind at Steventon with her father, give a vivid account of the manners, festivities and fashions of Bath during the last year of the eighteenth century.

As Edward lived for another fifty-three years and no further mention of his complaints is made in his sister's letters, it is presumed his ailments were cured by the bitter waters, and a round of pleasures. These included the purchase of a new pair of matching black coach horses for sixty guineas, escorting his family party to the theatre, and attending an outdoor Grand Gala at Sydney Gardens, belatedly held in honour of the King's birthday, where Edward and his party were entertained by a concert of vocal and instrumental music, including works by Haydn and Pleyel, bird imitations by a Mr Nimroide, and a capital display of fireworks.

Although as Jane Austen grew older she became increasingly critical and abhorrent of the average married woman's entrapment in what she termed 'mothering', she left no remaining comment on Edward's rapidly increasing family. Between 1791 and 1808 Elizabeth Austen presented him with eleven healthy children: Edward's favourite sister, Cassandra, was usually present at Godmersham to assist in the deliveries. Just before the birth of Elizabeth's last child, Jane Austen in the company of her brother James and his family paid a long summer visit to Godmersham. At that time she noted Elizabeth did not look well.[19] The baby, a boy who was named Brook John, was born in September 1808, after which his mother seemed to have made a normal recovery. Eleven days later Elizabeth became suddenly ill after eating a hearty dinner and died before the serious nature of her attack had been realized.

The sad news reached Jane Austen and her mother at Southampton in record time. Three days after Elizabeth's death, Jane wrote to Cassandra expressing her sympathy

> for dearest Edward, whose loss and whose sufferings seem to make those of every other person nothing. — God be praised! that you can say what you do of him — that he has a religious Mind to bear him up, & a Disposition that will gradually lead him to comfort.

Later, in speaking of Elizabeth Austen in the same letter, Jane continued,

> We need not enter into a Panegyric on the Departed — but it is sweet to think of her great worth — of her solid principles, her true devotion, her excellence in every relation of Life. It is also consolatory to reflect on the shortness of the sufferings which led her from this World to a better.[20]

Meanwhile, Jane Austen, being a practical person, made arrangements for Edward's young sons, Edward and George, who on the death of their mother had been taken from Winchester College to Steventon, to be sent to Southampton to be comforted. When they arrived by the stagecoach 'very well, but very cold, having by choice travelled on the outside, and with no great coat but what Mr Wise, the coachman, good-naturedly spared them of his', her efforts to amuse them and relieve their minds of their sorrow were tireless. These diversions ranged from 'bilbocatch, at which George is indefatigable, spillikins, paper ships, riddles, conundrums, and cards, with watching the flow and ebb of the river, and now and then a stroll out....'[21]

Jane's letter also contains the first intimation of Edward's future plan for his mother and sisters. This consisted of an offer to them of a house on his property at Godmersham or another house in Chawton. The decision was not hard to make, for Mrs Austen and her daughters did not want to leave Hampshire. By July 1809 they and their good friend Martha Lloyd had moved into the house in Chawton that Edward had renovated for them. In a letter in jog-trot verse written from Chawton on 26 July 1809 to her brother Francis, complimenting him on the birth of his eldest son, Jane Austen also expressed her delight in the new arrangement:

> As for ourselves, we're very well;
> As unaffected prose will tell. —
> Cassandra's pen will paint our state,
> The many comforts that await
> Our Chawton Home, how much we find
> Already in it, to our mind;
> And how convinced, that when complete
> It will all other Houses beat
> That ever have been made or mended,
> With rooms concise, or rooms distended....[22]

Posterity is greatly indebted to Edward for his generosity to his mother and sisters. By ensuring their security he also provided Jane Austen with the first permanent home she had enjoyed since reluctantly leaving Steventon rectory in May 1801. She began to write again. Her first published novels were the final reworkings of two manuscripts dating from her Steventon days. In November 1811 *Sense and Sensibility* was published. It had been begun in November 1797 as a rewriting of an earlier novel in letter form called *Elinor and Marianne.* It was popular in high society, for on 25 November 1811 the Countess of Bessborough, sister of Georgiana, the beautiful Duchess of Devonshire, wrote to Lord Granville Leveson-Gower, 'Have you read "Sense and Sensibility"? It is a clever Novel. They were full of it at Althorp, and tho' it ends stupidly, I was much amus'd by it.'[23]

Edward's reaction to his sister's first appearance in print has not been preserved, but he was fully aware it was about to take place. Two months before it was published his elder daughter Fanny made the following entry in her pocket diary under the date 28 September 1811, 'Letter from At. Cass. to beg we would not mention that Aunt Jane wrote *Sense and Sensibility.*'[24] But

Edward had other things besides novels to think about at that time. In October of the following year, Mrs Knight, his adoptive mother, died at her home in Canterbury. Her death automatically made him the sole heir of all the Knight properties. Shortly afterward he took the arms and surname of Knight: the surname of his children was also changed then from Austen to Knight. The change was noted by Jane Austen in a letter written to Martha Lloyd late in November 1812, in which she said: We have reason to suppose the change of name has taken place, as we have to forward a Letter to Edward Knight Esqre from the Lawyer who has the management of the business.' She then added a characteristic quip, 'I must learn to make a better K.[25]

Although Edward had enjoyed the revenues from Chawton Manor since 1797, he had never lived there as the Great House was usually let. Its tenant at the time of Mrs Knight's death was John Charles Middleton,[26] a relative by marriage of William Beckford of Fonthill Abbey, the author of the celebrated Oriental novel *Vathek*. When Middleton's lease expired in 1812 Edward decided to take over the manor house as a second home for his family rather than let it again. Since his mother and sisters were already in residence in Chawton, an easy walk from the manor house, the arrangement was even more attractive.

In April 1813, three months after the publication of *Pride and Prejudice*, Edward turned Godmersham over to painters[27] and moved his entire household to Chawton Manor, where they remained for five months until the smell of fresh paint had faded sufficiently to make their return a pleasant one. Although Jane Austen was busy at that time with *Mansfield Park*, she also thoroughly enjoyed the excitement of having Edward and his family nearby. In a letter written in July 1813 to her brother, Francis, then serving on board the *Elephant* in the Baltic, she gave a pleasant picture of the constant comings and going between the cottage and the Great House:

> The pleasure to us of having them here is so great, that if we were not the best creatures in the World we should not deserve it. We go on in the most comfortable way, very frequently dining together, & always meeting in some part of every day. — Edward is very well & enjoys himself as thoroughly as any Hampshire born Austen can desire. Chawton is not thrown away upon him.[28]

In mid-September Jane accompanied Edward and his family on their return to Kent. The journey was broken with a brief stay in London devoted to a whirlwind of shopping that included the purchase of a Wedgwood dinner service, pieces of which are now on exhibition at Jane Austen's House in Chawton. The stay in London also included several visits to the theatre. Jane wrote to Cassandra concerning the principal character in *Don Juan:* '. . . whom we left in hell at half past eleven,' adding later, 'I must say that I have seen nobody on the stage who has been a more interesting character than that compound of cruelty and lust.'[29]

Jane Austen's two-month stay at Godmersham, from September to November 1813, was her last visit there, and her surviving letters written to Cassandra during that period sparkle with word-pictures of the clever, the boring, the beautiful, and the graceless members of the landed gentry of Kent who took advantage of Edward's hospitality. As a keenly observant spectator, Jane enjoyed the kaleidoscopic human comedy that swirled around her from breakfast until bedtime. Any careful reader of her letters who is already familiar with *Emma*, begun in January of the following year, will have no trouble in recognizing the Kentish originals from which Miss Bates and her mother and Mrs Elton were taken.

As *Mansfield Park* had only recently been completed, it is safe to assume that the manuscript, or at least a part of it, travelled to Godmersham with Jane in her mahogany lap desk. If so, it was no doubt the novel that figured in the reminiscences of Edward's daughter, Marianne, who was twelve at the time of her aunt's last visit to Godmersham. Miss Knight, who never married and died in 1896 at the age of ninety-five, wrote:

> I remember that when Aunt Jane came to us at Godmersham she used to bring the MS of whatever novel she was writing with her, and would shut herself up with my elder sisters in one of the bedrooms to read them aloud. I and the younger ones used to hear peals of laughter through the door, and thought it very hard that we should be shut out from what was so delightful. . . . I also remember how Aunt Jane would sit quietly working beside the fire in the library, saying nothing for a good while, and then would suddenly burst out laughing, jump up and run across the room to a table where pens and paper were lying, write something down, and then come back

to the fire and go on quietly working as before.[30]

Sceptical critics have tried to discredit these pleasant recollections. But the disappointments of childhood, like the one mentioned in Miss Knight's first reminiscence, are long-lasting. Also, as Jane Austen plainly states in a letter to Cassandra written from Godmersham during this last visit: 'We live in the Library except at Meals & have a fire every Eveng.'[31], it is reasonable to suppose Marianne Knight was not only a member of the family party on those occasions, but was sufficiently impressed by her aunt's unusual behaviour not only to notice it at the time, but to remember it later.

Although both the elder and younger Thomas Knight had been Members of Parliament, Edward apparently never aspired to that distinction. But he was High Sheriff of Kent in 1801, and a magistrate for most of his adult life. In November 1813, Edward even took Jane on one of his official inspections in Canterbury. In describing the occasion to Cassandra, Jane wrote:

> He went to inspect the Gaol, as a visiting Magistrate, & took me with him. I was gratified — & went through all the feelings which People must go through — I think in visiting such a Building. — We paid no other visits — only walked about snugly together & shopp'd. — I bought a Concert Ticket & a sprig of flowers for my old age.[32]

When *Mansfield Park* was published, Edward's response was quietly approving. In jotting down his reactions, Jane wrote, 'Not so clever as P. & P. — but pleased with it altogether. Liked the character of Fanny. Admired the Portsmouth scene.'[33] But when *Emma* came out, Edward's country-squire knowledge of the seasons caused him to be amusedly critical of Jane's unintentional gaffe in her account of the strawberry party at Donwell Abbey. According to Caroline Austen, 'The first time my uncle Knight saw his sister after the publication of *Emma* he said, "Jane, I wish you would tell me where you get those apple-trees of yours that come into bloom in July." '[34]

Edward's comfortable routine was interrupted in 1814 by a lawsuit that not only cost him a great deal of time and money, but was settled only after Jane Austen's death.[35] It was unfortunate the litigation came when it did, for it coincided with Jane's failing health and no doubt caused additional anxiety. An unfavourable decision against Edward could possibly have deprived her of her Chawton home.

It will be remembered that when Thomas (Brodnax) May inherited the Chawton estates of Mrs Elizabeth Knight in 1738, he changed his surname to Knight. Later, in 1755, a disentailing deed was executed that guaranteed the possession of the Chawton property to the Brodnax line as long as it survived. On its failing, however, the heirs-at-law of Mrs Elizabeth Knight came in. Thomas Knight II, who had adopted Edward, was the last of the Brodnax line. When Edward came into possession of the Chawton property there were those who felt he had no legal claim to the estate. Not all the heirs-at-law of Mrs Elizabeth Knight wanted to assert their claims, but one of them, James Baverstock of Alton, Hampshire, decided to do something about it. Baverstock had married Jane Hinton, a daughter of the Revd John Hinton, rector of Chawton, whose first wife Martha was listed in Baverstock's claim as the 'sole representative of the Knights of Chawton'.[36] An amusing sidelight on the case is given by Lord Brabourne: 'There is a curious story connected with the law suit to the effect that an old, long-since deceased Mr Knight appeared twice or thrice in a dream to the claimant, and informed him that he was the rightful owner of Chawton.'[37]

Early in 1814 an attempt was made by Baverstock to force Edward to give up Chawton. In a letter to Cassandra in March of that year Jane wrote: 'Perhaps you have not heard that Edward has a good chance of escaping his Lawsuit. His opponent knocks under. The terms of agreement are not quite settled.'[38] But Jane was too optimistic, for instead of 'knocking under', Baverstock filed his suit and in October 1814 Edward was formally served with a writ of ejectment from Chawton. As the loss of his Chawton property would have deprived him of two-thirds of his annual income, Edward filed a countersuit. The court proceedings dragged on for several years, and were settled only when Edward paid £15,000 to the plaintiff 'that all claims on the estate should be for ever relinquished'.[39]

The severe financial loss to Edward, according to one of his nieces, 'occasioned the great gap in Chawton Park Wood, visible for 30 years afterwards, and probably not filled up again even now.'[40] The loss of so large a sum was also particularly crippling to Edward as he had already lost £20,000 when his brother Henry was declared a bankrupt in March 1816.

Edward was in Hampshire at the time of Jane's death and was present with his younger brothers, Henry and Francis, and his nephew James Edward, at her funeral in Winchester Cathedral. He was therefore among those whom his nephew remembered fifty-three years later:

> Her brothers went back sorrowing to their several homes. They were very fond and very proud of her. They were attached to her by her talents, her virtues, and her engaging manners; and each loved afterwards to fancy a resemblance in some niece or daughter of his own to the dear sister Jane, whose perfect equal they yet never expected to see.[41]

Edward, who lived on at Godmersham for thirty-five years after Jane's death, saw all his eleven children reach maturity. He died there on 19 November 1852, at the age of eighty-five. He had been able to take his usual drive on the previous day. Early on the morning of his death he asked his servant to leave him as he felt comfortable and wanted to rest. When the servant returned, he discovered that Edward had died in his sleep. In commenting on his peaceful death, one of his relations said,

> It strikes me as a characteristic end of a prosperous and placid life, and he will certainly leave on the minds of all who knew him an image of Gentleness and quiet Cheerfulness of no ordinary degree.[42]

He was buried beside his wife in the Knight family vault in Godmersham church. The inscription on his monument ends with these lines from the Book of Ecclesiasticus: 'Living peaceably in his habitation he was honoured in his generation. A merciful man, whose righteousness shall not be forgotten.'

Henry Thomas
Jane's favourite brother

JANE AUSTEN described him with amused resignation in four carefully chosen words — 'Oh, what a Henry!'[1] She was speaking of her favourite brother, Henry Thomas, allegedly the brightest, but the least stable of the otherwise solidly satisfactory Hampshire-born Austens. Tall and physically attractive, with the alert 'peculiar and bright' hazel eyes of his father, Henry was the best-looking of all Jane Austen's brothers.[2] According to his nephew he 'had great conversational powers, and inherited from his father an eager and sanguine disposition. He was a very entertaining companion, but had perhaps less steadiness of purpose, certainly less success in life, than his brothers.'[3] His niece, Anna Lefroy, remembered him as

> the handsomest of the family, and in the opinion of his own father, the most talented. There were others who formed a different estimate, but for the most part, he was greatly admired. Brilliant in conversation he was, and like his father, blessed with a hopefulness of temper which, in adapting itself to all circumstances, even the most adverse, served to create a perpetual sunshine.[4]

But these guardedly complimentary estimates of Henry's character and personality represent only the brighter side of the picture. There were others in the family, particularly those who had lost heavily when he was declared a bankrupt in 1816, who had reason to feel resentful at his 'almost exasperating buoyancy and sanguineness of temperament and high animal spirits which no misfortunes could depress and no failures damp.'[5] Henry's great-nephew, the first Lord Brabourne, remarked, '... his sister gauged his character pretty well, and did not anticipate much success for his career.'[6] Lord Brabourne also illustrated Henry's quixotic impetuosity with a characteristic anecdote:

133

He is said to have been driving on one occasion with a relation in one of the rough country lanes near Steventon, when the pace at which the postchaise was advancing did not satisfy his eager temperament. Putting his head out of the window, he cried out to the postillion, 'Get on, boy! get on, will you?' The 'boy' turned round in his saddle, and replied: 'I *do* get on, sir, where I can!' 'You stupid fellow!' was the rejoinder, 'Any fool can do that. I want you to get on *where you can't.*'[7]

Henry, who was four years older than Jane Austen, was privately baptized at Steventon on 8 July 1771. A year and a half later, his mother wrote to her sister-in-law, Mrs Walter: 'My little boy is come home from nurse, and a fine stout little fellow he is, and can run anywhere. . . .'[8] Three years later, she told the same correspondent,

> Henry has been in breeches some months and thinks himself near as good a man as his brother Neddy, indeed no one would judge by their looks that there was above three years and a half difference in their ages, one is so little and the other so great.[9]

Many years later, in describing one of her brother Edward's sons, Jane Austen recalled her own childhood recollections and wrote: 'George's enquiries were endless, and his eagerness in everything reminds me often *of his Uncle Henry.*'[10]

Like his brothers, Henry received his early education at home from his father. A retrospective glimpse of his early schooldays was given by him in a letter addressed to Warren Hastings in 1802:

> Your works of taste, both of the pencil & the pen were continually offered to my notice as objects of imitation & spurs to exertion. I shall never forget the delight which I experienced when on producing a translation of a well-known ode of Horace to my Father's criticism, he favoured me with a perusal of your manuscript and as a high mark of commendation said that he was sure Mr Hastings would have been pleased with the perusal of my humble essay.[11]

Henry's parents had expected he would become a clergyman, but their hopes were foiled, for a good many years at least, when Mr Austen's worldly niece Eliza, Comtesse de Feuillide, returned to England from France in 1786. Although only fifteen, Henry immediately attracted the attentions of his alluring cousin, ten years his senior and a self-acknowledged flirt. The attraction was apparently mutual, for in April 1787 Eliza wrote to her cousin Philadelphia Walter from London:

> ... it will not be in my power to receive you the latter end of the month, which my cousin Henry Austen is to spend with us, & this visit cannot be deferred because it is most probable he will soon be obliged to reside at Oxford.[12]

In July of the following year Henry went up to St John's College, Oxford, on a Founder's Kin scholarship. He had hoped to return to France with Eliza. His plans miscarried, for Philadelphia Walter in reporting the family news to her brother James at that time wrote: 'Henry Austen is sadly mortified that one of the Fellows of St John's choosing to marry or die, which vacancy he is obliged to fill up, and would totally prevent his accompanying his cousin to France, which was particularly harped upon on both sides....'[13] That did not prevent Eliza from continuing her flirtations. In August of the same year she dropped in on Henry and James Austen at Oxford, at which time she informed Philadelphia Walter, 'I do not think you would know Henry with his hair powdered and dressed in a very *tonish* style, besides he is at present taller than his father.'[14]

Apart from his regular studies at Oxford, Henry also helped his brother James with the publication of *The Loiterer;* it contained several essays by Henry, some of which were quite spirited and amusing. One of them, No. 47, warning its readers against an over-indulgence in romantic ideas, is of particular interest because of its influence on Jane Austen, who was then writing *Love and Freindship.*

In blaming the sentimental novel for the dispersal of 'degenerate and sickly refinement', Henry warned his readers that those who insisted on emulating the example set by the emotional heroines of fiction would 'be tortured by the poignant delicacy of their own feelings, and fall the Martyrs to their own Susceptibility'. Jane obviously made a note of Henry's observation, for in *Love and Freindship* she parodied her brother's admonition when she made her heroine declare, 'A sensibility too tremblingly alive to every affliction of my Freinds [*sic*], my Acquaintance and particularly to every affliction of my own, was my only fault, if a fault it could be called.'[15]

In 1792, the year Henry was awarded his Bachelor of Arts degree, he was also honoured by Jane with the dedication of one of her juvenilia, *Lesley Castle*, a rollicking burlesque that undoubtedly elicited hearty laughter when it was read aloud at Steventon rectory. Jane's dedication to Henry is interesting, as its wording suggests her brother had also been indulging in novel-writing. The significant sentence in the dedication reads: 'I am now availing myself of the Liberty you have frequently honoured me with of dedicating one of my Novels to you.'[16] Unfortunately no trace of any attempts at fiction by Henry has ever been discovered. That he was pleased with the dedication is apparent, for he added to it, 'Messrs Demand & Co. — please to pay Jane Austen Spinster the sum of one hundred guineas on account of your Humbl. Servant. H T Austen'.[17]

A few years before this joking took place, Eliza de Feuillide had fled with her mother and child to England to escape the upheaval of the French Revolution. The intimacy between Henry and herself was immediately resumed, and, although Eliza's husband was still alive, it is obvious she exerted considerable influence over her susceptible young male cousin. In 1791-2, the Comte de Feuillide had briefly visited his wife and returned to France. Eliza then went to Steventon. From there she wrote to Philadelphia Walter:

> Henry is now rather more than six foot high, I believe: He also is much improved, and is certainly endowed with uncommon abilities, which indeed seem to have been bestowed, tho' in a different way upon each member of this family — As to the coolness which you know had taken place between H. & myself, it has now ceased, in consequence of due acknowledgments   on his part, and we are at present on very proper relation-like terms, you know that his family design him for the Church.[18]

The last phrase is significant, for Eliza's distaste for the cloth as a suitable profession for a young man of spirit was well known.

When France declared war on Great Britain in 1793 Henry joined the Oxford Militia as a lieutenant. The next year brought the news of Eliza's husband's untimely death on the guillotine. Meanwhile Henry had been complimenting Warren Hastings in a pompous letter on the favourable outcome of his impeachment trial,[19] and at the same time was courting a girl named Mary

Pearson. She was a daughter of Sir Richard Pearson, one of the officers of Greenwich Hospital, who, earlier in his naval career, had been the commanding officer of the *Serapis* when she was defeated by John Paul Jones in the *Bonhomme Richard* during the American Revolution.[20] According to Eliza, Mary Pearson led Henry a merry chase, but Eliza was hardly an unprejudiced observer.

The period of Henry's courtship of Mary Pearson coincided with the earliest of Jane Austen's surviving letters. From them one is able to gather a good deal concerning Henry's movements. In January 1796, when he received his Master of Arts degree, he was 'hankering after the Regulars' and 'has got a scheme in his head about getting a lieutenancy and adjutancy in the 86th, a new-raised regiment, which he fancies will be ordered to the Cape of Good Hope,' Jane noted, adding, 'I heartily hope that he will, as usual, be disappointed in this scheme.'[21] Later in the year, when Jane wanted to return home from Kent where she had been visiting her brother Edward, Henry's inability to act as her escort proved difficult. At that time young women of Jane Austen's class did not travel alone in a public conveyance, but Henry, who was ailing and had gone off to seek a doctor's advice, came up with an idea that he was certain would solve the problem. Jane was coaxed into writing to Mary Pearson suggesting she would visit her at Greenwich for a few days, after which the two of them would be joined by a male member of the Austen family who would escort them to Steventon. Jane made the best of the situation by suggesting that her father would 'be so good as to fetch home his prodigal Daughter from Town ... unless he wishes me to walk the Hospitals, Enter at the Temple, or mount Guard at St James'.[22] The situation was also responsible for an allusion by Jane, showing how deeply her cultural roots were fixed in the eighteenth century. In expressing her mock fears of what might happen to her in London, she told Cassandra, '... if the Pearsons were not at home, I should inevitably fall a Sacrifice to the arts of some fat Woman who would make me drunk with Small Beer'.[23] This vividly suggests the first plate of Hogarth's *Harlot's Progress*, in which a country girl, newly arrived in London, is being cajoled by a fat, over-dressed procuress.

Eventually Jane grew tired of Henry's dilatory ways, comparing her predicament to 'waiting for *Dead men's Shoes*',[24] and returned to Steventon one way or another. Later, Eliza, who was in London, wrote to Philadelphia Walter in November of the same year:

> Our cousin Henry Austen has been in Town: he looks thin & ill. I hear his late intended is a most intolerable flirt, & reckoned to give herself great airs. The person who mentioned this to me says she is a pretty wicked looking girl with bright black eyes which pierce through & through. No wonder this poor young man's heart could not withstand them.[25]

Henry's parents' hopes for his becoming a parson were doomed, for in May of the next year Eliza provided Philadelphia with further details concerning her designs on Henry:

> ... Captn Austen has just spent a few days in town. I suppose you know that our cousin Henry is now Captain, Paymaster, & Adjutant. He is a very lucky young man & bids fair to possess a considerable share of riches & honours. I believe he has now given up all thoughts of the Church, & he is right for he certainly is not so fit for a parson as a soldier....[26]

Evidently Philadelphia Walter chided Eliza for her pursuit of Henry, for two months later Eliza answered obliquely:

> As to your enquiry concerning another youth I have to say that I believe his match with a certain friend of ours, which I know you looked upon as fixed will never take place. For my own part I think this young man ill-used but the lady is so well pleased with her present situation that she cannot find in her heart to change it, and says in her giddy way that independence and the homage of half a dozen are preferable to subjection and the attachment of a single individual.... I am more & more convinced that she is not at all calculated for sober matrimony.[27]

But Eliza was only putting up a smoke-screen for early in 1797, and obviously in preparation for her marriage to Henry, she persuaded John Woodman and Henry's father to relinquish their joint trusteeship of the £10,000 settled on her mother and herself by Warren Hastings.[28] Later in September she went to Lowestoft, ostensibly for the health of her child but mainly to be near Henry who was stationed at Norwich. By December the die was cast. In writing to Warren Hastings three days after Christmas she announced her intention to marry Henry.

I have consented to an Union with my Cousin Captn Austen who has the honour of being known to you. He has been for some time in Possession of a comfortable Income, and the excellence of his Heart, Temper, and Understanding, together with steady attachment to me, his Affection for my little Boy, and his disinterested concurrence in the disposal of my Property in favour of this latter, have at length induced me to an acquiescence which I have withheld for more than two years.[29]

Henry and Eliza were married on 31 December 1797 in Marylebone parish church, an 'edifice then almost in the open country, and because of the remoteness of its situation much favoured for hasty and secret marriages.'[30] Mrs Austen and her daughters had been staying in Bath with the Leigh Perrots:

On returning home for Christmas they received a piece of news which, even if it did not come entirely as a surprise, can hardly have given unmixed pleasure.... Though he [Henry] was endowed with many attractive gifts there was a certain infirmity of purpose in his character that was hardly likely to be remedied by a marriage to his very pleasure-loving cousin.[31]

Eliza's letter to Warren Hastings announcing her marriage was formal and circumspect, but she painted an entirely different picture of her marital arrangements when she wrote in February 1798 to Philadelphia Walter:

Unmixed felicity is certainly not the produce of this world, & like other people I shall probably meet with many unpleasant & untoward circumstances but all the comfort which can result from the tender affection & society of a being who is possessed of an excellent heart, understanding & temper, I have at least ensured — to say nothing of the pleasure of having my own way in everything, for Henry well knows that I have not been much accustomed to controul & should probably behave rather awkwardly under it, and therefore like a wise man he has no will but mine, which to be sure some people would call spoiling me, but I know it is the best way of managing me....[32]

Henry continued to serve with the Oxford Militia a little longer, during which time Eliza, according to her own account, enjoyed the adulation of her husband's fellow officers, although she assured Philadelphia Walter she had 'left off trade' as far as flirtation was concerned.[33] By June 1801 Henry had resigned his commission and he and Eliza had moved to London where, according to Philadelphia Walter,

> I spent one day with our cousins the Henry Austens. She is much the same, but talks of retiring into Wales — resigning the world, in which he seems perfectly to agree. He has given up the Army. They live quite in style in Upper Berkeley Street, Portman Square.[34]

By then, if there had been any resentment on the part of Henry's parents concerning his marriage, it had been smoothed over, for his sister Cassandra spent three weeks with the couple at that address earlier in the same year. During her visit Jane Austen wrote: 'I hope you will see everything worthy of notice, from the Opera House to Henry's office in Cleveland Court.' Then she added playfully, 'You will have a turkey from Steventon while you are there, and pray note down how many full courses of exquisite dishes M. Halavant converts it into.'[35] — Monsieur Halavant being Eliza's expensive French cook. An elegant carriage had also been added to the establishment to facilitate her getting around London.

It was while the couple lived in Upper Berkeley Street that Eliza's fifteen-year-old handicapped son, Hastings de Feuillide, died.

Henry's office in Cleveland Court was his first London business address as a banker and army agent, a firm he had founded with a former fellow officer named Henry Maunde. Later they moved to the Albany. In 1807 they were joined by another former officer of the Oxford Militia named James Tilson, at which time the firm was renamed Austen, Maunde and Tilson, with offices at 10 Henrietta Street, Covent Garden. Henry had also become an associate of the banking firm of Austen, Gray and Vincent of Alton, Hampshire.

Meanwhile, the Peace of Amiens in March 1802 had sent English tourists flocking across the Channel for a look at Napoleon's Paris. In the late spring of the next year they were followed by Henry and Eliza, who went to France hoping to be able to salvage something from the estate of Eliza's first husband. Nothing definite concerning these negotiations is known, but according to family tradition it was Eliza's perfect command of French that saved Henry and her from being detained in France with the hundreds of British subjects whom Napoleon ordered to be arrested when the short-lived peace with England was suddenly terminated in May 1803. Eliza's plan was a clever if risky one. Henry was relegated to an invalid's role in a corner of their travelling carriage, and Eliza gave the orders for fresh horses at the posting stations between Paris and the unknown port from which they eventually escaped to England.

Henry's residence in London exerted a culturally broadening influence on Jane Austen, for, although she apparently preferred the quiet routine of life in a country village for most of the year, she also enjoyed the excitement of her regular visits to London. Henry made sure Jane saw the latest art exhibitions and also highlighted her stays with frequent visits to the Covent Garden and Drury Lane theatres. On one occasion Henry made some blunder with the theatre tickets causing Jane to miss a performance by Mrs Siddons. This prompted her to remark, 'I should particularly have liked seeing her in Constance, & could swear at her with little effort for disappointing me.'[36] Henry made up later for disappointing Jane when he took her to Drury Lane to see Edmund Kean as Shylock in *The Merchant of Venice*. She wrote to Cassandra:

> I shall like to see Kean again excessively, & to see him with you too; — it appeared to me as if there were no fault in him anywhere; & in his scene with Tubal there was exquisite acting.[37]

Both Henry and Eliza had a wide acquaintance in the fashionable world. In Eliza's case, this included many of her French friends who had been fortunate enough to escape to England from the turmoil on the Continent. Among these were the Comte and Comtesse d'Antraigues and their musical son Julien, to whose home at Barnes in Surrey Henry and Eliza took Jane for an evening visit in 1811. The Comtesse, who before her marriage had been Mlle Saint-Huberty, was a celebrated dramatic soprano at the Paris Opera before the Revolution, while her husband, who claimed to be a distant relation of the ill-fated Bourbons, was then operating as a Russian secret agent in England. Jane was particularly impressed with the Comte, whom she described as 'a very fine looking man, with quiet manners, good enough for an Englishman....'[38] The Comte took particular pleasure in showing Jane his fine collection of paintings, which, she said, 'delighted Henry as much as the Son's music gratified Eliza — & among them, a Miniature of Philip 5. of Spain, Louis 14.s Grandson, which exactly suited *my* capacity.'[39] Unfortunately, the Comte and his wife were murdered a year later by a demented Italian servant who then committed suicide.[40]

At the time of her visit to the d'Antraigues, Jane was staying with Henry and Eliza at their fine house at 64 Sloane Street, where she was engaged in correcting the proofs of *Sense and Sensibility.* It was also during this visit that Eliza gave a grand evening musical party that was not only mentioned in the *Morning Post* for 25 April 1811, but also inspired one of Jane's most sparkling letters.[41] The affair was a fitting climax for Eliza's pleasure-loving life. Shortly afterwards she became gravely ill, possibly with cancer like her mother. She died after a long illness on 25 April 1813.

In commenting on Henry's reaction to Eliza's death in a letter to her brother Francis, Jane wrote:

> Upon the whole his Spirits are very much recovered. — If I may so express myself, his Mind is not a Mind for affliction. He is too Busy, too active, too sanguine. — Sincerely as he was attached to poor Eliza moreover, & excellently as he behaved to her, he was always so used to be away from her at times, that her Loss is not felt as that of many a beloved wife might be, especially when all of the circumstances of her long and dreadful Illness are taken into account. — He very long knew that she must die, & it was indeed a release at last.[42]

In September 1813, shortly after Eliza's death, Henry visited Warren Hastings at his Daylesford estate in Worcestershire. Later, in commenting on this visit in a letter to Cassandra, Jane Austen wrote, 'Mr Hastings never *hinted* at Eliza in the smallest degree.'[43] It may be suggestive that the word 'hinted' was underlined.

Henry's residence in London was also rewarding for Jane

Austen from a business standpoint. His first negotiations on her behalf took place early in 1803. Henry sent an employee named Seymour to Richard Crosby, the London publisher, with Jane's manuscript of a novel she had called *Susan*, for which Crosby paid £10. The novel was later advertised as *Susan: a Novel in 2 Volumes*, but was never published. Six years later, Jane wrote to Crosby under the assumed name of Mrs Ashton Dennis, asking if the manuscript had been lost. If it had been, she offered to provide a copy. Jane then said if no reply to her letter was received, she would feel at liberty to arrange for the novel's publication elsewhere. Crosby's reply was curt, telling his correspondent he still had the novel, but that no firm commitment had been made regarding its publication. He also said if it was published elsewhere he would instigate proceedings to stop the sale. Crosby then added, 'the MS. shall be yours for the same as we paid for it'.[44]

Crosby's rebuff was unnecessarily blunt, but Henry and Jane had the last laugh. After *Emma* was published, Henry bought back from Crosby the manuscript of *Susan* and the copyright. When the £10 had been paid, he had the pleasure of telling the publisher the manuscript he had just relinquished was by the author of *Pride and Prejudice*. The manuscript of *Susan*, with possible later alterations by Jane Austen, was finally published as *Northanger Abbey* after Jane Austen's death.

Henry conducted all the business arrangements for the publication of *Sense and Sensibility, Pride and Prejudice, Mansfield Park,* and *Emma,* the four novels that came out during Jane Austen's lifetime. He also supervised the publication of *Northanger Abbey* and *Persuasion* after his sister's death.

Henry's severe illness in late 1815, during which Jane nursed him for several months at his home in Hans Place, London, was also responsible for the most notable recognition she received during her lifetime. Caroline Austen, an old lady with a long and excellent memory, included the episode in her memoir of her aunt that was 'Written out, At Frog Firle — Sussex', in March 1867.

It was during this stay in London, that a little gleam of Court favour shone upon her. She had at first published her novels with a great desire of remaining *herself* unknown — but it was found impossible to preserve a secret that so many of the family knew and by this time, she had given up the attempt —

and her name had been made public enough — tho' it was never inserted in the title page —

Two of the great Physicians of the day attended my Uncle during his illness — I am not, at this distance of time, sufficiently sure *which* they were, as to give their names, but *one* of them had very intimate access to the Prince Regent, and continuing his visits during my Uncle's recovery, he told my Aunt one day, that the Prince was a great admirer of her novels: that he often read them, and had a set in each of his residences — That *he*, the physician had told his Royal Highness that Miss Austen was now in London, and that by the Prince's desire, Mr Clarke, the Librarian of Carlton House, would speedily wait upon her —

Mr Clarke came, and endorsed all previous compliments, and invited my Aunt to see Carlton House, saying the Prince had charged him to show her the Library there, adding many civilities as to the pleasure his R.H. had received from her novels — Three had then been published — The invitation could not be declined — and my Aunt went, at an appointed time, to Carlton House —

She saw the Library, and I believe, some other apartments, but the particulars of her visit, if I ever heard them, I have now forgotten — only *this*, I *do* well recollect — that in the course of it, Mr Clarke, speaking again of the Regent's admiration of her writing, declared himself charged to say, that if Miss Austen had any other novel forthcoming, she was quite at liberty to dedicate it to the Prince.

My Aunt made all proper acknowledgments at the moment, but had no intention of accepting the honour offered — until she was avised [*sic*] by some of her friends that she must consider the permission as a command —

Emma was then in the Publisher's hands — so a few lines of dedication were affixed to the 1st volume, and following still the instructions of the well-informed, she sent a copy, handsomely bound, to Carlton House — and I *suppose* it was duly acknowledged by Mr Clarke —

My Aunt, soon after her visit to *him*, returned home, where the little adventure was talked of for a while with some interest, and afforded some amusement — In the following Spring, Mr Henry Austen ceased to reside in London, and my

Aunt was never brought so near the precincts of the Court again — nor did she ever try to recall herself to the recollection of Physician, Librarian or Prince, and so ended this little burst of Royal Patronage.[45]

On another occasion when Jane Austen was staying with Henry in London, she received an invitation of a different kind.

Miss Austen was on a visit in London soon after the publication of *Mansfield Park*: a nobleman, personally unknown to her, but who had good reasons for considering her to be the authoress of that work, was desirous of her joining a literary circle at his house. He communicated his wish in the politest manner, through a mutual friend, adding, what his Lordship doubtless thought would be an irresistable inducement, that the celebrated Madame de Staël would be of the party. Miss Austen immediately declined the invitation. To her truly delicate mind such a display would have given pain instead of pleasure.[46]

Henry, whose extroverted assurance made it easy for him to meet anyone on his or her particular ground, was no doubt disappointed that Jane's shyness with strangers caused her to decline the invitation to meet the formidable Madame de Staël. But his brotherly pride in her accomplishments was not content until he had betrayed the secret that the anonymous 'Lady' who appeared on the title pages as the authoress of the novels was none other than his younger sister. The revelation apparently had already been made by 1813, when Henry was in Scotland, after which Jane, in a letter to her brother Francis wrote:

Henry heard P. & P. warmly praised in Scotland, by Lady Robt Kerr & another Lady; — & what does he do in the warmth of his Brotherly vanity & Love, but immediately tell them who wrote it! A Thing once set going in that way — one knows how it spreads! — and he, dear Creature, has set it going so much more than once.... I am trying to harden myself. After all, what a trifle it is in all its Bearings, to the really important points of one's existence even in this World![47]

Henry's 'dreams of affluence, nay of competence',[48] to use his own words, were about to end. In 1813 he had been made Receiver General for Taxes for Oxfordshire, at which time his uncle, James Leigh Perrot and his brother, Edward Knight, acted as his sureties for £10,000 and £20,000 respectively. The inflationary economy created by the war with France had also brought prosperity to the banking firm of which he was a member. After Waterloo, however, a severe economic depression brought ruin to many speculators. The failure of the Alton bank in which Henry was a partner brought down the London bank of Austen, Maunde and Tilson in March 1816. No personal extravagance was attributed to Henry, but his bankruptcy caused serious losses to several members of his family, particularly to his uncle and brother, both of whom lost the large sums of money they had pledged when he became Receiver General. Jane's losses were fairly light, amounting to a little over £13, part of her profits from *Mansfield Park*.[49] The strain of her worry over Henry's financial ruin came at the beginning of her critical illness, however, and added greatly to her physical distress.

Optimistic as ever, at the age of forty-five Henry decided to turn from banking to the church. By September 1816 Jane notified Cassandra at Cheltenham: '...he is decided for Orders'.[50] According to Caroline Austen's reminiscences, Henry went early in December 1816 to be examined by the Bishop of Winchester. Before setting out, Henry brushed up his Greek in order to be able to answer the bishop's questions. His efforts were unnecessary, however, for when the bishop had finished questioning him, he placed his hand on a Greek Testament lying on a nearby table and remarked, 'As for this book, Mr Austen, I dare say it is some years since either you or I looked into it.'[51] A few days later Henry was ordained deacon in Salisbury Cathedral by John Fisher, Bishop of Salisbury, on Letters Dismissory from the Bishop of Winchester.[52]

Henry, for whom London, according to Jane, had 'become a hateful place',[53] became curate for the Revd John Rawston Papillon, rector of Chawton, in December 1816. One month later, Jane wrote to her friend Alethea Bigg:

Our own new clergyman is expected here very soon, perhaps in time to assist Mr Papillon on Sunday. I shall be very glad when the first hearing is over. It will be a nervous hour for our pew, though we hear that he acquits himself with as much ease and collectedness, as if he had been used to it all his life.[54]

Henry was ordained priest in the Quebec Chapel of the Parish of St Marylebone in London, early in 1817.[55] In May of the same year he and his nephew William Knight rode in the rain beside the carriage that took Jane to Winchester for the last time. Henry visited her in Winchester many times during her last illness and may have assisted his brother James when their sister received the Sacrament some time before her death. He was also present with his brothers, Edward and Francis, and his nephew, James Edward, at Jane's funeral in Winchester Cathedral.

In the autumn of 1818, while he was still curate at Chawton, Henry served for a time as chaplain to the British Embassy in Berlin. While there he delivered a series of *Lectures upon some important passages in The Book of Genesis* in the chapel of the British Minister in Berlin. These were published in 1820, at which time Henry was described on the title page as being rector of Steventon and domestic chaplain to HRH the Duke of Cumberland and the Rt Hon the Earl of Morley.[56] Henry had become rector of Steventon in 1820, following the death of his elder brother James in December 1819. Henry also married for the second time in 1820, his wife being Eleanor Jackson, a niece of the Revd J. R. Papillon. Eleanor, who survived Henry, was an authoress of sorts, and published *An Epitome of the Old Testament* in 1831, which she dedicated to the Bishop of Winchester.[57]

In 1822 Henry became the curate of Farnham, Surrey, and later a master at the Farnham Grammar School. In 1824 he also became perpetual curate of Bentley, a village on the road from Farnham to Alton. While there he secured the erection of a cage for the drunk and disorderly that replaced the time-honoured stocks and whipping-post, a project to which he contributed out of his meagre income.[58]

In 1826 Henry published *A Sermon in aid of the fund-raising for the Vaudois,* following it three years later with another sermon based on the text, 'Ye know not what manner of spirit ye are'. Copies of these, together with his Berlin lectures on the Book of Genesis, are in the British Library.

Henry, who has been described as 'an earnest preacher of the evangelical school',[59] resigned his Farnham curacy in 1827, and his curacy at Bentley in 1839. He is said to have lived afterwards in France for a while. Henry attended the funeral of his sister

Cassandra at Chawton in March 1845, at which time J. E. Austen-Leigh noted, 'Uncle Henry struck me as very agreeable and not very old.'[60] He died five years later on 12 March 1850 in Tunbridge Wells, Kent, and is buried there in Woodbury Park Cemetery, where his well-preserved tombstone, bearing properly evangelical quotations from the Bible, may still be seen.

Cassandra Elizabeth
the beloved sister

THERE are two ways of regarding Cassandra Elizabeth, Jane Austen's beloved sister. One is to impugn her for her calculated destruction of her sister's intimate letters and other papers a few years before her own death in 1845. The other is to be thankful she spared as much as she did from the flames.

In the light of today's scholarly interest in the smallest facts concerning Jane Austen's tragically brief life, Cassandra's systematic destruction of her sister's papers seems almost criminal, but she had her own reasons for acting as she did.

Cassandra, who was almost three years older than Jane, was the fifth of the Hampshire-born Austens, and was privately baptized on 9 January 1773. In June of the same year her mother wrote to her sister-in-law, Mrs Walter:

> I want to show you my Henry and Cassy, who are both reckoned fine children. I suckled my little girl thro' the first quarter; she has been weaned and settled at a good woman's at Deane just eight weeks; she is very healthy and lively and puts on her short petticoats to-day.[1]

Two years later Cassandra's proud mother informed Mrs Walter: 'My little girl talks all day long, and in my opinion is a very entertaining companion.'[2] Mrs Austen was carrying Jane at that time, but instead of being born when expected, she surprised her parents by being a month overdue. When she arrived on 16 December 1775, her father wrote to Mrs Walter: 'We have now another girl, a present plaything for her sister Cassy and a future companion. She is to be Jenny, and seems to me as if she would be as like Henry, as Cassy is to Neddy.'[3]

In recalling his two aunts, J. E. Austen-Leigh wrote:

> Their sisterly affection for each other could scarcely be

exceeded. Perhaps it began on Jane's side with the feeling of deference natural to a loving child toward a kind elder sister ... This attachment was never interrupted or weakened. They lived in the same home, and shared the same bed-room, till separated by death. They were not exactly alike. Cassandra's was the colder and calmer disposition; she was always prudent and well judging, but with less outward demonstration of feeling and less sunniness of temper than Jane possessed. It was remarked in her family that 'Cassandra had the *merit* of having her temper always under command, but that Jane had the *happiness* of a temper that never required to be commanded.'[4]

But Cassandra's reserved nature was only a mask that covered very deep feeling. Her strong attachment to Jane during her lifetime, fortified by her belief that she would rejoin her younger sister in a better world when her own earthly life was ended, was the mainspring of her existence. That she was bitterly disappointed when the man to whom she was engaged died before they could be married is true. But Jane was there to help her endure her sorrow, and the deep-seated love and understanding that developed between the two sisters as the years passed was terminated only by Jane's untimely death. No one with the least claim to feeling can read the two letters Cassandra wrote to her niece Fanny Knight after Jane's death without being moved. For though Cassandra's stoicism enabled her to take the world in her quiet stride for twenty-eight years after Jane's body was buried in Winchester Cathedral, she never forgot the prediction her father made when Jane was born that she would be her 'present plaything' and 'a future companion'. Cassandra's fortitude was unconquerable, and the remembrance of the mutual intimacy that had existed between her sister and herself never faded. When a great-niece was staying at Chawton long after Jane's death she was 'greatly struck and impressed' by the way Cassandra spoke of her sister: '... there was such an accent of *living* love in her voice'.[5]

Altogether, Cassandra and Jane had only about five years of formal schooling, the rest of their education being obtained from their parents and elder brothers, and by well-regulated reading. Their first schoolmistress was Mrs Ann Cawley, widow of Dr Ralph Cawley, sometime Principal of Brasenose College, Oxford, and a sister of the Dr Edward Cooper who had married Mrs Austen's elder sister, Jane Leigh. At some time in 1782, when Mrs

Cawley opened a boarding-school in Oxford, Cassandra, aged nine, and Jane, aged six, were among her pupils. Fortunately Mrs Cawley's enrolment also included her niece, Jane Cooper, a first cousin of the Austen girls, whose quick and independent action a few months later saved Jane Austen from an untimely death. In 1783, when Mrs Cawley, who is remembered as a 'stiff-mannered person',[6] moved her school to Southampton, Cassandra and Jane and their cousin Jane Cooper accompanied her. Shortly afterwards the Austen girls became seriously ill from what was then called putrid fever — presumably typhus.[7] Tradition says Mrs Cawley refused to notify Mr Austen of the gravity of the situation, but Jane Cooper took matters into her own hands and sent off a letter that quickly brought Mrs Austen and Mrs Cooper to Southampton. Cassandra and Jane were taken back to Steventon, where Jane almost died. Unfortunately, Mrs Cooper had caught the infection and died in October 1783, shortly after her return home.

This experience apparently disturbed Mr Austen and his wife considerably, for their daughters were presumably taught at home for at least another year before being sent away to school again. This conjecture is supported by a child's primer of French fables, still preserved in the Austen family, that bears the inscription 'Miss Jane Austen, 5th Dec. 1783' in an adult hand on its outer cover. It was this book that was doubtless used by Mr Austen or some other member of the family to impart the elements of French grammar to eight-year-old Jane. The book, which also contains what is possibly Jane Austen's earliest known signature, also includes two diverting scrawls, 'Mothers angry fathers gone out', and 'I wish I had done', apparently scribbled by Jane during her inattentive moments.[8]

Other motives besides family connections were undoubtedly taken into consideration by Mr Austen when he decided to send his daughters away to school again, for the Abbey School at Reading, where they received their last formal education, was a well-recognized, although easy-going establishment. Earlier biographers of Jane Austen have stated her formal schooling ended in 1784, when she was nine, but that is not correct. Recently discovered banking records of the Revd George Austen prove conclusively that Cassandra and Jane continued their boarding-school education at least until 1787, when the former was fourteen and the latter eleven.[9] Although the banking records do not give a complete picture for the years involved, for Mr Austen doubtless made some of the tuition and board payments in cash, it is definitely known that he paid some of the instalments to 'S. La Tournelle' by cheque, beginning in August 1785 and continuing until January 1787. As usual, Jane insisted on accompanying Cassandra when the time came to depart for Reading, causing her mother to remark, 'If Cassandra were going to have her head cut off, Jane would insist on sharing her fate.'[10]

The Abbey School was founded some time before Cassandra, Jane and their cousin Jane Cooper became pupils.[11] Evidently they were regular scholars, for, according to the memoirs of another girl who was at the school in 1790, those fortunate enough to be styled 'parlour boarders' were rare.[12] Also, contrary to statements made by earlier biographers of Jane Austen, Sarah La Tournelle was not the wife or widow of a French *émigré*. According to her obituary her surname was spelled 'La Tournelle,' the way Mr Austen wrote it on his cheques, and not 'Latournelle,' the spelling used by these biographers:

> ... having early in life, been engaged as a French teacher, her employers thought it right to introduce her into the school under a foreign name. She accordingly took that of La Tournelle, and her real name was probably known only to a few of her numerous friends. ...[13]

The notice also gave her real name as Sarah Hackitt and stated she was a native of London and sixty years of age at the time of her death at Henley-on-Thames.

By the time Cassandra and Jane attended the school Mrs La Tournelle's partner was a Miss Pitts, a former parlour boarder at the school whose wealthy bachelor uncle had disinherited her, leaving his fortune to his housekeeper. Miss Pitts, a handsome young woman, was an excellent needlewoman, played and sang well, spoke fluent French, and 'danced remarkably well, but with too much of the Scotch style, which was then the fashion'.[14] Her partnership with Mrs La Tournelle gave the school a good reputation, and its enrolment was largely made up of young girls from the families of the landed gentry, professional classes and clergy. Later, after Cassandra and Jane had left the school, Miss Pitts married a French *émigré*, a M. St Quentin, and they subsequently moved the school to London, where Mary Russell Mitford and Lady Caroline Lamb were numbered among their pupils. After the fall of Napoleon the school was transferred to Paris, where Fanny Kemble was one of the scholars.[15]

The Abbey School was established in the still-extant thirteenth-century inner gatehouse of Reading Abbey, founded by Henry I in 1121. In Cassandra and Jane's time it was described as 'a gateway with rooms above, and on each side of it a vast staircase, of which the balustrades had been gilt.'[16] When the school continued to prosper, Mrs La Tournelle expanded her establishment by renting a large house next door that 'was encompassed by a beautiful old-fashioned garden, where the children played under tall trees in hot summer evenings.'[17]

Mrs La Tournelle was a stout conservative woman with a cork leg:

> She never had been seen or known to have changed the fashion of her dress; her white muslin handkerchief was always pinned with the same number of pins, her muslin apron always hung in the same form; she always wore the same short sleeves, cuffs and ruffles, with a breast bow to answer the bow on her cap, both being flat with notched ends.[18]

As headmistress, she presided in a wainscoted parlour hung round with chenille pieces representing tombs and weeping willows, with a clothwork screen in a corner and several miniatures over the lofty mantelpiece. When she was not engaged in teaching, making tea, ordering dinner, sorting out clothes for the laundress, or attending to her pupils' physical needs, she liked to hold forth concerning 'plays, and play acting, and greenroom anecdotes, and the private lives of actors'.[19]

Discipline at the school was relatively relaxed, for once the girls had said their lessons they were at liberty to lounge about the garden or gossip with their friends in the turrets flanking the abbey gateway. The permissiveness at the school is substantiated by an Austen family tradition that says Cassandra and Jane and their cousin, Jane Cooper, 'were allowed to accept an invitation to dine at an inn with their respective brothers, Edward Austen and Edward Cooper'.[20] That a general sense of well-being prevailed at the school is also evident from a remark made by Jane Austen in a letter written to Cassandra from Kent in September

1796: 'The letter which I have this moment received from you has diverted me beyond moderation. I could die of laughter at it, as they used to say at school.'[21]

In July 1788, after Cassandra and Jane had left the Abbey School for good, they accompanied their parents on a visit to their relations in Kent. At that time their cousin Philadelphia Walter reported her reaction to them in a letter to her brother James:

> As it's pure Nature to love ourselves I may be allowed to give the preference to the Eldest who is generally reckoned a most striking resemblance to me in features, complexion & manners. I never found myself so much disposed to be vain, as I can't help thinking her very pretty, but fancied I could discover *she* was not so well pleased with the comparison — which reflection abated a great deal of the vanity so likely to arise, & so proper to be supprest.[22]

Philadelphia was not impressed with Jane, considering her 'not at all pretty & very prim, unlike a girl of twelve ... whimsical and affected', but her admiration of Cassandra was unstinting, for she added, 'I continue to admire my amiable likeness the best of the two in every respect: she keeps up conversation in a very sensible & pleasing manner.'[23] It was the beginning of a lifelong mutual admiration, for Philadelphia (afterward Mrs George Whitaker) and Cassandra continued to be on friendly terms until the former's death in 1834.

Shortly after Cassandra and Jane returned home from the Abbey School, to ensure their greater privacy an upstairs sitting-room at Steventon rectory was arranged for them. In describing the room, Anna Lefroy, who played in it as a child, wrote:

> This room, the Dressing room, as they were pleased to call it, communicated with one of smaller size where my two Aunts slept: I remember the common looking carpet, with its chocolate ground that covered the floor, and some portions of the furniture. A painted press, with shelves above for books, that stood with its back to the wall next the Bedroom, and opposite the fireplace; my Aunt Jane's Pianoforte — and above all, on a table between the windows, above which hung a looking glass, 2 Tunbridge ware work boxes of oval shape, fitted up with ivory bands containing reels for silk — yard

measures &c. I thought them beautiful, & so perhaps in their day, & their degree they were. . . . But the charm of the room, with its scanty furniture and cheaply papered walls, must have been, for those old enough to understand it, the flow of native homebred wit with all the fun & nonsense of a clever family who had but little intercourse with the outer world.[24]

That the room was a snug refuge for the Austen girls and their ageing parents, particularly when the winter winds blew in from the North Hampshire Downs, is evident from a letter to Cassandra written in December 1798, in which Jane said, 'We live entirely in the dressing-room now, which I like very much; I always feel more elegant in it than in the parlour.'[25]

It was presumably in this room that Jane's first literary efforts were written, four of which, *The Beautiful Cassandra*; *The History of England* . . . . *By a partial, prejudiced, & ignorant Historian*; *Catharine or The Bower*; and an 'Ode to Pity', were dedicated to Cassandra, all being prefaced by facetious mock inscriptions.[26] Cassandra, who apparently had received drawing lessons while she was at school, or after her return home, painted thirteen water-colour caricatures of British royalty to illustrate her younger sister's tongue-in-cheek *History of England*. Cassandra was Jane's first critical audience of one, and her laughter and encouragement no doubt inspired her pert younger sister to write down her burlesques of the sentimental novels in the three surviving notebooks that Cassandra fortunately preserved when she destroyed many of her sister's other papers. Later, Cassandra's long memory, with the aid of original manuscripts and other memoranda no longer in existence, enabled her to record the dates of composition of her sister's six famous novels.

From the time of their return from school until early in 1797 life was carefree for Cassandra and Jane, both of whom had grown up to be handsome young women. Mrs Austen was still well enough to ensure the domestic arrangements at the rectory ran smoothly, and even if her daughters were occasionally required to assist with the supervision of the brewing and baking, there was plenty of time left over for relaxation. Both Cassandra and Jane enjoyed reading aloud to one another from the latest novels in their own collection or those from the lending library at Basingstoke. There were other diversions when they grew tired of reading. Cassandra drew or looked after her plants,[27] her bees,[28] or her flowers, of which she was very fond. Jane practised the lessons her master, William Chard, the assistant organist at Winchester Cathedral,[29] had assigned her, or played pieces of her own liking on her piano in the upstairs dressing-room. If these simple pleasures palled, there was always sewing for the poor, the making of fancy caps for themselves, or letter-writing to attend to. If the weather was fine they took long walks through the rolling Hampshire countryside, and if the lanes were muddy they minced about on pattens nearer home. During the full moon there was also the excitement of the monthly Assembly Balls at Basingstoke, or smaller but more exclusive dances or dinner parties in the houses of the nearby gentry, to which Cassandra and Jane usually rode in the rectory carriage.

But this serene routine was shortly overshadowed by tragedy. In 1795 Cassandra became engaged to the Revd Thomas Fowle, a former pupil of her father. Tom, as he was familiarly known at Steventon, was a younger son of the Revd Thomas Fowle, vicar of Kintbury, Berkshire. Born in 1766, Tom was seven years older than Cassandra and had lived at Steventon rectory while he was George Austen's pupil. He went up to St John's College, Oxford, in 1783, received a Bachelor of Arts degree in 1787, and a Master of Arts degree in 1794. In December 1793 he was instituted as rector of Allington, a not too lucrative living in Wiltshire, but there is no trace of his ever having done duty there, his presence having been supplied by a curate.[30]

Tom was a distant relation of William Craven (1770-1825), seventh Baron and first Earl of Craven of the second creation, of Hampstead Marshall and Ashdown Park, Berkshire, from whom he had a prospect of early preferment.[31] In 1795 Lord Craven was commanding officer of The Buffs (or 3rd of Foot). When his regiment was ordered to the West Indies as part of the military expedition headed by Sir Ralph Abercromby, Tom went along with his noble kinsman. Contrary to statements in earlier biographies of Jane Austen, however, he did not go along as the chaplain of Lord Craven's regiment. The chaplain at that time was the Revd Humphrey Jones, who was on continuous duty with the Buffs from 1776 to 1797, and is known to have accompanied the regiment to the West Indies.[32] There is also no mention of a Thomas Fowle in the Army Lists for 1793-7, or in the official records of the Buffs.

What happened was that Lord Craven did not in fact sail with Sir Ralph Abercromby and the forces under his command in November 1795 when the latter set out to reduce the French Sugar Islands. Instead, the official records of The Queen's Regiment, into which The Buffs were later incorporated, show that Lord Craven, as a founder of the Royal Yacht Squadron, sailed in his own private yacht to join Sir Ralph Abercromby in the West Indies.[33] Since it is definitely known Tom Fowle accompanied him, it seems likely that Lord Craven took him along as his private chaplain.[34]

That Cassandra expected to be married on Tom's return is evident from the mention of her wedding clothes in a letter written to her by Jane in September 1796.[35] But Cassandra was doomed to bitter disappointment, for Tom died of yellow fever in San Domingo in February 1797. In writing of the event to Philadelphia Walter in May 1797, Eliza de Feuillide said:

I have just received a letter from Steventon where they are all in great affliction (as I suppose you have heard) for the death of Mr Fowle, the gentleman to whom our cousin Cassandra was engaged. He was expected home this month from St Domingo, where he had accompanied Lord Craven, but alas instead of his arrival news were received of his death. This is a very severe stroke to the whole family, & particularly to poor Cassandra, for whom I feel more than I can express. Indeed I am most sincerely grieved at this event & the pain which it must occasion our worthy relations. Jane says that her sister behaves with a degree of resolution & propriety which no common mind could evince in so trying a situation.[36]

Later Cassandra learned Lord Craven was greatly disturbed by Tom's death, declaring that had he known of his engagement to Cassandra he would never have permitted him to venture into such a treacherous climate. Even so, Tom apparently anticipated something might happen to him while he was away from England, for in October 1795, before setting out with Lord Craven, he made his will in which he left £1,000 to Cassandra and the rest of his property to his father.[37]

It was preferable that such a tragedy should happen to Cassandra, whose philosophical acceptance of fate enabled her to survive, for the same situation might have permanently shattered

Jane, whose nature was more vulnerable. Although Cassandra, by her own admission late in life, had 'never been otherwise than a little ailing',[38] she was fundamentally a person of indomitable courage. She was also, by experience and necessity, a Christian stoic, a conviction she forcefully conveyed in a letter to her cousin, Philadelphia Walter (then Mrs George Whitaker), sixteen years after Jane's death. In it she said:

> ...but you & I have lived long enough not to expect perfection in this imperfect world & to be thankful for the blessings we are allowed to enjoy, without embittering them with vain wishes for what is unattainable.[39]

The loss of Tom Fowle was apparently so traumatic that Cassandra never again entertained the idea of marriage, although there are hints in Jane's surviving letters that there were those who would have been happy if she had considered them as prospective husbands. But that never happened, and Cassandra's strong sense of duty toward her family, coupled with the reciprocal love that had existed between the sisters since childhood, enabled her to conceal her heartbreak behind the routine of everyday existence. Her mother's increasingly poor health, coinciding with her own personal tragedy, made it necessary for Cassandra to take over the household management. From the time of his marriage in 1791, Cassandra also spent a great deal of time with Edward's family in Kent. These extended visits were fortunate for Jane Austen's biographers, for when Cassandra was away from home there was a frequent exchange of letters with Jane. Regrettably, none of Cassandra's letters to Jane have survived, and it is likely she destroyed them when she burned the greater part of Jane's more private correspondence.

The letters exchanged between the sisters, like countless other intimate personal communications of that or any other era, were not written with posterity in mind. Even if there is an occasional rumble of the distant thunder of the Napoleonic War in some of Jane's letters, most of them dealt chiefly with home and family events of primary interest to the writers, having no bearing on the historic events of the time.[40] It is also obvious to anyone who has carefully read Jane's letters to Cassandra that she used an elliptical style that enabled her to crowd as much news as possible into a limited space, realizing Cassandra's previous knowledge of the persons and events being discussed would enable her to fill in the necessary background. This does not mean Jane's letters are uninteresting, for they are endlessly diverting to anyone who takes the time to learn something concerning the persons, places and events mentioned in them. But they would have been relegated long since to the realm of Late Georgian social history had not the woman who wrote them also been the author of the six incomparable novels.

Jane's letters to Cassandra reveal many pleasing aspects of her elder sister's taste and character. Although Jane loved and respected her mother as a parent, she was much closer to Cassandra, and as she grew older was increasingly dependent on her, becoming restless when they were separated for any length of time. This almost childlike reliance was welcomed and encouraged by Cassandra, for from the time of Tom Fowle's death her own emotional life was increasingly centred on her younger sister — intensely so as time passed. Eventually, Cassandra and Jane, as their niece, Anna, expressed it, '... were everything to each other. They seemed to lead a life to themselves within the general family life which was shared only by each other. I will not say their true, but their full feelings and opinions were known only to themselves.'[41]

Although a great deal has been surmised concerning the romantic episodes in Jane Austen's life, few have taken the trouble to examine the part Cassandra undoubtedly played in them. Her vigilant prudence was always present to curb Jane's girlish spontaneous excesses, and although it would be unjust to accuse her of having been jealous, she nevertheless evidently regarded Jane's flirtations with trepidation, an attitude that was perhaps rooted in a secret fear of losing her younger sister to another person.

Until Cassandra inherited £1,000 from Tom Fowle, she was an attractive, but penniless, spinster, a situation Jane also shared until she began to make a little money with her novels. That was an unenviable position for young women of their class in a day when a girl's dowry was considered an important part of her marriage. The inheritance gave Cassandra a modest independence, enabling her to decide not to marry. On the other hand, Jane's lack of a dowry apparently did not keep her from hoping her cleverness, her good looks, and her gaiety might attract an eligible suitor who could afford to disregard the fact that her father could give her little in the way of a marriage portion. This over-confidence evidently shocked some of the more censorious Steventon matrons. It is also a matter of record that it aroused Cassandra's protective concern.

A great deal of indignation has been raised over a patently malicious remark made in 1815 by the mother of Mary Russell Mitford, that the youthful Jane Austen was 'the prettiest, silliest, most affected, husband-hunting butterfly' she ever remembered.[42] Those who reject the indictment claim that Mrs Mitford, the daughter of a former rector of Ashe, had left the Steventon area early in 1783 when Jane was only seven years old and therefore was in no position to make such a statement. They fail to realize Mrs Mitford had moved only fifteen miles away to Alresford, near Winchester, where she lived until 1791, when Jane was in her sixteenth year.[43] They also ignore the fact that she still had relations and friends living near Steventon who had ample opportunity to observe Jane's spontaneous gaiety at the Basingstoke balls and other social gatherings in the district. Mrs Mitford herself, as an occasional visitor to the neighbourhood, could have been present on any number of these occasions, in which case she could have made her own observations, passing them on, embellished with exaggerations and inaccuracies, to her daughter a few years later.

The point is that even the most casual reading of Jane Austen's letters of the Steventon period reveal her to have been a flirtatious, high-spirited, sharp-tongued girl who merited some if not all of Mrs Mitford's spiteful censure. And no one was more aware of Jane's girlish coquetry and the remarks it could elicit than her older and more circumspect sister. This is evident in the earliest known letter (dated 9 January 1796) from Jane to Cassandra, who was staying with the Fowles at Kintbury. In it Jane said, 'You scold me so much in the nice long letter which I have this moment received from you, that I am almost afraid to tell you how my Irish friend and I behaved.'[44] Jane was referring to her current flirtation with Thomas Langlois (Tom) Lefroy, a nephew of the rector of Ashe. The dalliance was also a source of concern to the rector's wife, who eventually sent the young man off to London before the affair could become serious. Jane took Cassandra's scolding in good part, and continued her letter with a good deal of bravado. But it is evident Cassandra had heard rumours of Jane's over-eager behaviour and had sent her a warning to be wary of the gossip it would cause among such sharp-eyed individuals as Mrs Mitford.

Cassandra was also fully aware of Jane's 'nameless and dateless' romance that took place later when she and her younger sister and their parents were staying at a seaside place.[45] But she did not reveal it until all the principals were dead — and guardedly even then. The same was true concerning Jane's overnight acceptance of a proposal from Harris Bigg-Wither of Manydown Park, Hampshire, when she and Cassandra were staying there with his family early in December 1802. Nothing is known concerning Cassandra's reaction when Jane told her of accepting the proposal. But one can easily surmise, from evidence provided by the published history of the Bigg-Wither family, that Cassandra possibly reminded Jane that Harris was the only surviving son of a doting father, with several adoring sisters, that he was quick-tempered, stammered badly and avoided society, promising little in the way of matrimonial happiness.[46]

In later years, one of Cassandra's younger nieces, Catherine, who had been permitted by her aunt to read some of Jane's letters which were subsequently destroyed, wrote:

> I gathered from the letters that it was in a momentary fit of self-delusion that Aunt Jane accepted Mr Wither's proposal, and that when it was all settled eventually, and the negative decisively given she was much relieved. I think the affair vexed her a good deal, but I am sure she had no attachment to him.[47]

Catherine saw a great deal of her Aunt Cassandra during her last years, and was apparently well acquainted with the details of the story from her aunt's telling; she knew that after Jane's rejection of the proposal she and Cassandra hastily departed from Manydown Park to Steventon the next morning.

As far as is known, that was the last time Jane Austen gave marriage any serious consideration. By the time she and Cassandra moved with their mother to Chawton in 1809, both sisters were confirmed spinsters, playfully referred to as 'the formidables' by Jane herself.[48] Later, their niece Caroline wrote, 'I believe my two Aunts were not accounted very good dressers, and were thought to have taken to the garb of middle age unnecessarily soon — but they were particularly neat, and they held all untidy ways in great disesteem.[49] That Jane regarded Cassandra as the wiser of the two is also evident in another observation of her niece:

> When I was a little girl, she would frequently say to me, if opportunity offered, that Aunt Cassandra could teach everything much better than *she* could — Aunt Cass. knew more — Aunt Cass. could tell me better whatever I wanted to know — all which, I ever received in respectful silence — Perhaps she thought my mind wanted a turn in that direction, but I truly believe she did always *really* think of her sister as the superior to herself. The most perfect affection and confidence ever subsisted between them — and great and lasting was the sorrow of the survivor when the final separation was made —[50]

The eight peaceful years at Chawton, aided by Cassandra's protective reassurance, provided Jane Austen with the security in which her genius came to fruition. But the era ended early in 1816, when Jane fell ill. In May Cassandra accompanied Jane to Cheltenham for the benefit of her health, but the trip did her no good. On their way back to Chawton the sisters stayed with the Fowles at Kintbury, where Caroline Austen recalled one of the family telling her later, 'Aunt Jane went over the old places, and recalled old recollections associated with them, in a very particular manner — looked at them, my cousin thought, as if she never expected to see them again.'[51]

Jane's condition continued to worsen and on 27 April 1817 she made her will. In it she left 'my dearest sister Cassandra Eliz'th every thing of which I may die possessed or which may hereafter be due to me subject to the payment of my funeral expenses and to a legacy of £50 to my brother Henry and £50 to Mde Bigion [*sic*]....'[52] It will be remembered that Henry had been declared a bankrupt in 1816, while the Madame Bigeon mentioned in the will was his faithful French servant who had apparently lost her savings when his bank had failed.

On 24 May 1817, when Jane was moved to a house in College Street, Winchester, for better medical treatment, Cassandra went with her in James Austen's carriage. Two months later, on Friday, 18 July 1817, as the great Norman tower of nearby

Winchester Cathedral was beginning to reflect the faint light of dawn, Jane Austen died. In writing of Jane's death to her niece Fanny Knight, Cassandra said:

> I *have* lost a treasure, such a Sister, such a friend as never can have been surpassed, — she was the sun of my life, the gilder of every pleasure, the soother of every sorrow, I had not a thought concealed from her, & it is as if I had lost a part of myself. I loved her only too well, not better than she deserved, but I am conscious that my affection for her made me sometimes unjust to & negligent of others, & I can acknowledge, more than as a general principle, the justice of the hand which struck this blow.[53]

Six days later, when Jane was buried in Winchester Cathedral, Cassandra told Fanny:

> Everything was conducted with the greatest tranquillity, and but that I was determined I would see the last, and therefore was upon the listen, I should not have known when they left the house. I watched the little mournful procession the length of the street; and when it turned from my sight, and I had lost her for ever, even then I was not overpowered, nor so much agitated as I am now in writing of it.[54]

Cassandra returned to Chawton, where she nursed her mother until the latter's death in 1827. In 1828, Martha Lloyd, who had lived with the Austens since 1806, became the second wife of Cassandra's brother Francis. After that Cassandra lived alone at Chawton with her memories until her death seventeen years later. Occasionally she left home for a visit to some member of the family, and it was on one of these visits that a great-niece saw her at a christening and remembered her as 'a pale, dark-eyed old lady, with a high arched nose and a kind smile, dressed in a long cloak and a large drawn bonnet, both made of black satin.'[55] But Cassandra was always happy to return to Chawton, for, as she wrote to Philadelphia Whitaker in 1833:

> ...home always ought to have its comforts, & it certainly has for me... I am likewise a great worker & have varieties of knitting & worsted work in hand. My garden is also a constant object of interest & at suitable seasons of the year of employ likewise....[56]

During these same years, John White, a Chawton farm worker who died in 1921 at the age of one hundred, remembered that when he was a boy:

> Miss Cassandra Austen lived at the corner house by the Pond. She took a great interest in young girls, and taught them reading, the catechism and sewing. I remember a nice dog, his name was 'Link', that she had. He always went with her manservant, William Littleworth, to Chawton House for milk, and carried it home in his mouth.[57]

Cassandra did not die at Chawton. She was visiting her brother Admiral Sir Francis Austen, who lived near Portsmouth, when he was sent out as Commander-in-Chief of the North American and West Indies Station. Shortly afterwards Cassandra died at his house, Portsdown Lodge, on 22 March 1845. Her body was brought back to her home in Chawton, where her coffin was placed in the dining parlour near the old piano on which Jane had played many years before.[58] The funeral procession was led by her brothers Henry and Charles, and her nephew Charles Knight conducted the service. In describing the funeral J. E. Austen-Leigh, who was also present, wrote to his half-sister Anna Lefroy:

> The day was fine, but the wind exceedingly boisterous, blowing the pall almost off the coffin, & quite sweeping away all sound of Charles' voice between the gate and church-door. It also struck me as remarkably emblematic of her age & condition that the wind whisked about us so many withered beech leaves, that the coffin was thickly strewed with them before the service closed.[59]

Francis William
'the officer who knelt in church'

SIR FRANCIS William Austen, the elder of Jane Austen's two naval brothers, who rose to the rank of Admiral of the Fleet and died greatly honoured at the age of ninety-one, was the sixth of the Hampshire-born Austens. His birth date is usually given as 23 April 1774, but the Steventon parish register states he was baptized on April 25, and it is likely the latter date is the correct one for his birth also. Known as Frank by his family, he was also nicknamed 'Fly' during his childhood because of his energetic liveliness.[1] His first appearance in the Austen family chronicle was on 20 August 1775, when his mother, in a letter to her sister-in-law, Mrs Walter, wrote: 'My last boy is very stout [healthy], and has run alone these two months, and he is not yet sixteen months old.'[2] Thirty-four years later, in a poem written by Jane Austen to congratulate Francis on the birth of his eldest son, she recalled her brother during his own childhood as having been a sturdy, curly-haired little fellow who could be intimidated only by a donkey's bray.[3]

Like all the Austen boys, Francis was an enthusiastic follower of the hounds 'in a scrambling sort of way, upon any pony or donkey that they could procure, or, in default of such luxuries, on foot.'[4] But Francis was not content with such makeshift arrangements. At the age of seven he bought a bright chestnut pony on his own account, naming it 'Squirrel', although to tease him his older brothers usually referred to it as 'Scug'. By then, the scarlet riding habit that had been a part of his mother's trousseau had seen better days, but according to family tradition there was still enough good material left to fashion a coat of hunting pink for Francis, who by that time was jumping everything his pony could get its nose over. The future Admiral of the Fleet also proved to be a sharp horse-trader. After having ridden the pony for two years, he sold it for almost twice as much as he had paid for it.[5]

Francis's carefree boyhood in the Hampshire hunting field ended in April 1786 when he entered the Royal Naval Academy at Portsmouth a few days before his twelfth birthday.[6] Why his father chose to launch him on a naval career is uncertain, for so far as its known, Francis was the first Austen to go to sea. The fact that once a boy was accepted board and tuition at the Academy were free no doubt influenced Mr Austen's decision to send Francis there.

The Academy, which was established by an Order in Council in 1729 and opened its doors to 'forty young gentlemen, sons of noblemen and gentlemen' in 1733, was regarded from its inception with jaundiced eyes by naval officers who felt the Admiralty's endorsement of the institution undermined their entrenched privilege of patronage.[7] Contemporary evidence also shows the place had a long-standing evil reputation for bullying, idleness, and debauchery. One of Francis's contemporaries at the Academy later recalled, 'The name of the Master of this school was Orchard, a very good man he was; but who the devil taught him navigation is more than I can say. He was a great disciplinarian and used to flourish with direful sway an infernal horsewhip, that I have reason to remember.'[8] Still another scholar who was at the Academy with Francis remembered the place 'was not well conducted' and thought 'there was a screw loose somewhere'.[9]

But Francis was not among those who idled away their time, and 'having attracted the particular notice of the Lords of the Admiralty by the closeness of his application, and being in consequence marked out for early promotion', he left the Academy late in December 1788 and sailed as a volunteer aboard the *Perseverance* for the East Indies to learn the ways of the sea at first hand.[10] Before his departure, his father prepared a '*Memorandum* for the use of Mr F. W. Austen on his going to the East Indies on board his Majesty's ship *Perseverance* (Captain Smith)' which impressed his fourteen-year-old son so forcibly that he treasured it until his death, when it was found among his private papers.[11] The letter is far too long to quote in its entirety. However, the following excerpt not only provides insight into Mr Austen's own character but also indicates the moral climate in which Francis and his brothers and sisters were reared:

Your behaviour, as a member of society, to the individuals around you may be also of great importance to your future well-doing, and certainly will to your present happiness and comfort. You may either by a contemptuous, unkind and selfish manner create disgust and dislike; or by affability, good humour and compliance, become the object of esteem and affection; which of these very opposite paths 'tis your interest to pursue I need not say.

The little world, of which you are going to become an inhabitant, will occasionally have it in their power to contribute no little share to your pleasure or pain; to conciliate therefore their goodwill, by every honourable method, will be the part of a prudent man. Your commander and officers will be most likely to become your friends by a respectful behaviour to themselves, and by an active and ready obedience to orders. Good humour, an inclination to oblige and the carefully avoiding every appearance of selfishness, will infallibly secure you the regards of your own mess and of all your equals. With your inferiors perhaps you will have but little intercourse, but when it does occur there is a sort of kindness they have a claim on you for, and which, you may believe me, will not be thrown away on them. Your conduct, as it respects yourself, chiefly comprehends sobriety and prudence. The former you know the importance of to your health, your morals and your fortune. I shall therefore say nothing more to enforce the observance of it. I thank God you have not at present the least disposition to deviate from it. Prudence extends to a variety of objects. Never any action of your life in which it will not be your interest to consider what she directs! She will teach you the proper disposal of your time and the careful management of your money, — two very important trusts for which you are accountable. She will teach you that the best chance of rising in life is to make yourself as useful as possible, by carefully studying everything that relates to your profession, and distinguishing yourself from those of your own rank by a superior proficiency in nautical acquirements.[12]

That Francis heeded the precepts set down by his father is apparent, for he grew up to be a quiet-spoken, dignified, self-reliant man who was remembered by his nephew as possessing great firmness of character, with a strong sense of duty, whether due from himself to others, or from others to himself. He was consequently a strict disciplinarian, but, as he was a very religious man, it was remarked of him (for in those days, at least, it was remarkable) that he maintained this discipline without ever uttering an oath or permitting one in his presence.[13]

But Francis Austen was no authoritarian prude, for beneath his official exterior he was a warm-hearted man, a considerate son and brother, and a devoted husband and father who revelled in the comforts of home and family when he was ashore. Although Henry was Jane Austen's favourite brother because of their reciprocal gaiety of temperament, Francis also stood high in Jane's estimation for his quiet humour, his pride in her literary accomplishments, his neatness (a characteristic they both shared), and his brotherly affection.

This empathy and admiration between Francis and his younger sister were of long standing, for two of Jane's juvenilia, *Jack and Alice*[14] and *The Adventures of Mr Harley*,[15] were dedicated to him when he was serving as a midshipman aboard the *Perseverance*. Later, in 1791, while he was still stationed in the East Indies, Jane also made an oblique reference to him in her *History of England*. In her account of Queen Elizabeth I, Jane wrote:

> It was about this time that Sir Francis Drake the first English Navigator who sailed round the World, lived, to be the ornament of his Country & his profession. Yet great as he was, & justly celebrated as a Sailor, I cannot help foreseeing that he will be equalled in this or the next Century by one who tho' now but young, already promises to answer all the ardent & sanguine expectations of his Relations & Friends, amongst whom I may class the amiable Lady to whom this work is dedicated [Cassandra Austen], & my no less amiable Self.[16]

In December 1792 Francis was commissioned a lieutenant. His return to England one year later coincided with the declaration of war by France on Great Britain, a conflict that was to continue, with only a brief respite during the Peace of Amiens (1802-3), for twenty-two years. As a naval officer Francis served throughout the period, and his letters home and his conversations when ashore provided Jane Austen with first-hand accounts of the conflict. That she used only those portions of them in her writings germane to her purpose is indicative of her selective artistic integrity.

From 1793 to 1796 Francis was assigned to vessels attached to the home station. In March 1795, as senior lieutenant in the *Lark*, he accompanied the naval squadron dispatched across the North Sea in Arctic weather to bear Princess Caroline of Brunswick from Cuxhaven to England for her ill-fated marriage to the Prince of Wales:[17] Although Francis's duties aboard the vessels attached to the home station were routine, he at least had opportunities for occasional visits ashore to his family and friends. In September 1796 Jane Austen was with him at Rowling, her brother Edward's home in Kent, at which time she recorded the first instance of his delight in working with his hands. In a letter to Cassandra, Jane said, 'He enjoys himself here very much, for he has just learnt to turn, and is so delighted with the employment, that he is at it all day long,'[18] later adding he had turned 'a very nice little butter-churn' for Edward's eldest daughter, Fanny.

Francis's manual skills were to afford him continuous pleasure throughout his long lifetime, and he was never happier than when he was making tiny gold-decorated ivory boxes, creating sturdy toys for his children, or fashioning nets to protect his Morello cherries and currants from predatory birds at Portsdown Lodge, his home ashore near Portsmouth.[19] Although Henry Austen stated in his biographical sketch of Jane: 'She drew from nature, but, whatever may have been surmised to the contrary, never from individuals,'[20] this is disproved by a statement made by Francis in a letter written to an American lady in 1852. In it, he said:

I do not know whether in the character of Capt. Wentworth the authoress meant in any degree to delineate that of her Brother: perhaps she might — but I rather think parts of Capt. Harville's were drawn from myself. At least some of his domestic habits, tastes and occupations bear a strong resemblance to mine.[21]

In a period when influence in high places was a necessity for advancement in military and naval circles, Francis was particularly fortunate in belonging to a family with important social connections. A year after he returned to England from the East

Indies his father solicited the help of Warren Hastings on his son's behalf.[22] But the man who eventually became Francis's patron was Admiral James Gambier (1756-1833), a friend of General Edward Mathew, whose daughter Anne had married Francis's eldest brother James in 1792. Gambier, a very religious man, regarded as 'a canting and hypocritical methodist' by many of his more turbulent naval contemporaries, was a member of the all-powerful Admiralty Board.[23] It was through his influence that Francis was eventually placed in a position to prove his mettle.

In 1796, Francis was appointed to the *Triton.* The next year, when Spain allied herself with France in the war against Great Britain, he was transferred to the *Seahorse,* in which he served until February 1798, when he was appointed to the *London,* one of the vessels engaged in blockading Cadiz. Francis's service aboard the *London* coincided with Napoleon's Egyptian campaign and Nelson's victory over the French fleet at the Battle of the Nile. Meanwhile, events were taking place in England that were to ensure Francis the command of his own vessel, in which it would be possible to enrich himself with prize money from captured enemy vessels, the dream of every ambitious naval officer of the period.

On Christmas Eve 1798 Jane Austen gleefully assured Cassandra that Admiral Gambier had just informed her father Francis's promotion was imminent, adding, 'There! I may now finish my letter and go and hang myself, for I am sure I can neither write nor do anything which will not appear insipid to you after this.'[24] Two days later Jane continued in the same vein: 'Frank is made. — He was yesterday raised to the Rank of Commander & appointed to the Petterel [*sic*] Sloop, now at Gibraltar.'[25]

As commanding officer of the *Peterel,* Francis was responsible for the capture and destruction of upward of forty enemy vessels of various descriptions.[26] He also gained distinction, and promotion to the rank of post captain, as the result of an encounter off Marseilles in March 1800 with three French vessels. Two of these he drove on the rocks. The third, *La Ligurienne,* a splendid new brig that was to have followed Napoleon to Egypt, was captured in a fierce fight within point-blank range of two shore batteries. The action was fought without the loss of a man aboard the *Peterel,* thirty of whose crew, including the first lieutenant and the gunner, were at that time absent in prizes.[27]

Francis next participated in the blockade of Genoa, after which he joined the squadron of Sir Sidney Smith on the coast of Egypt. While there, he prevented a Turkish line-of-battle ship from falling into the hands of the French. Although this necessitated the burning of the vessel, the Capitan Pasha was so pleased with Francis's action that he presented him with a handsome sabre and pelisse.[28] It was during this same period that Francis first came to the attention of Lord Nelson, who was then at Palermo, where he had taken the royal Neapolitan family when Naples fell to the French in December 1798. An important dispatch from Lord St Vincent at Gibraltar concerning the movements of the French fleet, which had put to sea from Brest and had entered the Mediterranean, had been given to the captain of the *Hyena* for delivery to Nelson. As the *Hyena* was a slower vessel than the *Peterel* the dispatch was entrusted to Francis and was taken by him from Minorca to Palermo in less than two days, an act that gained him Nelson's gratitude.[29]

Although Francis's promotion to post-captain in recognition of his capture of *La Ligurienne* was known by his family at Steventon, it was not until late in 1800 that the good news reached him in the Mediterranean. Apparently Jane had a letter from him describing the change of command, for she mentioned it in a letter to Cassandra in January 1801:

> What a surprise to him it must have been on the 20th of Octr [sic] to be visited, collar'd & thrust out of the Petterell [sic] by Captn. Inglis! — What a pity it is that he should not be in England at the time of this promotion, because he certainly would have had an appointment.[30]

An appointment was not long in coming after Francis arrived home. In the autumn of 1801, he became flag-captain to his patron Admiral Gambier, in the *Neptune*, a post which he held at the time of the Peace of Amiens in March 1802. On 23 August 1802, he had the pleasure of entertaining his proud parents on board the *Neptune*, then anchored at Portsmouth.[31]

The resumption of hostilities early in 1803 was accompanied by the fear that England would be invaded from the French maritime provinces where Napoleon had concentrated the Army of England; he had even had the Bayeux Tapestry displayed to excite enthusiasm for what he hoped would be a triumphant crossing of the Channel.[32] Although England still trusted to the Channel Fleet to turn back the flat-bottomed barges in which Napoleon hoped to transport his troops during favourable weather, measures were also taken to establish a second line of defence. This was known as the Sea Fencibles, a home guard to be used to repel a French landing on the English beaches.

Francis Austen was assigned to command the North Foreland unit of the Sea Fencibles, with headquarters at Ramsgate, Kent. It was there that he met his first wife, Mary Gibson, a lady ten years younger than himself, whom he married in 1806. It was also in Ramsgate that his devout demeanour was remarked on and gained him the designation of '*the* officer who knelt in church'.[33]

But fate had more exciting assignments in store for Francis than the drilling of units of fishermen and country bumpkins on the Kentish cliffs. In May 1804 he was appointed to the *Leopard,* the flagship of Rear-Admiral Thomas Louis, who then held a command in the squadron engaged in blockading Napoleon's Boulogne flotilla. In March of the next year Francis accompanied Admiral Louis to the Mediterranean Station when he hoisted his flag in the *Canopus.* At that time Lord Nelson, in a letter to Lord Moira, wrote:

> You may rely upon every attention in my power to Captain Austen. I hope to see him alongside a French 80-gun ship, and he cannot be better placed than in the *Canopus,* which was once a French Admiral's ship, and struck to me. Captain Austen I knew a little of before; he is an excellent young man.[34]

With the army of England poised to strike, Napoleon ordered the French fleets at Toulon, Brest, and Rochefort to assemble in the West Indies, recross the Atlantic, and overpower the British Channel Fleet, thereby making it possible for his army to cross the Channel. But that never took place. Although the Rochefort squadron did reach the West Indies, the Brest fleet was unable to escape the tight British blockade. Early in 1805, when the Toulon fleet under Admiral Villeneuve headed westward through the Straits of Gibraltar, Francis in the *Canopus* was among those who followed Nelson to the West Indies in pursuit of the French vessels. Later, Villeneuve abandoned the plan of meeting Napoleon's other squadrons and sailed back to Europe, where he joined the Spanish fleet in Cadiz harbour.[35]

That was the prelude to Trafalgar, but the high hopes Francis entertained of participating in the imminent conflict were doomed to disappointment. The *Canopus* was one of the English squadron that had been assigned to keep a close watch on the French and Spanish ships at Cadiz, and Francis had every reason to believe that he would join in the battle once the enemy tried to escape. But these hopes came to nothing. On 28 September 1805 Nelson arrived from England in the *Victory* and three days later dispatched the *Canopus* and four other vessels to Tetuan and Gibraltar for supplies and water.[36] In that way the *Canopus* missed the Battle of Trafalgar a little less than one month later. When Francis received the news of the victory he wrote to Mary Gibson:

> Alas! my dearest Mary, all my fears are but too fully justified. The fleets have met, and, after a very severe contest, a most decisive victory has been gained by the English twenty-seven over the enemy's thirty-three. Seventeen of the ships are taken and one is burnt, but I am truly sorry to add that this splendid affair has cost us many lives, and amongst them the most invaluable one to the nation, that of our gallant, and ever-to-be regretted, Commander-in-Chief, Lord Nelson, who was mortally wounded by a musket shot, and only lived long enough to know his fleet successful... As a national benefit I cannot but rejoice that our arms have been once again successful, but at the same time I cannot help feeling how very unfortunate we have been to be away at such a moment, and, by a fatal combination of unfortunate though unavoidable events, to lose all share in the glory of a day which surpasses all which ever went before, is what I cannot think of with any degree of patience; but, as I cannot write upon that subject without complaining, I will drop it for the present, till time and reflection reconcile me a little more to what I know is now inevitable.[37]

Although Francis never ceased to regret having missed the Trafalgar action, his disappointment was temporarily mitigated by participation in the Battle of San Domingo in February 1806. In it, he reported, the first broadside from the *Canopus* 'brought our opponent's three masts down at once, and towards the close of the business we also had the satisfaction of giving the three-

decker a tickling which knocked all *his sticks* away.'[38] For his part
in the action Francis was presented with a gold medal, in common
with others, the thanks of both Houses of Parliament, and a vase
worth £100 from the Patriotic Society of Lloyds.[39] In June of the
same year he went on leave, and on 24 July 1806, he married Mary
Gibson at Ramsgate. She became the 'Mrs F.A.' of Jane Austen's
letters to differentiate her from 'Mrs J.A.', the wife of Jane's
eldest brother James, whose name was also Mary.

Jane and her mother and sister continued to live in Bath after
the death of Mr Austen in 1805, but by the autumn of 1806 they
had joined forces with Francis and his bride and had moved to
Southampton, within easy distance of Portsmouth. At first they
lived in lodgings, but in March 1807 they moved into a large old-
fashioned house in Castle Square. Before that took place, Jane
wrote in February to Cassandra, who was then in Kent:

> Frank & Mary cannot at all approve of your not being at home
> in time to help them in their finishing purchases, & desire me
> to say that, if you are not, they shall be as spiteful as possible &
> chuse everything in the stile most likely to vex you, knives that
> will not cut, glasses that will not hold, a sofa without a seat, & a
> Bookcase without shelves.[40]

Later, Jane reported, 'Frank has got a very bad cough, for an
Austen; — but it does not disable him from making very nice
fringe for the Drawingroom Curtains.'[41]

But Francis was not to enjoy life ashore for long. Early in 1807
he took command of the *St Albans,* in which he continued to
serve until September 1810. His years of service in the *St Albans*
coincided with the outbreak of the Peninsular War in Spain.
During that period he escorted a division of transports to the
coast of Portugal, where they arrived on the eve of the Battle of
Vimeiro in August 1808, which Francis watched through a
telescope from the deck of the *St Albans.* Early in the next year he
superintended the disembarkation at Portsmouth of the
remnants of Sir John Moore's army on their return from
Corunna. After that he was engaged in convoying East Indiamen
to China, where he remained in the vicinity of Canton from
September 1809 to March 1810. As difficulties arose there
between the English and the Chinese over the murder of a native
by a British sailor, it appeared for a time that the convoy of tea

ships would not be permitted to sail early enough to avoid encountering bad weather on the long voyage home. But the quiet yet forceful diplomacy of Francis finally secured the Chinese officials' permission for the convoy to sail. When it arrived home safely, Francis was honoured with the approval of the Admiralty, and a gratuity of one thousand guineas from the grateful East India Company.[42]

While Francis was in China two important family events had taken place in England. First, Mrs Austen and her two daughters and their good friend Martha Lloyd, who was later to become Francis's second wife, had left Southampton and moved to Chawton. Second, Francis's wife had given birth in July 1809 to his eldest son and second child. Fourteen days after the event, Jane dispatched a congratulatory poem to Francis in which she reminisced concerning his own childhood.

> My dearest Frank, I wish you joy
> Of Mary's safety with a Boy,
> Whose birth has given little pain
> Compared with that of Mary Jane. —
> May he a growing Blessing prove,
> And well deserve his Parents' Love! —
> Endow'd with Art's & Nature's Good,
> Thy name possessing with thy Blood,
> In him, in all his ways, may we
> Another Francis William see! —
> Thy infant days, may he inherit,
> Thy warmth, nay insolence of spirit; —
> We would not with one fault dispense
> To weaken the resemblance.
>
> May he revive thy Nursery sin,
> Peeping as daringly within,
> His curley Locks, but just descried,
> With, 'Bet, my be not come to bide.' —
> Fearless of danger, braving pain,
> And threaten'd very oft in vain,
> Still may one Terror daunt his soul,
> One needful engine of Controul
> Be found in this sublime array,

A neighbouring Donkey's aweful Bray.
So may his equal faults as Child,
Produce Maturity as mild!
His saucy words & fiery ways
In early Childhood's pettish days,
In Manhood, shew his Father's mind
Like him, considerate & kind;
All Gentleness to those around,
And eager only not to wound.

Then like his Father, too, he must
To his own former struggles just,
Feel his Deserts with honest Glow,
And all his self-improvement know. —
A native fault may thus give birth
To the best blessing, conscious Worth. —[43]

After returning from China Francis took leave in order to be with his family, but by December 1810 he was off again to serve as flag captain to his patron, Admiral Gambier, in the *Caledonia*, then engaged in blockading the French coast. In April 1811, when Jane was in London correcting the proofs of *Sense and Sensibility*, his wife presented him with another son, at which time Jane wrote to Cassandra: 'I give you joy of our new nephew, & hope if he ever comes to be hanged, it will not be till we are too old to care about it.'[44]

In July 1811 Francis took command of the *Elephant*, attached to the North Shore Fleet. When war was declared the next year between the United States and Great Britain, he was dispatched with two other vessels to cruise off the Western Islands where he captured the *Swordfish*, an American privateer. Later, the *Elephant* was stationed in the Baltic where Francis was engaged in convoy duty. Two of Jane's letters to Francis from that period have survived. As they are in a much more expanded style than the chatty sisterly communications she wrote to Cassandra, it is a matter of regret that the many others she sent to him during the long periods when he was away from England were not saved.

Jane was then engaged in writing *Mansfield Park*. On 3 July 1813, she told Frank:

I have something in hand & which I hope on the credit of P. & P. will sell well, tho' not half so entertaining. And by the bye — shall you object to my mentioning the Elephant in it, & two or three other of your old Ships? I *have* done it, but it shall not stay, to make you angry. — They are only just mentioned.[45]

The permission was granted by Francis by return post.

In 1815, one year after his return from the Baltic, Francis was made a Companion of the Bath. From then on, Jane saw a great deal of him as he was living with his family either at Chawton Manor House or in nearby Alton. Francis was therefore at home when *Mansfield Park* was published, and his evaluation of the novel led the list of criticisms that Jane compiled under the heading of 'Opinions of Mansfield Park'. He said,

We certainly do not think it as a *whole*, equal to P. & P. — but it has many & great beauties. Fanny is a delightful Character! and Aunt Norris is a great favourite of mine. The Characters are natural & well supported, & many of the Dialogues excellent — You need not fear the publication being considered as discreditable to the talents of its Author.[46]

One year later, when *Emma* was published, Francis showed himself again a perceptive critic. Although his actual words were not jotted down by Jane in her 'Opinions of Emma', she paraphrased them thus: 'Captn Austen — liked it extremely, observing that though there might be more Wit in P & P — & an higher Morality in M P — yet altogether, on account of it's peculiar air of Nature throughout, he preferred it to either.'[47]

When Jane died in 1817, Henry brought the sad news back from Winchester to Chawton. From there it was communicated to Francis at Alton. Methodical from years of quarter-deck training, he sent a brief note to his niece Anna's husband, Ben Lefroy, then living at Wyards, near Alton:

I do not know if you have heard how very unfavourable the accounts which were yesterday brought from Wincr [Winchester] by my brother were, if not you and Anna will be the more shocked to learn that all is over — my dear Sister was seized at 5 yesterday Evening with extreme faintness and on Mr Lyfords arriving soon after he pronounced her to be dying — She breathed her last abt. ½ past 4 this morning, and went off without a struggle — My mother bears the shock as well as can be expected.[48]

Early in the morning of 24 July 1817, Francis joined his brothers, Edward and Henry, and their nephew, James Edward, who had ridden over from Steventon to represent his ailing father. Together they walked behind the coffin from Mrs David's house in College Street to Winchester Cathedral. There the service was conducted by the Revd Thomas Watkins, Precentor of the cathedral and Chaplain of Winchester College.[49]

Francis's subsequent history can be briefly summarized. His first wife, who had borne him six sons and five daughters, died in 1823. Five years later he married Martha Lloyd, whom Jane and Cassandra, as early as 1798[50], had hoped that he would marry. She died in 1843 leaving no issue. Francis became a rear-admiral in 1830, was made a Knight Commander of the Bath in 1837, and vice-admiral in 1838. In 1848 he became a full admiral. Meanwhile, he was appointed to the command of the North American and West Indies Station, with his flag in the *Vindictive*.[51]

Two delightful anecdotes epitomizing Francis's character are included in Lord Brabourne's edition of Jane Austen's letters.

During his later years, Francis paid a visit to a well-known watchmaker, one of whose chronometers he had taken with him during an absence of five years. After examining the instrument, which to all appearances was still in excellent order, the watchmaker, beaming with conscious pride, remarked, 'Well, Sir Francis, it seems to have varied none at all,' to which the admiral very slowly and very gravely replied, 'Yes, it *has* varied — *eight seconds!*'[52]

He was exceedingly precise, and spoke always with due deliberation, let the occasion be what it might, never having been known to hurry himself in speech for any conceivable reason. It so fell out, then, that whilst in some foreign seas where sharks and other similar unpleasant creatures abound, a friend, or sub-officer of his (I know not which), was bathing from the ship. Presently Sir Francis called out to him in his usual tone and manner. 'Mr Pakenham you are in danger of a shark — a shark of the blue species! You had better return to the ship.' 'Oh, Sir Francis, you are joking, are you not?' 'Mr Pakenham, I am not given to joking. If you do not immediately return, soon will the shark eat you.' Whereupon Pakenham, becoming alive to his danger, acted upon the advice thus deliberately given, and, says the story, saved himself 'by the skin of his teeth' from the shark.[53]

In 1862 Francis became Rear-Admiral and Vice-Admiral of the United Kingdom. Three years later he was promoted to Admiral of the Fleet. When he died on 10 August 1865, at the age of ninety-one, he was the last of the Hampshire-born Austens. He had already paid a belated tribute to his beloved sister Jane who had died forty-eight years earlier. In a letter written in January 1852 to Miss Eliza Quincy of Boston, daughter of a former president of Harvard College, he looked back over the years and remembered Jane Austen thus:

Of the liveliness of her imagination and playfulness of her fancy, as also of the truthfulness of her description of character and deep knowledge of the human mind, there are sufficient evidence in her works; and it has been a matter of surprise to those who knew her best, how she could at a very early age and with apparently limited means of observation, have been capable of nicely discriminating and pourtraying such varieties of the human character as are introduced in her works. — In her temper, she was chearful and not easily irritated, and tho' rather reserved to strangers so as to have been by some accused of haughtiness of manner, yet in the company of those she loved the native benevolence of her heart and kindness of her disposition were forcibly displayed. On such occasions she was a most agreeable companion and by the lively sallies of her wit and good-humoured drollery seldom failed of exciting the mirth and hilarity of the party.[54]

Charles John
'our own particular little brother'

FANNY BURNEY's third novel, *Camilla, or A Picture of Youth*, to which Jane Austen subscribed when it was published in 1796, provided her sister Cassandra and herself with a favourite phrase to use regarding their youngest brother, Charles John, then a handsome seventeen-year-old at the beginning of a distinguished naval career. Sir Hugh Tyrold, one of the principal characters in *Camilla*, refers to the heroine as 'my own particular little niece'. The aptness of the phrase was appropriated by Charles's admiring sisters, and from then on he was referred to as 'our own particular little brother'.[1] The designation was especially appropriate in Charles's case as he was greatly beloved by his family for his manly charm and affability. The impression was also long-lasting, for almost twenty years after Charles's death in 1852 of cholera in Burma his nephew remembered him thus:

> His sweet temper and affectionate disposition, in which he resembled his sister Jane, had secured to him an unusual portion of attachment, not only from his own family, but from all the officers and common sailors who served under him.[2]

Charles, privately baptized at Steventon on 23 June 1779, was the youngest of the Hampshire-born Austens. Like his brothers, he received his earliest schooling from his father. His childhood also coincided with Jane Austen's first attempts at authorship, and two of her juvenilia, written between the time he was eight and eleven, were dedicated to him. These were *Sir William Mountague* [3] and the *Memoirs of Mr Clifford*,[4] the latter being inscribed: 'Your generous patronage of the unfinished tale, I have already taken the Liberty of dedicating to you, encourages me to dedicate to you a second, as unfinished as the first.'[5] The sentence still echoes the high spirits and fun that prevailed at Steventon rectory during Jane Austen's childhood.

In July 1791, when Charles was twelve, he followed his brother Francis to the Royal Naval Academy at Portsmouth. In December of the next year his cousin, Jane Cooper, was married to Captain Thomas Williams in Steventon Church. As the wedding took place when Charles would have been home from the Academy for the Christmas holidays, he presumably attracted Captain Williams's attention at that time. In any event, when he left the Academy at the age of fifteen in September 1794 and embarked as a midshipman aboard the *Daedalus,* Captain Williams was his first commanding officer. From then on Charles was an active participant in the long war with France, and served throughout the conflict until Napoleon was banished to St Helena in 1815. He subsequently served in the *Unicorn* and the *Endymion,* also under Captain Williams's command. On 8 June 1796, while attached to the *Unicorn,* he assisted in the capture of the French frigate *La Tribune* in home waters after a running fight of several hours.[6] Captain Williams was knighted as the result of this action, and as Charles's benefactor continued to assist in his advancement.

Charles followed his patron when the latter was transferred from the *Unicorn* to the *Endymion* in March 1797. In December of the same year he was made a lieutenant after distinguishing himself when the *Endymion* assisted in driving the Dutch line-of-battle ship *Brutus* into Helvoetsluys following Admiral Duncan's naval victory over the Dutch at Camperdown.[7] Because of his promotion, Charles was removed from the friendly command of Sir Thomas Williams, under whom he had served for three exciting years, and was posted to the *Scorpion,* a much smaller vessel in which his duties were less arduous. Charles, who was impulsive by nature, fretted at the lack of action and complained bitterly in his letters home, causing Jane Austen to comment, 'I am sorry that our dear Charles begins to feel the Dignity of Ill-usage.'[8]

Charles's father, who was always willing to ease an unpleasant situation by appealing to the proper authorites, sent off a letter to Admiral Gambier, his son Francis's patron and a member of the Admiralty Board, asking that Charles be transferred to a frigate. Gambier replied that Charles should be content for the time being to serve in a small vessel for the sake of the valuable experience to be gained in such an assignment. But Charles, impatient of delay, took the matter into his own hands and aired his grievances to Lord Spencer, the First Lord of the Admiralty. This prompted Jane to observe, 'I am afraid his Serene Highness will be in a passion, and order some of our heads to be cut off',[9] an expedient that was not necessary, as Lord Spencer soon acted favourably on Charles's request.

Like his brother Francis, when attached to vessels of the home station Charles had occasional opportunities to come ashore to visit his family, and Jane's surviving letters of that period contain numerous references to his being at Steventon. Early in January 1799, when she expected him to arrive in time to conduct her to a ball given by Lord and Lady Dorchester at Kempshott Park (to which she wore a borrowed Mameluke cap, a style of millinery made fashionable by the Battle of the Nile), Charles disappointed her by not coming.[10] Later in the month he arrived unexpectedly, at which time his good looks and affability contributed greatly to the social life of the Steventon neighbourhood. Charles even gained the critical approval of Jane's good friend Madam Lefroy, the charming wife of the rector of Ashe, who, Jane reported, 'never saw anyone so much improved in her life, and thinks him handsomer than Henry', adding, 'He appears to far more advantage here than he did at Godmersham, not surrounded by strangers and neither oppressed by a pain in his face or powder in his hair.'[11]

Like many of the other young men of his generation then engaged in the war, Charles's days of 'powder in his hair' were at an end, for about that time he had his hair cropped short for convenience on shipboard. When he left Steventon for Deal late in January 1799 to take up his new appointment aboard the *Tamar,* Jane wrote playfully to Cassandra, who was nursing her sick brother at Godmersham, 'I thought Edward would not approve of Charles being a crop, and rather wished you to conceal it from him at present, lest it might fall on his spirits and retard his recovery.'[12]

Fortunately for Charles, the Admiralty decided not to refit the *Tamar,* and in February 1799 he was reappointed to the *Endymion* in which, under the command of Sir Thomas Williams and others, he subsequently came into frequent combat with enemy gunboats off Algeciras near Gibraltar and assisted in making prizes of several privateers. On one occasion, the capture of the *Scipio,* Charles's bravery under fire received special commendation from his superiors. When the *Scipio* surrendered during a violent gale, Charles put off from the *Endymion* in an open boat with only four men. Boarding the vessel, he held her until reinforcements arrived the following day.[13]

During the same period the *Endymion* was also engaged in convoying East Indiamen home from St Helena, which gave Charles opportunities for quick visits to his family. In November 1800 his return home coincided with the annual ball given by the eccentric Lord Portsmouth of Hurstbourne Park, a former pupil of Mr Austen, on the anniversary of his marriage. Jane, who had hoped her brother would arrive in time to accompany her to the ball, finally despaired of his coming. But Charles, impulsive as ever, surprised his sister by riding up to the rectory at 2 o'clock in the morning on the day before the ball on a nag he had hired in Gosport. In commenting on Charles's unconventional arrival and the ball in one of her most sparkling letters, Jane said, 'His feeling equal to such a fatigue is a good sign, & his finding no fatigue in it a still better. — We walked down to Deane to dinner, he danced the whole Evening, & today is no more tired than a gentleman ought to be.'[14] The Austen party did not get back to Deane until around five in the morning, and Jane later confessed to immoderation the night before when she told Cassandra:

> I believe I drank too much wine last night at Hurstbourne; I know not how else to account for the shaking of my hand today; — You will kindly make allowance therefore for any indistinctness of writing by attributing it to this venial Error.[15]

Another of Jane's letters, written in February 1801 before she left Steventon with her parents to settle in Bath, contains a passage that shows the Hampshire-born Austens were well aware of scandal in high places — even in the Royal Family: 'Charles spent three pleasant days in Lisbon. — They were very well satisfied with their Royal Passenger, whom they found fat, jolly & affable, who talks of Ly Augusta as his wife & seems much attached to her.'[16]

The 'Royal Passenger' was Augustus Frederick, Duke of Sussex, sixth son of George III, whose asthma had obliged him to take passage in the *Endymion* early in 1801 for the milder climate of Portugal. Prince Augustus had made the acquaintance in

Rome in 1793 of Lady Augusta Murray, whom he usually referred to as 'my amiable Goosey'. One year later they were married there by a Protestant clergyman. Still later they were married again, under assumed names, in St George's Church, Hanover Square, London. When the news reached George III he declared the marriage void. But Prince Augustus held out and lived with his 'Goosey', by whom he had a son and a daughter, until after he returned from Lisbon in 1801. Subsequently, he is said to have 'preferred the solid worth of a Dukedom and £12,000 a year to the charms of a forty-year-old wife'.[17]

It was also at this time that Charles presented each of his sisters with a topaz cross, a characteristic act of generosity on his part that undoubtedly provided Jane Austen with the genesis of the amber cross episode in *Mansfield Park* a decade later. In a letter to Cassandra written from Bath in 1801, Jane said,

> He has received 30£ for his share of the privateer & expects 10£ more — but of what avail is it to take prizes if he lays out the produce in presents to his sisters. He has been buying gold chains & Topaze crosses for us; — he must be well scolded.

Then, after telling Cassandra the *Endymion* had received orders to transport troops to Egypt, Jane continued, 'He will receive my yesterday's letter today, and I shall write again by this post to thank & reproach him. — We shall be unbearably fine.'[18]

When the Peace of Amiens became effective in March 1802, Charles returned to England. That summer he accompanied his parents on a tour of Wales.[19] When hostilities were resumed in May 1803 he rejoined the *Endymion* as her first lieutenant until he was promoted in October 1804 to command the *Indian,* on the recommendation of his captain as the reward for his conduct during the capture of three men-of-war and two privateers. From then until 1810 Charles served on the North American Station, his principal duty being to keep neutrals from trading with France.[20] In 1807 he married Frances Fitzwilliam Palmer, a daughter of John Grove Palmer, a former Attorney General of Bermuda.[21] Charles's affability and good looks continued to serve him well, for in writing to Cassandra in December 1808, Jane Austen said, 'I must write to Charles next week. You may guess in what extravagant terms of praise Earle Harwood speaks of him. He is looked up to by everybody in all America.'[22]

Charles was well-provided with creature comforts and
intellectual pleasures while away from home, for in January of the
next year Jane wrote: 'Charles's rug [coverlet] will be finished today, and sent tomorrow to Frank, to be consigned by him to Mr
Turner's care; and I am going to send *Marmion* out with it. —
very generous of me, I think. —'[23] Jane's desire that Charles be
provided with Scott's latest poem, published only the year before,
is an indication of the literary interests she and her brother
shared. The 'Mr Turner' mentioned was the man who ran a
nautical clothing store in the Portsmouth High Street, and
whom she later referred to in connection with William Price in
Mansfield Park,.

After more than five years on the North American station,
Charles returned to England in 1811 with his wife and their two
small daughters, Cassandra Esten and Harriet, who had been
born in Bermuda. While staying with the Henry Austens in
London and engaged in correcting the proofs of *Sense and
Sensibility* Jane heard rumours of Charles's impending arrival in
April aboard the *Cleopatra*. Later, she informed Cassandra that
at a grand evening musical party given by Eliza Austen, she had
met a Captain Simpson who 'told us, on the authority of some
other Captn just arrived from Halifax, that Charles was bringing
the Cleopatra home, & that she was probably by this time in the
Channel,' adding, 'but as Capt S. was certainly in liquor, we must
not quite depend on it.'[24]

But the tipsy Captain Simpson proved right, for the Charles
Austens arrived shortly afterward in the *Cleopatra*. Of Charles's
first visit to his mother and sisters at Chawton, Cassandra wrote
to her cousin Mrs Whitaker, the former Philadelphia Walter:

After an absence from England of almost seven years you may
guess the pleasure which having him amongst us again
occasion'd. He is grown a little older in all that time, but we
had the pleasure of seeing him return in good health and
unchanged in mind. His Bermudan wife is a very pleasing little
woman, she is gentle and amiable in her manners and appears
to make him very happy. They have two pretty little girls.
There must be always something to wish for, and for Charles
we have to wish for rather more money. So expensive as every
thing in England is now, even the necessaries of life, I am afraid
they will find themselves very, very poor.[25]

Once more Sir Thomas Williams came to Charles's rescue, and made him flag-captain aboard the *Namur* at the Nore anchorage at the mouth of the Thames. Charles was given the responsibility of regulating all men recruited for the Navy in the Thames and eastern ports, and also the task of manning the warships fitted out in the Thames and Medway.[26] For the sake of economy, Charles and his family lived aboard the *Namur,* a pleasant enough nautical abode under normal conditions but confining and conducive to seasickness in rough weather. Life aboard the *Namur* was varied by visits ashore to Charles's wife's family in London. In 1813 he and his family were with Jane during her last visit to Godmersham. At that time, Jane felt Charles was almost too devoted a husband, and deliberately 'extracted' him from his wife and children so that he might engage in field sports, of which there were plenty at Godmersham.[27]

Frances Austen bore Charles two more children between their return to England and her death in childbed on 6 September 1814 at the age of twenty-four. The first, Frances Palmer, was delivered in London in 1812, but when the time came for the last child to be born a violent storm arose which prevented Charles's wife from leaving the *Namur.*[28] She and her infant daughter, Elizabeth, who survived her mother for only a few days, are commemorated by a marble wall tablet decorated with a weeping willow and an anchor in St John the Baptist Church, Kentish Town, London, where the Palmer family had lived for several generations. The epitaph to Charles's wife bears a rhymed tribute ending with the couplet:

> Sleep on dear fair one, wait the Almighty's will,
> Then rise unchanged and be an Angel still.[29]

Fortunately Frances Austen had an elder sister Harriet, who lived with her father in London, and she took charge of the three little girls after their mother's death. Meanwhile, Charles had become restless at the Nore and yearned to be at sea. A little less than a month after his wife's death he was appointed to the *Phoenix* and sailed for the Mediterranean. On the renewal of hostilities after Napoleon's escape from Elba in March 1815, the *Phoenix* and two other vessels under Charles's orders were sent in pursuit of a Neapolitan squadron supposed to be in the Adriatic. After the surrender of Naples in May, Charles instigated a close blockade of the port of Brindisi and was instrumental in persuading the castle and two of the enemy's largest frigates in the harbour to hoist the colours of the restored King of Naples. For this action Charles received a special commendation.[30] He was then sent in search of a French squadron, and after the cessation of hostilities in 1815 was engaged in the suppression of piracy in the Greek Archipelago.[31]

When *Emma* was published late in 1815 a copy was dispatched immediately to Charles. His response was all Jane Austen could wish for. Earlier in the year he had written from Palermo:

> Books became the subject of conversation, and I praised 'Waverley' highly, when a young man present observed that nothing had come out for years to be compared with 'Pride and Prejudice,' 'Sense and Sensibility,' &c. As I am sure you must be anxious to know the name of a person of so much taste, I shall tell you it is Fox, a nephew of the late Charles James Fox. That you may not be too much elated at this morsel of praise, I shall add that he did not appear to like 'Mansfield Park' so well as the two first, in which, however, I believe he is singular.[32]

Charles had apparently forgotten that he too had not cared particularly for *Mansfield Park*, thinking it 'wanted Incident.'[33] but his enthusiastic praise for *Emma* more than made up for his earlier lapse. He wrote: 'Emma arrived in time to a moment. I am delighted with her, more so I think than even my favourite Pride & Prejudice, & have read it three times in the Passage.'[34]

In the meantime Charles had more important things to do than the reading of novels. At Smyrna he had received orders to join an expedition to the coast of Barbary, and had put to sea immediately. Unable to clear the Archipelago before the commencement of a violent gale, Charles sought shelter for his ship in the port of Chisme on the coast of Asia Minor. Scarcely had the vessel anchored when the wind veered from the southwest to the north and blew a perfect hurricane. Everything possible was done to save the *Phoenix*, but she was driven on the shore even after her masts had been cut away. Fortunately no lives were lost, and because of the strenuous exertions of the crew the guns and stores were saved. It was Charles's good fortune that the disaster was later attributed to the ignorance of the Greek pilots, for he was fully acquitted of all blame by a court-martial held on board the *Boyne* in the Bay of Tunis in April 1816.[35]

Charles's return home to his three motherless little daughters was additionally saddened by his brother Henry's bankruptcy and Jane's illness and death. Her last letter to him was written from Chawton on 6 April 1817, and was endorsed by Charles as 'My last letter from dearest Jane.'[36] Most of its contents dealt with Jane's sickness and the disappointment of the family over the will of their rich uncle James Leigh Perrot. But the old Jane shines through in the playful postscript, 'Tell dear Harriet [Charles's sister-in-law] that whenever she wants me in her service again, she must send a Hackney Chariot all the way for me, for I am not strong enough to travel any other way, & I hope Cassy will take care that it is a green one.'[37]

Charles, who did not attend Jane's funeral, was at Eastbourne with his children at the time of his sister's death on 18 July 1817. Two days later he wrote in his pocket diary: 'a letter from Henry announced my Dear Sister Janes death on the morning of the 18th — a sad day — wrote to my Mother & Henry.' On July 23 he made another entry: 'My trunk of Mourning arrived from Town,' and on July 24, he added, 'a very fine day. Dr [Dear] Janes Funeral.'[38]

Charles outlived Jane for thirty-five years. In 1820 he married Harriet Palmer, his first wife's elder sister who had cared for his three daughters since their mother's death. Harriet bore him three sons and a daughter and died in 1869.

Charles did not go to sea again until 1826 when he went out to the West Indies in the *Aurora*. His tactics in securing the appointment were characteristic of his impulsive nature. The *Aurora* was anchored at Spithead ready for a cruise to the West Indies when Charles, who was conning the roads off Gosport with his spyglass, noted the captain's flag was flying at half-mast. Charles, who was awaiting a commission at that time, took a boat out to the ship and learned that the captain had just died. Returning ashore, he took a postchaise to London, and was the first to report the vacancy to the Admiralty. He then requested the appointment. Asked when he could take command of the ship, he replied, 'Tomorrow'. He was given the post.[39] In commenting on his good fortune in a letter to a friend, he admitted his 'poor wife suffered much from the suddenness of [my] leaving her', and although he too keenly felt the abrupt separation from his family, he resolved the difficult situation philosophically by adding, '...but Sailors are bound for all weathers.'[40]

Charles served in the *Aurora* on the West Indies station until December 1828; he was principally engaged in suppression of the slave trade. It was remarked that his concern for the physical welfare of the officers and crew had been so vigilant there had not been the loss of a man by sickness or otherwise during the period of his command. In gratitude the officers and crew presented him with a silver snuff box and a silver salver.[41] Earlier, in March 1827, he had also received an inscribed naval sword from Simon Bolivar, the South American soldier, statesman and revolutionary leader.[42] So favourable was the official report of the state of discipline and efficiency aboard the *Aurora* that Charles was made flag captain of the *Winchester* on the North American and West Indies station, a post he held until he was severely injured in an accident in December 1830. He returned to England, settling at Anglesey near Gosport, where his sister Cassandra visited him frequently. In one of her letters she said, 'I wish he were richer, but fortune has not yet smiled on him.'[43] But Charles recovered from his accident and lived to continue his naval career for another fourteen years.

In 1838, still a captain after nearly thirty years in that rank, he was appointed to the *Bellerophon* (known by the seamen as the 'Billy Ruffian'). He returned in her to the Mediterranean and participated in the joint French and English campaign against Mehemet Ali, Viceroy of Egypt. After engaging in the bombardment of St Jean d'Acre in November 1840, the *Bellerophon* ran into difficulties one month later when she encountered a violent storm and barely escaped destruction on the coast of Syria. For his share in the Levant campaign Charles was made a Companion of the Bath. He was awarded a good service pension in 1840. Five years later he was present at the funeral of his sister Cassandra at Chawton, and was described at the time by a nephew as 'kind, grave & thoughtful'.[44]

In November 1846 Charles was promoted to rear-admiral. In January 1850 he was appointed Commander-in-Chief of the East India and China station with headquarters at Trincomalee. Charles left England in the steamer *Ripon* for Alexandria and crossed the desert to Suez, the usual overland route before the opening of the Suez Canal.[45] Two years later trouble broke out between British traders and Burmese officials. At Calcutta the Governor-General of India ordered a combined military and naval expedition against Burma. Charles then shifted his flag from the *Hastings* to the steam sloop *Rattler* and proceeded to the mouth of the Rangoon River, where in April 1852 he commanded the naval forces at the capture of Rangoon.[46]

Charles had given Captain Spencer Ellman, the commander of the *Salamander*, permission to open the attack, which he did by firing the shot himself in a highly theatrical manner. Seeing the *Rattler* would shortly be between him and Rangoon, Ellman trained the gun on a large pagoda and waited until the *Rattler* was in the direct line of fire. At that point he fired the shot over the Admiral's head and hit the pagoda, prompting Charles to remark, 'The man who fired that shot is looking for promotion.'[47]

Charles contracted cholera during the Rangoon campaign and was moved to Calcutta, where he gradually recovered. Returning to Rangoon, he transferred his flag to the steam sloop *Pluto* and led the combined force up the Irrawaddy River to Prome on reconnaissance. The region was unhealthy and Charles suffered a relapse. On 6 October 1852 he recorded his last actions in line of duty: 'Received a report that two steamers had been seen at anchor some miles below, wrote this and a letter to my wife, and read the lessons of the day.'[48] He died the following morning at the age of seventy-three.

An officer who was with Charles at the time of his death wrote:

Our good Admiral won the hearts of all by his gentleness and kindness while he was struggling with disease, and endeavouring to do his duty as Commander-in-chief of the British naval forces in these waters. His death was a great grief to the whole fleet. I know that I cried bitterly when I found he was dead.[49]

The importance of being a good aunt

The importance of being a good aunt

AT the time of her death Jane Austen had eleven nephews and thirteen nieces living, ranging in age from two months to young adulthood — a goodly number even at a time when fecundity was regarded as a primary domestic virtue. Her eldest brother James had three children; Edward had sired eleven before his wife's death at the age of thirty-five; Francis had begotten seven, and Charles, who had married later than the others, was the father of three. Jane was interested in all of them, for she placed great importance on being a good aunt. Her eldest and favourite niece, Fanny Catherine Knight, made a splendid marriage in 1820 when she became the second wife of Sir Edward Knatchbull (1781-1849), of Provender, Kent, the year after he succeeded his father as the ninth baronet. It was to Fanny that Cassandra Austen left the original manuscript of *Lady Susan* as well as the greater part of those of Jane's letters that she saved when she destroyed most of her sister's correspondence some years before her own death. It was also to Fanny that Cassandra wrote the two heart-rending letters describing Jane's death and burial. To Fanny's credit, she saved this precious legacy and the letters were edited and published after her own death by her son, the first Lord Brabourne.[1]

Fanny had been regarded by Jane as 'almost another sister', but after Jane and Cassandra were long dead the memory of her aunts' Georgian forthrightness apparently offended her Victorian proprieties. If she had kept her thoughts to herself she would still be safe from the accusation of ungratefulness. But she made the mistake of revealing her thoughts in a letter to a younger sister, never thinking they would be made public. The letter was preserved, however, and remains as an indictment of her ingratitude. It reads:

> Yes my love it is very true that Aunt Jane from various circumstances was not so *refined* as she ought to have been from her *talent*, & if she had lived 50 years later she would have

been in many respects more suitable to *our* more refined tastes. They were not rich & the people around with whom they chiefly mixed, were not at all high bred, or in short anything more than *mediocre & they* of course tho' superior in *Mental powers & cultivation* were on the same level as far as *refinement* goes — but I think in later life their intercourse with Mrs Knight (who was very fond of & kind to them) improved them both & Aunt Jane was too clever not to put aside all possible signs of 'common-ness' (if such an expression is allowable) & teach herself to be more refined, at least in intercourse with people in general. Both the Aunts (Cassandra & Jane) were brought up in the most complete ignorance of the World & its ways (I mean as to fashion, &c) & if it had not been for Papa's marriage which brought them into Kent, & the kindness of Mrs. Knight, who used often to have one or the other of the sisters staying with her, they would have been, tho' not less clever and agreeable in themselves, very much below par as to good Society and its ways. If you hate all this I beg yr. pardon, but I felt it at my *pen's end* & it chose to come along & speak the truth. It is now nearly dressing time. . . .[2]

But there were three who repaid their aunt's devotion by providing posterity with much of the first-hand information that has enabled later biographers to present Jane Austen as a living personality. These were the Revd James Edward Austen-Leigh, his sister Caroline Mary Craven Austen, and their half-sister Jane Anna Elizabeth Lefroy, all children of Jane's eldest brother James. They all had known their Aunt Jane intimately from childhood and eventually came to realize that the beloved aunt so appreciated during their early years had ceased to be merely a pleasant family memory, but had become a literary celebrity during their own lifetimes.

Apart from the biographical notice of his sister provided by Henry Austen in 1817 as a preface to the posthumous publication of *Northanger Abbey* and *Persuasion*, nothing of a personal nature had been published concerning Jane Austen until Richard Bentley, the London publisher, brought out his edition of her novels in 1833. At that time Henry added a few additional facts to his 1817 notice. An edition of the novels had been published in the United States in 1832-3 by Carey & Lea of Philadelphia, but this provided no further glimpses of Jane Austen. Even before these two editions appeared, however, Jane Austen had attracted many enthusiastic admirers on both sides of the Atlantic. One of these was John Marshall, Chief Justice of the United States, who wrote in 1826: 'Her flights are not lofty, she does not soar on eagles' wings, but she is pleasing, interesting, equable, and yet amusing.'[3] But for a little over half a century, apart from Henry Austen's 1817 notice and its amplification in 1833, nothing in the way of a biography of Jane Austen was available.

By the late 1860s James Austen's son and two daughters were elderly, but that did not deter them from undertaking the task of providing biographical information about their celebrated aunt. Fortunately, each had a long and accurate memory. With the help of other members of the family, particularly the daughters of Admiral Charles Austen, they began to collect the material that J. E. Austen-Leigh incorporated in his *Memoir of Jane Austen.*[4]

Jane Anna Elizabeth (1793-1872), later Mrs Benjamin Lefroy, was James Austen's only child by his first wife, Anne Mathew. She knew Jane intimately from her early childhood, and even though her wilfulness and instability during adolescence annoyed her aunt at times, she matured into a sensible and intelligent woman. Long before Jane Austen was accorded her rightful place in literature Anna began to write down her reminiscences of her aunt and the other Steventon Austens. She also fulfilled another important role. As a gifted amateur artist she left behind the only surviving sketches of Steventon rectory where Jane was born as well as sketches of many other scenes and buildings no longer existing in the Steventon area, thus providing an invaluable record of the physical world in which Jane was reared.

Anna's acquaintance with Steventon rectory began at the age of two. She was brought there from Deane by her father after the death of her mother in 1795, to be comforted by her two young aunts. Jane was then engaged in writing *First Impressions* (later *Pride and Prejudice*), and Anna, being a quick-witted child, 'caught up the names of the characters' as Jane read the manuscript aloud to Cassandra in their upstairs dressing- room, 'and talked about them so much downstairs that her aunts feared she would provoke inquiry, for the story was still a secret from the elders.'[5]   It was at that time or a little later that the short play *Sir Charles Grandison or the Happy Man* was written. A dramatization of some of the scenes from Samuel Richardson's

The History of Sir Charles Grandison, one of Jane's favourite novels, it is based on an attempt by the wicked Sir Hargrave Pollexfen to force a marriage on Harriet Byron, the heroine, who is rescued by Sir Charles Grandison and eventually becomes his wife. The play was long believed to have been written down by Jane Austen from the dictation of Anna, who was frequently at Steventon rectory from the time of her mother's death in May 1795 until her father's second marriage. This tradition, which had never been questioned until recently, was recorded by Fanny Lefroy, one of Anna's daughters, thus: 'I have still in my possession, in Aunt Jane's writing, a drama my mother dictated to her, founded on 'Sir Charles Grandison', a book with which she was familiar at seven years old.'[6] This was later amplified by Mary Augusta Austen-Leigh: 'Anna composed stories of her own long before she was old enough to write them down, and had always a vivid recollection of the way her kind Aunt Jane performed that office for her. On reaching the age of seven she dictated to her aunt a drama founded on "Sir Charles Grandison", which still exists in Jane Austen's handwriting.'[7]

These family recollections however, have recently been disputed by Brian Southam, the Jane Austen scholar, who maintains that the earliest part of the manuscript of the comedy was written by Jane Austen before Anna was born in 1793, while the rest of the play was completed no later than 1800, when Anna was six or seven years of age. This is a somewhat unconvincing argument as Anna Lefroy's daughter, in writing of the play, clearly stated her mother was already familiar with Richardson's novel 'at seven years old'. In dismissing the tradition of Anna's authorship of the play, which Southam suggests was possibly written for an intimate family theatrical at Steventon, he says:

> It is quite possible that during Anna's later visits to Steventon, between 1796 and 1800, Jane Austen was working intermittently on 'Grandison', revising and continuing the early pages, with the young niece at her elbow, offering and even being allowed, as a special privilege, to write on the manuscript itself — inserting a word or two here and there, changing a phrase, bringing a character on stage. That, almost certainly, was the extent of Anna's contribution; and if we grace it with the name of collaboration, that is the sum of it.[8]

Anna's troubles began when her father remarried in 1797 and she was taken back to Deane rectory to be cared for by her step-mother. The situation was not helped when Mary presented her husband with a son and heir the following year. From then on, until she married at the age of twenty-one, there was constant friction between Anna, who had developed into a pretty, high-spirited young woman, and her strong-willed step-mother. To be fair to Mary Austen, it is only proper to say that Anna could be very trying at times. As an example, she deliberately cut off her long hair on one occasion before attending a ball in order to attract attention. It was also remarked she could not always be relied on to behave properly and sometimes caused embarrass-ment when she was in company. Jane was always happier when the adolescent Anna was not present at social gatherings. As she pithily observed, Anna could always be counted on to 'be doing too little or too much'.[9]

Even so, Jane tried to be tolerant. Once having had a good report concerning Anna from old Mrs Austen and Martha Lloyd, with whom her niece had been staying at Chawton while her aunts were away, Jane confided to Cassandra: 'She is quite an Anna with variations — but she cannot have reached her last, for that is always the most flourishing & shewey — she is at about her 3rd or 4th which are generally simple & pretty.'[10]

Matters came to a head when Anna, at the age of twenty, announced her engagement to Ben Lefroy, a moody young man. Not even the fact that he was the youngest son of Jane's much-admired Madam Lefroy, wife of the Rector of Ashe, could make her regard the match with anything but trepidation. In a letter to her brother Francis, she wrote:

It came upon us without much preparation; — at the same time, there was *that* about her which kept us in a constant preparation for something. There is an unfortunate dissimi-larity of Taste between them in one respect which gives us some apprehensions, he hates company & she is very fond of it; — this, with some queerness of Temper on his side & much unsteadiness on hers is untoward.[11]

Ben also offended Anna's family by refusing to take holy orders and accept a curacy which would give him an income and so enable him to marry. When Anna's father approached him on the subject, he declared he would rather give up Anna than do something of which he did not approve. Jane's comment on Ben's stubbornness was to the point: 'He must be maddish' she said.[12] Nevertheless, the couple were married the following year and lived for a few months in Ben's brother's house at Hendon near London where Jane visited them in 1814. At that time she noted that Anna's impracticality had lured her into the extravagance of buying a piano for twenty-four guineas, rather than saving the money for essential household necessities. Later, the young Lefroys rented part of Wyards, a farmhouse near Chawton. From then on Anna saw a great deal of her aunt until the latter's death.

According to Anna's reminiscences, the relationship between her aunt and herself grew closer as she grew older. In recalling that period of her life, she wrote:

> The two years before my marriage and the three afterwards, during which we lived near Chawton, were the years in which my great intimacy with her was formed; when the original seventeen years between us seemed reduced to seven, or none at all. It was my amusement during part of a summer visit to the cottage to procure novels from the circulating library at Alton, and after running them over to narrate and turn into ridicule their stories to Aunt Jane, much to her amusement, as she sat over some needlework which was nearly always for the poor. We both enjoyed the fun, as did Aunt Cassandra in her quiet way though, as one piece of nonsense led to another, she would exclaim at our folly, and beg us not to make her laugh so much.[13]

Anna's improvement as she grew older even inspired Jane to write a mock panegyric in her honour. As far as is known it is the only poem Jane ever wrote with a niece or nephew in mind.

> In measured verse, I'll now rehearse
>   The charms of lovely Anna:
> And, first, her mind is unconfined
>   Like any vast savannah.
>
> Ontario's lake may fitly speak
>   Her fancy's ample bound:
> Its circuit may, on strict survey
>   Five hundred miles be found.

Her wit descends on foes and friends
   Like famed Niagara's Fall;
And travellers gaze in wild amaze,
   And listen, one and all.

Her judgment sound, thick, black, profound.
   Like transatlantic groves,
Dispenses aid, and friendly shade
   To all that in it roves.

If thus her mind to be defined
   America exhausts,
And all that's grand in that great land
   In similes it costs —

Oh how can I her person try
   To image and portray?
How paint the face, the form how trace
   In which those virtues lay?

Another world must be unfurled,
   Another language known,
Ere tongue or sound can publish round
   Her charms of flesh and bone.[14]

Before Anna's marriage, and after some hesitation, Jane had taken her niece into her confidence concerning her own authorship. This encouraged Anna to write a novel of her own which she intended to call either *Which is the Heroine?* or *Enthusiasm.*[15] As each chapter was completed, Anna sent it to her aunt for criticism. Fortunately the letters containing Jane's reactions to Anna's manuscript and her suggestions for its improvement were carefully preserved. They provide revealing insights into Jane's own self-imposed rules of composition:

Devereux Forester's being ruined by his Vanity is extremely good; but I wish you would not let him plunge into a 'vortex of Dissipation.' I do not object to the Thing, but I cannot bear the expression; — it is such thorough novel slang — and so old, that I dare say Adam met with it in the first novel he opened.'[16]

Unfortunately Anna destroyed the manuscript of her unfinished novel after Jane's death. One of her daughters recalled:

> The story was laid by for years, and then one day, in a fit of despondency, burnt. I remember sitting on the rug watching its destruction, amused with the flame and the sparks which kept bursting out in the blackened paper. In later years, when I expressed my sorrow that my mother had destroyed her story she said she could never have borne to finish it.[17]

Anna had very decided opinions concerning her aunt's novels. When *Mansfield Park* was published she liked it better than *Pride and Prejudice* but not so well as *Sense and Sensibility*. Even so, Fanny Price was not to her taste, but she was delighted with Mrs Norris, the scenes at Portsmouth, and 'all the humourous parts'.[18] When *Emma* came out, she ranked it with *Sense and Sensibility*, although she felt it was not as brilliant as *Pride and Prejudice*, or 'so *equal*' as *Mansfield Park*. Anna preferred *Emma* to all of Jane Austen's heroines. Although she had the temerity to tell her aunt that some of the conversations were too long, she qualified her boldness by adding: 'The Characters like all the others [are] admirably well drawn & supported — perhaps rather less strongly marked than some, but only the more natural for that reason.'[19] Along with countless others who have read and enjoyed *Emma* since that time, Anna was particularly fond of Mr Knightley, Mrs Elton, and Miss Bates.

Ben Lefroy finally decided to seek ordination the year Jane Austen died. In writing of it later, one of his daughters said:

> I have heard my mother say that when he returned from being ordained he told her that the Bishop had only asked him two questions — first, if he was the son of Mrs Lefroy of Ashe, and secondly, if he had married a Miss Austen. I suppose the chaplain's examination extended a little further but my impression is that having passed through Oxford was considered a sufficient guarantee of fitness, and that his questions were not much more troublesome than the Bishop's.[20]

After acting as curate at Compton, near Guildford, Ben Lefroy succeeded his brother as rector of Ashe from 1823 until his death in 1829 at the age of thirty-eight, at which time Anna was left a widow with one son and six daughters. She never remarried. She subsequently published two books for children: *The Winter's Tale: To which is Added Little Bertram's Dream* (1841), and *Springtide* (1842). Meanwhile, she carefully preserved anything relating to Jane, and when her half-brother was writing his *Memoir* she was one of his principal helpers and advisers. She died at the age of seventy-nine in 1872 and is buried in Ashe churchyard. She is commemorated by a marble tablet in the nave of the church.

As far as posterity is concerned, James Edward Austen (Austen-Leigh after 1837), was Jane's most important nephew. With the publication of his *Memoir of Jane Austen* it was he who laid the foundation upon which all future biographies of his aunt have been built. Before beginning it, he wrote:

> I was young when we lost her; but the impressions made on the young are deep, and though in the course of fifty years I have forgotten much, I have not forgotten that 'Aunt Jane' was the delight of all her nephews and nieces. We did not think of her as being clever, still less as being famous; but we valued her as one always kind, sympathising, and amusing. To all this I am a living witness, but whether I can sketch out such a faint outline of this excellence as shall be perceptible to others may be reasonably doubted. Aided, however, by a few survivors who knew her, I will not refuse to make the attempt. I am the more inclined to undertake the task from a conviction that, however little I may have to tell, no one else is left who could tell so much of her.[21]

Jane knew 'Edward', as he was called, from the time of his birth at Deane on 17 November 1798. She wrote a few days afterward, 'I had only a glimpse at the child, who was asleep; but Miss Debary told me his eyes were large, dark, and handsome.'[22] Not only was this true, but Edward grew up to be a strikingly good-looking and charming man. He visited his grandmother and aunts frequently when they lived in Bath and Southampton, but it was only after he had become a commoner of Winchester College in 1814 that he assumed an important part in the Jane Austen story. In that year, when he was sixteen, he was let into the family secret

of his aunt's authorship. So delighted was he with the revelation
that he sent her his congratulations in the form of a poem:

To Miss J. Austen

No words can express, my dear Aunt, my surprise
Or make you conceive how I opened my eyes,
Like a pig Butcher Pile has just struck with his knife,
When I heard for the very first time in my life
That I had the honour to have a relation
Whose works were dispersed through the whole of the nation.
I assure you, however, I'm terribly glad;
Oh dear, just to think (and the thought drives me mad)
That dear Mrs. Jennings's good-natured strain
Was really the produce of your witty brain,
That you made the Middletons, Dashwoods and all,
And that you (not young Ferrars) found out that a ball
May be given in cottages never so small.
And though Mr. Collins so grateful for all
Will Lady de Bourgh his dear patroness call,
'Tis to your ingenuity really he owed
His living, his wife, and his humble abode.
Now if you will take your poor nephew's advice,
Your works to Sir William pray send in a trice;
If he'll undertake to some grandees to show it,
By whose means at last the Prince Regent might know it,
For I'm sure if he did, in reward for your tale,
He'd make you a countess at least without fail,
And indeed, if the princess should lose her dear life,
You might have a good chance of becoming his wife.[23]

The prospect of the last two lines must have made Jane
shudder, for she had voiced her dislike of the Prince Regent in a
letter to her friend Martha Lloyd a year earlier.[24] But the rest of
the poem must have delighted her. From then on her future
biographer was one of her favourite relations.

By the time Edward left Winchester College at eighteen for
Exeter College, Oxford, he had begun a novel of his own. It was
in reference to this work that Jane included the now famous
passage concerning her own way of writing in a letter she sent to
him in December 1816:

By the bye, my dear Edward, I am quite concerned for the loss your Mother mentions in her Letter; two Chapters & a half to be missing is monstrous! It is well that *I* have not been at Steventon lately, & therefore cannot be suspected of purloining them; — two strong twigs & a half towards a Nest of my own, would have been something — I do not think however that any theft of that sort would be really very useful to me. What should I do with your strong, manly, spirited Sketches, full of Variety and Glow? — How could I possibly join them on to the little bit (two Inches wide) of Ivory on which I work with so fine a Brush, as produces little effect after much labour?[25]

That Jane and Edward had reached a delightful level of empathy is also evident from another passage in the same letter:

One reason for my writing to you now is that I may have the pleasure of directing to you *Esqre.* — I give you Joy of having left Winchester — Now you may own, how miserable you were there; now, it will gradually all come out — your Crimes & your Miseries — how often you went up by the Mail to London & threw away Fifty Guineas at a Tavern, & how often you were on the point of hanging yourself — restrained only, as some illnatured aspersion upon poor old Winton has it, by the want of a Tree within some miles of the City.[26]

But the pleasant compatibility between Edward and his aunt, which had promised to be so rewarding, ended shortly afterwards with her sickness and death. Even after her removal to Winchester in May 1817 for better medical treatment Jane was still capable of the light touch when she wrote to him:

Mr Lyford says he will cure me, & if he fails I shall draw up a Memorial and lay it before the Dean & Chapter, & have no doubt of redress from that Pious, Learned, and Disinterested Body.[27]

Even so, the letter ended on a sad note, for she added:

God bless you my dear Edward. If ever you are ill, may you be as tenderly nursed as I have been, may the same Blessed alleviations of anxious, simpathising friends be yours, & may you possess — as I dare say you will — the greatest blessing of all, in the consciousness of not being unworthy of their Love. *I could not feel this.*[28]

It was Jane's valediction to Edward. Two months later he was the youngest mourner at her funeral in Winchester Cathedral. In 1828, two years after his graduation from Oxford, he married Emma Smith. They were the parents of eight sons and two daughters. In 1837 he assumed the additional name of Leigh, having inherited the property of his great-uncle's widow, Mrs Leigh Perrot. From 1852 until his death in 1874 he was vicar of Bray in Berkshire, where his grave is marked by a tall granite cross.[29] But his real monument is his *Memoir of Jane Austen,* first published in 1870 and reprinted the following year. In the preface to the second edition he remarked:

> The Memoir of my Aunt, Jane Austen, has been received with more favour than I had ventured to expect. The notices taken of it in the periodical press, as well as letters addressed to me by many with whom I am not personally acquainted, show that an unabated interest is still taken in every particular that can be told about her.[30]

Last of James Austen's children was Caroline Mary Craven Austen, whose memoir, *My Aunt Jane Austen,* written in 1867 when she was an old lady, is one of the seminal biographical works concerning her famous aunt. Although brief, it is the most detailed first-hand account of the Chawton period — with the exception of Jane's surviving letters — that has come down to us from a person who knew and loved her.

Caroline, born at Steventon, was a frequent visitor to her grandmother's house at the time Jane was revising her earlier novels for publication and composing the later ones. She was evidently an appealing child, and early attracted the attention of her Aunt Jane. Caroline had the enviable knack of remembering all sorts of intimate but tellingly important details concerning her aunt and the Chawton household. Although her brother used some of her reminiscences in the *Memoir* many of those that he did not use are important for the vivid relationship they describe between a much-loved aunt and a perceptive little niece.

In recalling Jane Austen, Caroline said:

> Her charm to children was great sweetness of manner — she
> seemed to love you, and you loved her naturally in return —
> This as well as I can now recollect and analyse, was what I felt in
> my earliest days, before I was old enough to be amused by her
> cleverness — But soon came the delight of her playful talk —
> *Everything* she could make amusing to a child — Then, as I got
> older, and when cousins came to share the entertainment, she
> would tell us the most delightful stories chiefly of Fairyland,
> and her Fairies had all characters of their own — The tale was
> invented, I am sure, at the moment, and was sometimes
> continued for 2 or 3 days, if occasion served —[31]

In another place, Caroline wrote:

> When staying at Chawton, if my two cousins, Mary Jane and
> Cassy were there, we often had amusements in which my Aunt
> was very helpful — *She* was the one to whom we always looked
> for help — She would furnish us with what we wanted from her
> wardrobe, and she would often be the entertaining visitor in
> our make believe house — She amused us in various ways —
> *once* I remember in giving a conversation as between myself
> and my two cousins, supposed to be grown up, the day after a
> Ball.[32]

Jane's relationship with Caroline and all well-behaved children
was never marred by condescension. When Anna Lefroy's first
child was born in 1815, thereby making little Caroline an aunt,
Jane, who was then in London preparing *Emma* for the press,
wrote:

> Now that you are become an Aunt, you are a person of some
> consequence & must excite great Interest whatever you do. I
> have always maintained the importance of Aunts as much as
> possible, & I am sure of your doing the same now. — Believe
> me my dear Sister-Aunt, Yours affectly J. Austen[33]

Like her brother and half-sister, Caroline began to write poems
and stories of her own at an early age, and Jane patiently corrected
and commented on them. In recollecting the time when she first
began writing herself, however, Jane tempered her criticism with

other advice. In remembering her aunt's reactions to her efforts, Caroline recalled:

> She said — how well I recollect it! that she *knew* writing stories was a great amusement, and *she* thought a harmless one — tho' many people, she was aware, thought otherwise — but that at my age it would be bad for me to be much taken up with my own compositions — Later still — it was after she got to Winchester, she sent me a message to this effect — That if I would take her advice, I should cease writing till I was 16, and that she had herself often wished she had *read* more, and written *less*, in the corresponding years of her own life.[34]

Caroline also won her aunt's heart by being fond of music, and when Jane played the piano at Chawton, Caroline often stood beside her in rapt attention. Later, after Caroline began to play herself, Jane permitted her to use her 'instrument', but cautioned her in a letter from London not to 'allow anything to be put on it, but what is very light'.[35] In January 1817, when Jane's last illness was becoming critical, she still continued her playfulness with Caroline when she wrote: 'The Piano Forté often talks of you; in various keys, tunes, & expressions I allow — but be it Lesson or Country Dance, Sonata or Waltz, *you* are really its constant Theme.'[36]

Caroline visited Jane in the company of her half-sister Anna Lefroy, just before her aunt was taken to Winchester. At that time, she recalled, Jane, who was confined to her bedroom, mustered up enough of her old gaiety to say, 'There's a chair for the married lady, and a little stool for you, Caroline.'[37] That was the last time Caroline ever saw her aunt, but when her brother was collecting material for the *Memoir* her accurate memory added many colourful details to its pages. She outlived her half-sister and brother and died at Alfriston in Sussex in 1880.

Jane Austen's epitaph in Winchester Cathedral is a formal affirmation of the 'benevolence of her heart, the sweetness of her temper, and the extraordinary endowments of her mind'. But it was Caroline who unconsciously wrote the epitaph her aunt would have appreciated:

> For most of us therefore, the memorial on the perishing tombstone is enough — and more than enough — it will tell its tale longer than anyone will care to read it — But not so for all

— Every country has had its great men, whose lives have been and are still read — with unceasing interest; and so in *some* families there has been *one* distinguished by talent or goodness, and known far beyond the home circle, whose memory ought to be preserved through more than a single generation — Such a one was my Aunt — Jane Austen.[38]

Acknowledgments

Although a lack of space prevents my acknowledgment of all of the individuals and institutions, both in England and the United States, who have assisted me in the research for this book, the following should be specifically named: Oxford University Press for permission to quote from *Jane Austen's Letters to her sister Cassandra and others*, and the *Memoir of Jane Austen* by the Revd James Edward Austen-Leigh, both edited by the late Dr R. W. Chapman, and from other publications relating to Jane Austen; the Bodley Head for permission to quote from *Jane Austen's Sailor Brothers* by J. H. and Edith C. Hubback, and *Jane Austen, Her Homes & Her Friends* by Constance Hill; Paul Yeats-Edwards, Fellows' Librarian of Winchester College for permission to quote James Austen's poem on the death of Jane Austen, for his unfailing help in obtaining original source material, and for his friendly encouragement; Mr and Mrs Lawrence Impey for permission to quote from the invaluable *Austen Papers 1704-1856*, and other important family publications; Sir Hugh Smiley, Bt, chairman and honorary secretary of the Jane Austen Society, for his interest, and for permission to quote from *Annual Reports;* the Trustees of the Jane Austen Memorial Trust for permission to quote from manuscripts; the Earl of Powis and the India Office Library and Records, London, for permission to quote from a letter written by Lord Clive of Plassey; Lord Leigh for providing me with a pedigree of the Leigh family, information concerning Stoneleigh Abbey, and permission to quote from the *History of the Leigh Family of Adlestrop, Gloucestershire;* Mrs Joyce Bown for copying entries from the Steventon parish registers; the late Mrs Gwen Beachcroft for permitting me to quote from a letter of Dr Theophilus Leigh; David J. Gilson for constant encouragement and bibliographical information; J. David Grey for unfailing help and enthusiasm; Gilbert P. Hoole for invaluable help concerning the Austen family of Kent, the early career of the Revd George Austen, and the history of Tonbridge School; Mrs Joan Mason Hurley (Joan Austen-Leigh) for critical help and encouragement; the great-grandsons of Admiral Sir Francis Austen for permission to quote from manuscripts of Anna Lefroy; Dr A. Walton Litz of Princeton University for constant help and encouragement; Roland Q. Nicholson, librarian, Virginia Wesleyan College, and his assistant, Mrs Dorothy Hilliard, for securing rare and out-of-print books concerning the Austens through inter-library loan; John A. Parker, jr, head of the general reference department, Kirn Memorial Library, for obtaining copies of Austen-related articles from magazines and other publications through inter-library loan; Miss Deirdre Le Faye for her constant help and encouragement; my good friends, Ms Ruth Walker and James R. Henderson III, both of Norfolk, Virginia, for reading and correcting the manuscript, and for suggestions for its improvement; and Elizabeth B. (Beth) Williams of Norfolk, Virginia, for making the final typescript.

Abbreviations

AP *Austen Papers, 1704-1856,* edited by R. A. Austen-Leigh (privately printed by Spottiswoode, Ballantyne & Co Ltd, 1942).

AR *Annual Reports of the Jane Society.* These have been bound in two volumes, each with an Introduction by Elizabeth Jenkins: *Collected Reports of the Jane Austen Society 1949-1965* (William Dawson, 1967); *Collected Reports... 1966-1975* (William Dawson, 1977).

Aunt *My Aunt Jane Austen: a memoir,* Caroline Mary Craven Austen (Alton: Jane Austen Society, 1952).

Brabourne *Letters of Jane Austen,* edited with an Introduction and Critical Remarks by Edward, Lord Brabourne, 2 vols. (Richard Bentley & Son, 1884).

Chawton MSS Manuscript album of James Austen's miscellaneous works owned by the Jane Austen Memorial Trust, Chawton.

DNB *The Dictionary of National Biography,* edited by Sir Leslie Stephen and Sir Sidney Lee, 63 vols. (Smith, Elder & Co, 1885-1900; 1921-2).

Hill *Jane Austen: her homes and her friends,* Constance Hill (John Lane, 1902; 1923).

LCR 'Lady Chandos' Register', C. H. Collins Baker (*Genealogists' Magazine* 10 (1947-50) 255-64, 299-309, 339-52).

Letters *Jane Austen's Letters to her Sister Cassandra and Others,* collected and edited by R. W. Chapman, 2 vols. (Oxford: Clarendon Press, 1932; second edition 1952, reprinted in one volume, 1972).

Life and Letters *Jane Austen, her Life and Letters: a family record,* W. and R. A. Austen-Leigh (Smith, Elder & Co, 1913 1965).

Memoir *Memoir of Jane Austen,* J. E. Austen-Leigh (Richard Bentley, 1870); reprint of the second edition, 1871, with Introduction, Notes and Index by R. W. Chapman (Oxford: Clarendon Press, 1926; 1967).

MW The Works of Jane Austen, vol. 6: *Minor Works,* edited by R. W. Chapman (Oxford University Press, 1954; 1972, with revisions by B. C. Southam).

OFH 'An Old Family History', the Hon. Agnes Leigh, *National Review* 49 (1907), 277-86.

Pedigree Pedigree of Austen of Horsmonden, Broadford, Grovehurst, Kippington, Capel Manor, etc, R. A. Austen-Leigh (privately printed by Spottiswoode, Ballantyne & Co Ltd, 1940).

Sailor Brothers Jane Austen's Sailor Brothers, J. H. and E. C. Hubback, (John Lane The Bodley Head, 1906).

Trial The Trial of Jane Leigh Perrot, John Pinchard (Taunton: Thomas Norris, 1800).

Notes

The Austens of Kent

1 *Life and Letters*, 1.
2 *Burke's Genealogical and Heraldic History of the Peerage, Baronetage and Knightage* (1967) 1480; and *DNB*, XI, 879.
3 *AP*, 18.
4 Crouch, Marcus, *Kent* (Batsford, 1966) 95.
5 Kaye-Smith, Sheila, *Weald of Kent and Sussex* (Robert Hale, 1953) 1.
6 *Pedigree*, iii.
7 Cottle, Basil, *The Penguin Dictionary of Surnames* (1967) 38.
8 *Pedigree*, iii.
9 Cronk, Anthony, *St Margaret's Church, Horsmonden* (1967) 38-9.
10 Kaye-Smith, 153.
11 Defoe, Daniel, *A Tour Through the Whole Island of Great Britain* (1724-7).
12 Warner, Richard, *Excursions from Bath* (1801).
13 Chapman, R. W., 'Jane Austen's Library', *Book Collectors' Quarterly*, XI (July-Sept 1933) 32.
14 *AR* (1962) 'The Sources of Jane Austen's Kentish Ties', Canon S. Graham Brade-Birks.
15 *Letters* (74.1) 500.
16 *AP*, 3-16.
17 Hoole, Gilbert P., *The Priory and the Red House in Bordyke*, n.d., 4.
18 Information supplied June 1977 by A. R. Tammadge, Headmaster, Sevenoaks School.
19 *DNB*, VI, 1186-7.
20 *Pedigree*, 5.
21 *Pedigree*, 3, 5, 6.
22 *Pedigree*, 11-12.
23 *DNB*, XVII, 1214.
24 Baddeley, John James, *The Aldermen of Cripplegate Ward 1276-1900* (1900) 57.
25 *Burke's Peerage* (1970) 1227-8.
26 Information supplied April 1977 by Sir Robin Mackworth-Young, KCVO, HM Librarian, Windsor Castle.
27 *AP*, 43.
28 Hoole, Gilbert P., *Tonbridge Associations of Jane Austen's Family* (1977) 2.
29 Hoole, *Tonbridge Associations*, 3.

The Rector of Steventon and Deane

1 *Letters* (40) 144-5.
2 *Letters* (41) 146-7.
3 *MW,* 2.
4 *Hill,* 31.
5 *AP,* 16.
6 Rivington, S., *The History of Tonbridge School* (Rivingtons, 1925) 4th edition, 157.
7 Hargreaves-Mawdsley, W. N., *Woodford at Oxford 1759–1776* (Oxford Historical Society, new series, XXI, 1969) 11, 302.
8 *Memoir,* 19.
9 *AR* (1978) 'The Rev. Thomas Bathurst', William Jarvis.
10 *AP,* 333.
11 Freeman, Jean, *Jane Austen in Bath* (Alton, 1969) 9.
12 *Memoir,* 7-8.
13 Feiling, Keith, *Warren Hastings* (Macmillan, 1954; 1966).
14 Grier, Sydney C., ed., *The Letters of Warren Hastings to his Wife* (William Blackwood, 1905).
15 Diocesan Records, Hampshire Record Office, Winchester, *A true and perfect Terryer of the Rectory of Steventon in the Diocese of Winchester, 1696.*
16 *AR* (1976) 'Some Information about Jane Austen's clerical connections', William Jarvis.
17 *AR* (1975) 'Description of Steventon Rectory in the Rev. George Austen's time', Anna Lefroy.
18 Austen-Leigh, Emma, *Jane Austen and Steventon* (Spottiswoode, Ballantyne, 1937) 2-3.
19 Austen-Leigh, 10.
20 *Memoir,* 9.
21 Diocesan Records, Hampshire Record Office. Original record of gift is dated 23 March 1773.
22 Lambeth Palace archives. Original record is dated 27 March 1773.
23 *AP,* 29-30.
24 *Letters* (26) 88.
25 Cokayne's *Peerage,* X, 612.
26 *Letters* (Other Persons Index).
27 Hill, 83.
28 *AP,* 132.
29 Brabourne, I, 151.
30 *Letters* (9) 21.
31 *MW,* 76.

32 Photocopy of the original supplied by the Librarian, St John's College, Oxford.
33 Hill, 91.
34 Chapman, R. W., *Jane Austen: facts and problems* (Clarendon Press, Oxford, 1948; 1970) 46.
35 *Letters* (39) 141.
36 *Letters* (41) 146.
37 *AR* (1968).

Friends of Warren Hastings

1   *AP*, 34.
2   Ibid.
3   *AP*, 66.
4   Grier, *Letters of Warren Hastings*, 452-9.
5   Bence-Jones, Mark, *Clive of India* (Constable, 1974) 68, 316.
6   Davies, A Mervyn, *Clive of Plassey* (Nicholson & Watson, 1939) 121.
7   Bence-Jones, 72.
8   *AP*, 36.
9   *MW*, 194.
10 *AP*, 67.
11 Crawford, D. G., *A History of the Indian Medical Service 1600-1913*, 2 vols, (W. Thacker, 1913) I, 169-71.
12 *AP*, 77.
13 Bence-Jones, 200.
14 Feiling, *Warren Hastings*, 54.
15 Bence-Jones, 220.
16 Bence-Jones, 342.
17 *AP*, 74.
18 *AP*, 40.
19 *AP*, 60.
20 *AR* (1954) 'Some banking accounts of the Austen family', Elizabeth Jenkins.
21 *AP*, 101.
22 *AP*, 64-5.
23 *AP*, 68.
24 *AP*, 78-9.
25 *AR* (1956) 'Miniature of Mrs Philadelphia Hancock', T. Edward Carpenter.
26 *AP*, 82.
27 *AP*, 83.
28 *AP*, 92.

29 *Memoir*, 26.
30 *AP*, 98.
31 *AP*, 97-8.
32 *AP*, 100.
33 Gilson, D. J., 'Jane Austen's books', *Book Collector* XXIII (Spring 1974) 1, 32.
34 *MW*, 76.
35 *AP*, 118.
36 *AP*, 123.
37 *AP*, 129.
38 *AP*, 126.
39 *AP*, 133.
40 *AP*, 137.
41 *AP*, 139-40.
42 *AP*, 143-4.
43 *AP*, 321-3.
44 *Letters* (133), 465.

The aristocratic Leighs

1   Kaines Smith, S. C., *Stoneleigh Abbey*, n.d.
2   Orridge, B. B., *Some Account of the Citizens of London and their Rulers* (1867) 182-4, 187-9.
3   *Burke's Peerage* (1967) 1480-81.
4   *DNB*, XI, 878-9.
5   *DNB*, IX, 861-2.
6   Collins, Arthur, *The Peerage of England* (1735) III, 231.
7   *Burke's Peerage* (1967) 1480.
8   *DNB*, XI, 878-9.
9   Hayward, Sir John, *Annals of the first four years of the reign of Queen Elizabeth* (Camden Society, 1840).
10 Holinshed, Raphael, *Chronicles of England, Scotland and Ireland*, 6 vols, (1808; reprinted AMS Press, New York, 1965) IV, 158.
11 Holinshed, IV, 176.
12 Collins, III, 231.
13 *DNB*, XI, 878-9.
14 Watney, Sir John, *Some Account of the Hospital of St Thomas of Acon... and of the Plate of the Mercers' Company* (1891) 186.
15 *Burke's Peerage* (1967) 1480.
16 Information supplied July 1978 by the Shakespeare Birthplace Trust; also Throckmorton, C. Wickliffe, *A Genealogical and Historical Account of the Throckmorton Family* (Old Dominion Press, Richmond, Virginia, 1930) 123.

17 *DNB,* VI, 122-4.
18 Collins, III, 233.
19 Orridge, 183, 187.
20 Orridge, 183, 188.
21 Orridge, 183, 189.
22 *Burke's Peerage* (1967) 1480.
23 *OFH,* 278.
24 Ibid.
25 *Short description 'of the parish and village of Adlestrop in Gloucestershire with rough plan of the village* (1975) 7.
26 *OFH,* 278-9.
27 *DNB,* XIII, 608.
28 *OFH,* 279.
29 *OFH,* 284.
30 *OFH,* 280.
31 *OFH,* 283.
32 Ibid.
33 *LCR* (March 1949) 299.
34 *LCR* (December 1948) 257.
35 Young, Percy M., *Handel* (Dent, 1947; 1965) 33.
36 *LCR* (December 1948) 255.
37 Collins, I, 355.
38 Information supplied June 1976 by MSS Department, British Library.
39 *LCR* (March 1949) 301.
40 Kaines Smith, *Stoneleigh Abbey.*
41 Ward, W. R., *Georgian Oxford: University politics in the eighteenth century* (Clarendon Press, 1958) 209.
42 *Memoir,* 6.
43 Ibid.
44 *Memoir,* 7.
45 *Life and Letters,* 8.
46 *Life and Letters,* 6.
47 Original pedigree (Mun LIV/45), Library St John's College, Oxford.
48 Fuller, Thomas, *The Worthies of England* (1662).
49 *AR* (1977) 'The Austens and Oxford: "Founder's Kin"', D. J. Gilson.
50 Hearne, Thomas (1678-1735), *Remarks and Collections,* entry for 3 June 1722, ed. C. E. Doble *et al.* (Oxford Historical Society, 1885-1921).
51 Bloxom, John Rouse, *A register of the Presidents, Fellows... and other members of Saint Mary Magdalen College,* II (1857), 182-7; also Barnwell, Edward Lawry, *Perrot notes: some account of the various*

branches of the Perrot family (1867), 101-06.
52 *DNB.* XV, 914.
53 Austen-Leigh, Emma, *Jane Austen and Steventon,* 10.
54 *AP,* 272.
55 *MW,* 33.
56 *MW,* 149.
57 *Letters* (133) 467.

The Rector's sprack-witted wife

1 Hill, 31-2.
2 *Memoir,* 11.
3 *AP,* 228.
4 Watts, Canon A. J., *A guide to the parish church of St Margaret V. M. Harpsden cum Bolney, Oxon,* 5.
5 Quoted from the original letter of Dr Theophilus Leigh.
6 Lefroy, Fanny Caroline, 'Is it just?' *Temple Bar,* (February 1883) 273.
7 *Memoir,* 12.
8 *Memoir,* 20.
9 Freeman, Jean, *Jane Austen in Bath* (1969) 9.
10 *Memoir,* 43.
11 *Memoir,* 9.
12 *Sailor Brothers,* 9-10.
13 *AR* (1975) 'Description of Steventon Rectory in the Rev. George Austen's time', Anna Lefroy.
14 *Memoir,* 21.
15 *AP,* 29.
16 Austen-Leigh, Emma, *Jane Austen and Steventon,* 23.
17 *AP,* 32-3.
18 Lefroy, 274.
19 *AP,* 24.
20 *MW,* 47.
21 *AP,* 131.
22 *Memoir,* 17-18.
23 *Letters* (14) 39.
24 *Letters* (10) 22.
25 *Letters* (29) 99-100.
26 *Letters* (29) 101-02.
27 *Letters* (35) 122.
28 *Letters* (35) 125.
29 *Life and Letters,* 173.

30 Wright, R. W. M., *A pictorial history of Bath Abbey* (Pitkin, 1967) 20.
31 *AP*, 235.
32 *AP*, 246.
33 *Memoir*, 82.
34 *Memoir*, 83.
35 *Letters* (49) 178.
36 *Aunt*, 4, 6.
37 *Aunt*, 7.
38 Hill, 177.
39 Martha Lloyd's Household Book, Jane Austen's House, Chawton.
40 *Life and Letters*, 256-7.
41 *MW*, 423.
42 Grigson, Geoffrey, 'New letters from Jane Austen's home', *Times Literary Supplement* (19 August 1955) 493.
43 *MW*, 436.
44 *Aunt*, 13.
45 *Letters* (145) 495.
46 Lefroy, 284.
47 *Memoir*, 11-12.

Mrs Leigh Perrot stands accused

1 *Life and Letters*, 126.
2 *AP*, 291.
3 *Memoir*, 71.
4 *AP*, 196.
5 Gilson, D. J., 'Jane Austen's books', 27-39.
6 *AP*, 207.
7 'Account of the Trial of Mrs Leigh Perrot', *Lady's Magazine* (April 1800) 172.
8 *Trial*, 18.
9 Mackinnon, Sir Frank Douglas, *Grand Larceny: being the Trial of Jane Leigh Perrot, Aunt of Jane Austen* (Oxford University Press, 1937) 127.
10 *AP*, 184.
11 *AP*, 190.
12 *AP*, 193-5.
13 *AP*, 199.
14 *AP*, 197-8.
15 *AP*, 205-06.
16 *AP*, 219.

17 'Account of the Trial', 176.
18 *Bath Chronicle,* 3 April 1800.
19 'Account of the Trial', 171.
20 *AP,* 210-11.
21 *Trial,* 38.
22 *Trial,* 41.
23 *AP,* 211.
24 *AP,* 213.
25 *AP,* 207.
26 *Letters* (27) 92.
27 *AP,* 290.
28 *AP,* 222-4.
29 *Letters,* (61) 238.
30 *AP,* 332-3.
31 *Letters* (144) 491-2.
32 *AP,* 264.
33 Austen-Leigh, Mary Augusta, *James Edward Austen-Leigh: a memoir* (privately printed, 1911) 39.
34 *AP,* 259.
35 *AP,* 280.
36 Hickman, Peggy, 'Jane Austen's uncle and aunt', *Country Life* (18 April 1963) 842-3.

James – the poet of the family

1 *AP,* 265.
2 *Chawton MSS.* (Numbers have been assigned to the individual poems as they appear in sequence in the volume.)
3 *AR* (1977), 'The Austens and Oxford'.
4 *Memoir,* 6-7.
5 *Chawton MSS,* poems 11, 12, 13.
6 Poems 1, 2.
7 Poems 3, 4.
8 Poems, 14-19.
9 Brydges, Sir Egerton, *The Autobiography, Times, Opinions, and Contemporaries of Sir Egerton Brydges* (1834), 137.
10 *Chawton MSS,* poems 52,53.
11 *AP,* 128.
12 *AP,* 110.
13 *Chawton MSS,* poem 8.
14 Church of Wales Records, SD/SB/5, 63.
15 *AP,* 124.
16 *Chawton MSS,* poems 5, 6.

17 Poems 7, 8, 9.
18 *AP*, 133.
19 *MW*, 49.
20 *Memoir*, 12.
21 Cope, Sir Zachary, 'Who was Sophia Sentiment? Was she Jane Austen?' *Book Collector*, 15 (1966) 143-57.
22 *AP*, 138; also *Life and Letters*, 66.
23 *Chawton MSS*, poem 10.
24 *AP*, 138.
25 *Letters*, (27) 91-2.
26 *Letters* (1) 3.
27 *AP*, 156-7.
28 *AP*, 228.
29 Austen-Leigh, M. A., *James Edward Austen-Leigh: a memoir*, 17.
30 Thomson, C. Linklater, *Jane Austen: a survey* (Horace Marshall, 1929) 14-15.
31 Austen-Leigh, 17.
32 *Letters* (10) 23.
33 *Chawton MSS*, poem 20.
34 *Letters* (49) 181.
35 *Chawton MSS*, poem 27.
36 *Chawton MSS*, poem 28.
37 *Letters* (82) 325.
38 *MW*, 432.
39 *MW*, 436.
40 *Letters* (145) 494.
41 Austen, Henry, 'Biographical Notice of the Author' prefixed to the first edition of *Northanger Abbey* and *Persuasion* (1818); reprinted in *The Novels of Jane Austen*, edited by R. W. Chapman, (Oxford: Clarendon Press, 1923; 1972), vol. 5.
42 Austen-Leigh, 9-10.
43 *Aunt*, 17.
44 *Memoir*, 1.
45 The original manuscript is in the Fellows' Library, Winchester College, Hampshire.
46 *Chawton MSS*, poems 37, 38, 39.
47 Austen-Leigh, 133.
48 Austen-Leigh, 129.

George – the unfortunate brother

1 *AP*, 334.
2 *AP*, 66.

3 *AP*, 23.
4 *AP*, 27.
5 *AP*, 66.
6 *AP*, 130.
7 *Letters* (62) 242.
8 *AP*, 334.
9 Information supplied February 1977 by the Revd J. E. Gurnos Davies, Rector of All Saints' Church, Monk Sherborne.
10 *AR* (1976) 'Some information about Jane Austen's clerical connections', William Jarvis.

Edward – the squire of Godmersham

1 *Memoir*, 13.
2 *Hampshire Chronicle* (27 November 1852).
3 Brabourne, I, 20.
4 *AP*, 230.
5 Austen-Leigh, William, and Knight, Montagu George, *Chawton Manor and its owners* (Smith, Elder, 1911) 157-8.
6 Ibid.
7 Ibid.
8 Brabourne, II, 357.
9 *AP*, 141.
10 *AP*, 144.
11 *MW*, 57.
12 *AP*, 229.
13 *AP*, 230-31.
14 Hussey, Christopher, 'Godmersham Park, Kent, II', *Country Life* (23 February 1945) 332.
15 Cousins, Zechariah, *Tour through the Isle of Thanet* (1793).
16 *AR* (1962) 'The sources of Jane Austen's Kentish ties', Canon S. Graham Brade-Birks.
17 *Letters* (51) 189.
18 *Letters* (15) 44.
19 *Letters* (51) 188.
20 *Letters* (57) 219-20.
21 *Letters* (59) 225.
22 *Letters* (68) 266.
23 Leveson-Gower, Lord Granville, *Private Correspondence, 1781-1821*, 2 vols, (John Murray, 1916) II, 418.
24 Brabourne, II, 117.
25 *Letters* (74.1) 500.
26 *Letters* (Other Persons Index).

27 Brabourne, II, 119.
28 *Letters* (81) 314.
29 *Letters* (82) 321, 323.
30 Chapman, R. W., *Jane Austen: facts and problems*, 133-4.
31 *Letters* (84) 333.
32 *Letters* (90) 365.
33 *MW*, 431.
34 Pollock, Walter H., *Jane Austen: her contemporaries and herself —
    an essay in criticism* (Longmans Green, 1899) 90-91.
35 Austen-Leigh and Knight, 171.
36 *Letters* (Other Persons Index).
37 Brabourne, II, 219-20.
38 *Letters* (93) 383-4.
39 Austen-Leigh and Knight, 171.
40 Ibid.
41 *Memoir*, 176.
42 Austen-Leigh and Knight, 172.

Henry Thomas – Jane's favourite brother

 1 *Letters* (97) 390.
 2 Hill, 31.
 3 *Memoir*, 13.
 4 Hill, 48-9.
 5 Austen-Leigh and Knight, *Chawton Manor and its owners*, 163-4.
 6 Brabourne, I, 34.
 7 Brabourne, I, 35-6.
 8 *AP*, 28.
 9 *AP*, 31.
10 *Letters* (59) 229.
11 *AP*, 177.
12 *AP*, 122.
13 *AP*, 130.
14 *AP*, 133.
15 *MW*, 78.
16 *MW*, 109.
17 *MW*, 110.
18 *AP*, 148.
19 *AP*, 153-4.
20 *DNB*, XV, 619-20.
21 *Letters* (1) 3.
22 *Letters* (7) 17.
23 *Letters* (7) 18.

24   Ibid.
25   *AP*, 155.
26   *AP*, 159-60.
27   *AP*, 162.
28   *AP*, 160-61.
29   *AP*, 168.
30   Quennell, Peter, *Hogarth's Progress* (Collins, 1955).
31   *Life and Letters*, 106-7.
32   *AP*, 169.
33   *AP*, 170.
34   *AP*, 174.
35   *Letters* (33) 118.
36   *Letters* (70) 275.
37   *Letters* (93) 381.
38   *Letters* (70) 276.
39   Ibid; also Piggott, Patrick, *The Innocent Diversion: a study of music in the life and writings of Jane Austen* (Clover Hill, 1979) 23.
40   *Gentleman's Magazine* (July-December 1812) LXXXII, 78-9.
41   *Letters* (70) 272-7.
42   *Letters* (81) 315.
43   *Letters* (82) 324.
44   *Letters* (67a) 264.
45   *Aunt*, 11-13.
46   Austen, Henry Thomas, 'Memoir of Miss Austen', prefixed to the edition of Jane Austen's novels published by Richard Bentley, 1833, ix.
47   *Letters* (85) 340.
48   *AP*, 283.
49   *Life and Letters*, 332.
50   *Letters* (132) 461.
51   *Life and Letters*, 333.
52   Information supplied November 1978 by the Diocesan Registrar, Salisbury, Wiltshire.
53   *Letters* (142) 489.
54   *Letters* (139) 476.
55   See note 52.
56   *AR* (1976), 'Some information about Jane Austen's clerical connections', William Jarvis.
57   *AR* (1978) 'The Revd Henry and Mrs Eleanor Austen', Winifred Midgley.
58   Ibid.
59   *Life and Letters*, 333.
60   *AP*, 294.

Cassandra Elizabeth – the beloved sister

1 *AP*, 29.
2 *AP*, 31.
3 *AP*, 33.
4 *Memoir*, 16-17.
5 Hill, 258.
6 *Life and Letters*, 25.
7 *Oxford Universal Dictionary* (1953), 1629.
8 *AR* (1975) illustration.
9 *AR* (1964) 'Some banking accounts of the Austen family', Elizabeth Jenkins.
10 *Memoir*, 16.
11 Darton, F. J. Harvey, *The Life and Times of Mrs Sherwood, 1775-1851* (Wells, Gardner, 1910) 123.
12 Darton, 125.
13 *Gentleman's Magazine* (1797) 983.
14 Cooper, J. J., *Some Worthies of Reading* (Swarthmore Press, 1923) 72.
15 *Life and Letters*, 27.
16 Darton, 124.
17 Ibid.
18 Cooper, 72.
19 Darton, 128.
20 Hill, 33.
21 *Letters* (4) 8.
22 *AP*, 131.
23 Ibid.
24 *AR* (1975) 'Description of Steventon Rectory in the Rev. George Austen's time', Anna Lefroy.
25 *Letters* (13) 35.
26 *MW*, 44, 74, 138, 192.
27 *Letters* (23) 75.
28 *Letters* (29) 103.
29 Piggott, Patrick, *The Innocent Diversion*, 5-6, 167.
30 *AR* (1976) 'Some information about Jane Austen's clerical connections', William Jarvis.
31 *Letters* (Other Persons Index).
32 Information supplied July 1977 by Lieut. Col. C. C. E. Crew, curator of the Museum, Royal Army Chaplains' Department, Bagshot, Surrey.
33 Information supplied August 1977 by Major G. U. Weymouth, MBE, Regimental HQ, The Queen's Regiment, Canterbury.

34 See note 33.
35 *Letters* (4) 10.
36 *AP*, 159.
37 *AP*, 330.
38 *AP*, 284.
39 *AP*, 287.
40 *Aunt*, 9.
41 Austen-Leigh, M. A., *Personal Aspects of Jane Austen*, 147-8.
42 *Memoir*, 209.
43 Watson, Vera, *Mary Russell Mitford* (Evans, 1949) 10.
44 *Letters* (1) 1-2.
45 Chapman, R. W., *Jane Austen: facts and problems*, 63-9.
46 Bigg-Wither, Revd Reginald, *The Wither Family* (Warren, Winchester, 1907) 58.
47 Chapman, 62.
48 *Letters* (90) 367.
49 *Aunt*, 5.
50 *Aunt*, 11.
51 *Aunt*, 14.
52 *AP*, 332.
53 *Letters*, 513-14.
54 *Letters*, 517.
55 *Life and Letters*, 402.
56 *AP*, 288-9.
57 *Aunt*, 20.
58 Hill, 258.
59 *AP*, 294.

Francis William – 'the officer who knelt in church'

1 *Letters* (6) 15.
2 *AP*, 31.
3 *Letters* (68) 265.
4 *Memoir*, 39.
5 *Life and Letters*, 23-4.
6 O'Byrne, William R., *A Naval Biographical Dictionary* (new edition, 1861) I, 29.
7 Lloyd, Christopher, 'The Royal Naval Colleges at Portsmouth and Greenwich', *Mariners' Mirror* (1966) 145.
8 Lloyd, 146.
9 Ibid.
10 O'Byrne, I, 29.
11 *Sailor Brothers*, 16.

12 *Sailor Brothers*, 17-19.
13 *Memoir*, 14.
14 *MW*, 12.
15 *MW*, 40.
16 *MW*, 146.
17 O'Byrne, I, 29.
18 *Letters* (4) 8, 10.
19 *Sailor Brothers*, viii.
20 See note 42, *James – the poet of the family.*
21 *AP*, 303.
22 *AP*, 226-7.
23 *DNB*, VII, 833-5.
24 *Letters* (15) 42.
25 *Letters* (16) 47.
26 O'Byrne, I, 29.
27 Ibid.
28 Ibid.
29 *Sailor Brothers*, 60-64.
30 *Letters* (32) 112.
31 Austen-Leigh, Emma, *Jane Austen and Bath* (Spottiswoode, Ballantyne, 1939) viii.
32 *Sailor Brothers*, 112-16.
33 *Sailor Brothers*, 114.
34 Marshall, John, *Royal Naval Biography* (1824) II, 278.
35 *Sailor Brothers*, 131-43.
36 *Sailor Brothers*, 148.
37 *Sailor Brothers*, 155-6.
38 *Sailor Brothers*, 176.
39 O'Byrne, I, 29.
40 *Letters* (49) 177-8.
41 *Letters* (50) 184.
42 *Sailor Brothers*, 212-26; also O'Byrne, I, 29.
43 *Letters* (68) 264-6.
44 *Letters* (70) 272.
45 *Letters* (81) 317.
46 *MW*, 431.
47 *MW*, 436.
48 Grigson, Geoffrey, 'New letters from Jane Austen's home', 484.
49 Bussby, Frederick, *Jane Austen in Winchester* (Winchester, 1973) 5.
50 *Letters* (15) 42.
51 O'Byrne, 29.
52 Brabourne, I, 38.
53 Brabourne, I, 37.

54 Howe, M. A. DeWolfe, 'A Jane Austen letter, with other "Janeana" from an old book of autographs', *Yale Review* (January 1926) 321-2.

Charles John – 'our own particular little brother'

1 Bush, Douglas, *Jane Austen* (Macmillan, New York, 1975) 17.
2 *Memoir*, 15.
3 *MW*, 40.
4 *MW*, 43.
5 *MW*, 42.
6 *Sailor Brothers*, 21-2.
7 O'Byrne, *A Naval Biographical Dictionary*, 26-7.
8 *Letters*, (14) 38.
9 *Letters* (15) 46.
10 *Letters* (17) 49.
11 *Letters* (18) 54.
12 *Letters* (18) 57.
13 O'Byrne, 26-7.
14 *Letters* (27) 90.
15 Ibid.
16 *Letters* (34) 120.
17 Fulford, Roger, *The Royal Dukes: the father and uncles of Queen Victoria* (Duckworth, 1933) 253-60.
18 *Letters* (38) 137.
19 Austen-Leigh, E., *Jane Austen and Bath*, viii.
20 *Sailor Brothers*, 205.
21 Wilkinson, Henry C., *Bermuda in the old empire* (Oxford University Press, 1950) 441.
22 *Letters* (62) 243.
23 *Letters* (63) 248.
24 *Letters* (70) 275.
25 *AP*, 249.
26 Marshall, J., *Royal Naval Biography*, Supplement, (1828), II, 75.
27 *Letters* (88) 357.
28 'Captain Charles Austen and some others', *Notes and Queries* (28 June 1947), 273.
29 Information supplied April 1976 by the Revd W. G. Knapper, vicar of St John the Baptist Church, Kentish Town, London NW5.
30 O'Byrne, 26-7.
31 *Sailor Brothers*, 270.
32 Ibid.
33 *MW*, 434.
34 *MW*, 439.

35 Marshall, 76.
36 *Letters* (144) 491.
37 *Letters* (144) 492.
38 Austen, Charles, Diaries (1815-52), National Maritime Museum, Greenwich (AUS/109).
39 Hubback, John H., 'Pen portraits in Jane Austen's novels', *Cornhill* (July 1928) 32-3.
40 Llewelyn, Margaret, *Jane Austen: a character study* (William Kimber, 1977) 157.
41 *Bicentenary 1775-1975 Loan Exhibition Catalogue* (Chawton, 1975) items 30 and 31.
42 *Bicentenary Catalogue*, item 18.
43 *AP*, 285.
44 *AP*, 294.
45 *Sailor Brothers*, 278.
46 *Sailor Brothers*, 279.
47 *AR* (1970) 'Travels of a temple bell'.
48 *Sailor Brothers*, 281.
49 *Memoir*, 15.

The importance of being a good aunt

1 Brabourne, I, Introduction, ix and xii.
2 'Aunt Jane', *Cornhill*, 973 (Winter 1947-8) 72-3.
3 Beveridge, A. J., *The Life of John Marshall*, 2 vols (Houghton Mifflin, Boston, 1916) II, 79-80.
4 *Memoir*, 3.
5 Hill, 86.
6 Southam, Brian, ed., *Jane Austen's 'Sir Charles Grandison'* (Clarendon Press, Oxford, 1980) 5.
7 Austen-Leigh, M.A., *Personal Aspects of Jane Austen*, 113.
8 Southam, 10-11.
9 *Letters* (72) 282.
10 *Letters* (70) 275.
11 *Letters* (85) 340-41.
12 *Letters* (89) 363.
13 Hill, 194-5.
14 *MW*, 442-3.
15 *Letters* (98) 393.
16 *Letters* (101) 404.
17 Hill, 227.
18 *MW*, 432.
19 *MW*, 438.

20 Hill, 243-4.
21 *Memoir*, 2-3.
22 *Letters* (12) 31.
23 Austen-Leigh, Mary Augusta, *James Edward Austen-Leigh: a memoir*, 7.
24 *Letters* (78.1) 504.
25 *Letters* (134) 468-9.
26 Ibid.
27 *Letters* (146) 496.
28 *Letters* (146) 497.
29 Austen-Leigh, 309.
30 *Memoir* (preface), 2nd edition (1871).
31 *Aunt*, 5.
32 *Aunt*, 10.
33 *Letters* (112) 428.
34 *Aunt*, 10.
35 *Letters* (112) 428.
36 *Letters* (137) 473.
37 *Aunt*, 14-15.
38 *Aunt*, 1.

Index

231

234   *Index*